"A scarifying dive into China's pernicious spy state. . . . A prescient, alarming work on the overreach of technology and state power."
—*Kirkus* (starred review)

"*The Perfect Police State* should come with a warning: the scope of the Chinese surveillance state is deeper, broader, more insidious and terrifying than you can imagine. Geoffrey Cain deftly details how China has used global businesses, global aid, unabashed censorship at home, and alliances with authoritarian regimes to create an ever-expanding police state. Cain doesn't lose sight of the people entrapped by the system, most memorably a woman named Maysem whose trials keep the focus on the real human cost. *The Perfect Police State* is a tour-de-force."
—Elizabeth Becker, author of *When the War Was Over*

"In an exposé that is as timely as it is distressing, Geoffrey Cain shows how China is using artificial intelligence and totalitarian repression to turn its westernmost region into a human-rights hellhole. After reading *The Perfect Police State*, it is impossible to regard the Chinese leadership with anything other than contempt—and fear."
—Blaine Harden, author of *Escape from Camp 14*

"The future has arrived and it is beyond anything George Orwell could have imagined. In this important new book, Cain details exactly how the Chinese Communist Party deployed twenty-first-century technology—facial recognition, DNA tracking, artificial intelligence—to trap millions of its own citizens in a terrifying dystopia."
—Barbara Demick, author of
Nothing to Envy: Ordinary Lives in North Korea

THE
PERFECT
POLICE
STATE

THE PERFECT POLICE STATE

An Undercover Odyssey into
China's Terrifying Surveillance Dystopia
of the Future

GEOFFREY CAIN

PUBLICAFFAIRS
New York

PublicAffairs
Hachette Book Group
1290 Avenue of the Americas, New York, NY 10104
www.publicaffairsbooks.com
@Public_Affairs

Printed in the United States of America

First Edition: June 2021

Published by PublicAffairs, an imprint of Perseus Books, LLC, a subsidiary of
Hachette Book Group, Inc. The PublicAffairs name and logo is a trademark
of the Hachette Book Group.

The Hachette Speakers Bureau provides a wide range of authors for speaking events.
To find out more, go to www.hachettespeakersbureau.com or call (866) 376-6591.

The publisher is not responsible for websites (or their content) that are not owned
by the publisher.

Print book interior design by Jane Raese
Set in 12.5-point Whitman

Editorial production by Christine Marra, *Marra*thon Production Services.
www.marrathoneditorial.org

Library of Congress Cataloging-in-Publication Data has been applied for.

ISBN 978-1-5417-5703-5 (hardcover); ISBN 978-1-5417-5701-1 (e-book)

LSC-C

Printing 1, 2021

FOR MOM,
WHO TAUGHT ME TO CARE ABOUT
THE STATE OF THE WORLD

Contents

Note on Research and on Uyghur and Han Chinese Names

From August 2017 to September 2020, I interviewed 168 Uyghur refugees, technology workers, government officials, researchers, academics, activists, and a former Chinese spy who was preparing to defect. Most requested that I use pseudonyms if I published their interviews.

This was the only way I could write an accurate book on the Uyghurs, Kazakhs, and other ethnic groups that are oppressed in western China. Their families, who are still in China, can easily be harassed or tortured by the police or intelligence services. Some interviewees, public figures whose stories have already been widely published, requested that I use their real names.

The protagonist's name in this book, "Maysem," is a pseudonym for a young Uyghur woman I met in Ankara, the capital of Turkey, in October 2018. I interviewed her fourteen times from October 2018 to February 2021.

As I researched this book, I questioned myself about the wisdom of interviewing refugees who, under the cover of fake names, could take license to stretch their stories, or change their accounts to cope with unbearable trauma.

In fact, there is a long tradition among journalists and scholars of relying on refugee testimony when documenting political upheavals and human rights atrocities, sometimes withholding their names and identifying information. Researchers and writers have long relied on the testimony of "White" Russian, Jewish, Cuban, Chinese, and North Korean refugees.

Like some of these other writers, I spent my career as a foreign correspondent interviewing refugees and people in sensitive situations, whose careers or lives were at risk. I knew how to get around the downsides.

I rigorously cross-checked the statements of key characters with people who knew them and had heard their stories before. I also cross-checked my interviewees' statements with other refugee accounts, media reports, the chronology of events on the public record, the Uyghur victim database at shahit.biz, the speeches in state media of Chinese leaders, human rights reports from Human Rights Watch, the Uyghur Human Rights Project, the US Congress and US State Department, and the work of a small group of researchers who analyze satellite imagery, computer data, and Chinese corporate reports.

For key interviews, I spoke with each person in anywhere from four to twenty-five sessions, spending between eight and sixty hours with each one, revisiting the same questions, and listening carefully for inconsistencies or omissions. In 2 out of 168 interviews, I found the stories changed in minor ways. In one other interview, I found that the interviewee withheld information that reflected poorly on him; he was attempting to convince me he was a victim and not a perpetrator.

I didn't use these three interviews.

In all other interviews, the stories remained consistent down to fine details, in dates, places, addresses, and names. Most of these details were verifiable on Google Maps satellite imagery, in leaked Chinese state documents and online tender documents the interviewees provided to me, in annual reports published online by Chinese corporations, and in my own observations and travels inside Xinjiang.

From December 2020 to February 2021, I worked with a rigorous fact-checker, Wen-yee Lee, a Taiwanese technology journalist and native Mandarin Chinese speaker, to double-check the material in this book. She reviewed interview recordings and transcripts, called the interviewees and double-checked their stories, listened to their stories an additional time for changes or omissions, and rigorously checked the original Mandarin Chinese sources cited and translated in English-language press reports and research. I further checked passages on the mechanics of artificial intelligence, facial recognition, semiconductors, DNA collection, and other technical fields with academic experts. These experts, some well known in their fields, vouched for the technological validity of what Uyghurs witnessed and told me about China's surveillance state. I take responsibility for any remaining errors.

Since China's surveillance state is growing in sophistication, I withheld or obscured some pieces of identifying information, such as the exact chronology, locations, ages, and the amount of time that transpired between events. When writing the story of the protagonist Maysem—the pseudonym is also the name of a historical Uyghur heroine—I removed identifying dates and places, and obscured the amount of time that passed between events during her imprisonment. This was the only way to protect my sources while remaining true to their stories. If I'd revealed too much, the intelligence services would have no problem tracking down whom I spoke with, along with their families and friends.

Uyghur names consist of the individual's name first and the family name second. Han Chinese names follow the reverse standard of family name first, individual's name second. Out of respect for the people who appear in this book, I've written their names in English as they prefer to write it themselves. Some prefer to write their Han Chinese names in English with the given name first and family name second (Kai-fu Lee), as opposed to the usual convention (Xi Jinping). When writing Han Chinese words and names in our alphabet, the pinyin system, the international standard for the romanization of Standard Chinese, is used throughout.

The Situation

In the region of Xinjiang in western China, people call their dystopia "the Situation."[1]

Since 2017, an estimated 1.8 million Uyghurs, Kazakhs, and people from other primarily Muslim minorities have been accused by the government of harboring "ideological viruses" and "terrorist thoughts," and taken away to hundreds of concentration camps. Many of the camps were repurposed high schools and other buildings, turned into detention centers for torture, brainwashing, and indoctrination. It is the largest internment of ethnic minorities since the Holocaust.

Even if you don't end up in a camp, daily life is hellish. If you're a woman, you might wake up every morning next to a stranger appointed by the government to replace your partner whom the police "disappeared" to a camp. Every morning before work, this minder will teach your family the state virtues of loyalty, ideological purity, and harmonious relations with the Communist Party. He'll check on your progress by asking you questions, ensuring you haven't been "infected" with what the government calls the "viruses of the mind" and the "three evils": terrorism, separatism, and extremism.

After your morning indoctrination, you may hear a knock on the door. The local neighborhood watch official, appointed by the state to keep an eye on a block of ten homes, will check your house for "irregularities," such as having more than three children or owning religious books. She may ask why you were late for work yesterday.

She'll probably say that "the neighbors reported you."

For the crime of forgetting to set the alarm, you must now report to the local police station for an interrogation, where you must explain the irregularity.

After her daily inspection, the neighborhood watch official scans a card against a device hoisted on your door. It indicates she has completed her survey.

Before work, if you drive to the gas station or the grocery store to grab something for dinner, at each place you go you scan your ID card at the entrance, in front of armed guards. After you scan it, a display next to the scanner shows the word "trustworthy," meaning the government has declared you a good citizen, and you'll be permitted entry.

A person who receives the notification "untrustworthy" is denied entry, and after a quick check of his statistical data records may face further problems. Maybe the facial recognition cameras caught him praying in a mosque. Or the cameras recorded him buying a six-pack of beer and the artificial intelligence (AI) suspects he has an alcohol problem. He may never know the reason. But everyone knows that any little hiccup can cause the state to lower your trustworthy ranking.

Police officers approach and question him. They double-check his identity on their smartphones with a program called the Integrated Joint Operations Platform, which consists of mass data the government has gathered on every citizen using millions of cameras, court records, and citizen spies, all of it processed by AI.

Under the "predictive policing program," the AI determines he will commit a crime in the future and recommends sending him to a camp. The police officers concur. They take him away in their police car. He may return at some point after a period of "reeducation," or he may never be seen again.

After standing in a segregated checkout line for minorities, you pay for your groceries. Government cameras and your WeChat messaging app monitor your purchases. You exit the grocery store and drive to work. On the way you pass a dozen police checkpoints, called "convenience police stations." Convenient for whom? At two checkpoints the police stop you, demand to see your identification documents, and ask where you're headed.

Satisfied, they whisk you through, but only because you're "trust-worthy."

At the office, your coworkers watch you constantly. Before the day starts, you all stand and sing the national anthem, then watch a short propaganda film on how to spot a terrorist. It explains that a terrorist "is likely to stop smoking and drinking, doing so suddenly." You want to laugh. But your colleagues might report such disrespectful behavior, hoping for a reward from the government or a stronger trust ranking. You stay quiet throughout the film.

At noon each day, if you're female, you're required to take a government-mandated birth control pill. Still, you are one of the lucky ones: the government frequently summons female coworkers to a local clinic for mandatory sterilization. The government says it wants to cut down on minority birth rates, claiming lower birth rates will lead to prosperity.

After work is finished, you drive home, pass another dozen police checkpoints, and then scan your ID card to pass through the gate at the entrance of your neighborhood, a ghetto surrounded by a fence or concrete wall, where no one can enter or leave without scanning their card. At home, your children tell you about the party virtues of patriotism and harmony they learned that day in school. You don't debate their lessons. The teacher told the students to report parents who didn't agree with them.

After eating dinner and watching the evening news, in front of a government camera installed in the corner of the living room, you lie down in bed with your government minder. Hopefully, you can fall asleep. You remember that he has the power to do whatever he wants here in bed, because he was sent by the state. If you resist his advances, he'll invent an allegation and report you, and you'll be sent to the camps.

Luckily, tonight you're okay. But your luck might not last. You fall asleep, then repeat your routine the next morning. This is a day in the life of a Uyghur, Kazakh, or other ethnic minority in Xinjiang.

[ ]

This book tells the story of how Xinjiang became the world's most sophisticated surveillance dystopia—how the Situation came to be and what it means for our future as we embrace unprecedented advances in AI, facial recognition, surveillance, and other technologies.

When, in September 2001, the Twin Towers fell in New York it was the most visible terrorist act the world had ever seen. More than sixty-eight hundred miles away, the Chinese government in Beijing saw this as an opportunity to elevate its authoritarian rule. One month later, China commenced its own war on terror, and its main focus was extremist groups consisting of Muslim Uyghurs from Xinjiang.

Xinjiang, however, enjoyed relative peace and prosperity from 2001 to 2009, as a result of oil wealth and a construction boom. But China didn't distribute the fruits of prosperity fairly among Xinjiang's minorities, who had a historical claim to this land, and settlers from the Han Chinese majority group, who had arrived from the east seeking riches and opportunity.

After nearly a decade of simmering resentment, Uyghur rioters took to the streets of Xinjiang's regional capital, Urumqi, in July 2009. The government responded by shutting down the internet and communication lines, and disappearing untold numbers of young Uyghur men. Some were executed, accused of fomenting a violent separatist plot.

From 2009 to 2014, thousands of Muslim Uyghur men, having encountered persecution, traveled to Afghanistan and Syria, training and fighting with groups connected to ISIS, hoping to one day return to China and wage a *jihad*, or "holy war," against it. These new terrorists launched a campaign of shoot-outs, assassinations, knife attacks, and an attempted airplane hijacking in China.

From 2014 to 2016, China escalated its counterterrorism tactics to unseen levels of brutality. It resorted to old-school, heavy-handed policing, and "community policing" efforts that in reality amounted to recruiting snitches in households, schools, and workplaces. But this was not enough, the government felt, to completely squash the terrorist threat.

In August 2016, a strongman named Chen Quanguo became the region's highest leader, taking on the role of Communist Party chief of Xinjiang. He deployed new technologies to surveil and control the population. Using mass data, he introduced a predictive policing program in which a suspect could be detained because the AI predicted he or she *would* commit a crime. He opened hundreds of concentration camps, officially called "detention centers," "vocational training centers," and "reeducation centers." By 2017, the number of people imprisoned within them swelled to 1.5 million, out of a Uyghur population of 11 million.

China's goal was to erase one people's identity, culture, and history and to achieve a total assimilation of millions of people.

"You can't uproot all the weeds hidden among the crops in the field one by one—you need to spray chemicals to kill them all," one official said in January 2018. "Reeducating these people is like spraying chemicals on the crops."[2]

And with that, China created the perfect police state.

CHAPTER 1

The New Dominion

Long Live the Great, Glorious and Correct
Communist Party of China!
—GOVERNMENT PROPAGANDA SLOGAN

"See a terrorist, strike a terrorist!" shouted the policeman.

Near an outdoor market three tall, burly counterterrorism officers dressed in black SWAT uniforms, sunglasses, and bullet-proof vests stood in front of a line of shop owners. The shop owners were rehearsing a drill, and each of them wielded a wooden baton. At a policeman's mark, an alarm bell sounded. They began the drill: strike hard, strike fast, and pin an imaginary terrorist on the ground.

"Love the Party, love the Country!" they shouted together.

I casually snapped a photo of the scene with my cell phone, and started to walk away. One of the police officers was wearing sunglasses with a built-in camera linked to China's Sky Net surveillance database; the camera was connected by a wire to a minicomputer in his pocket. He turned left and glanced at me. If I were a local resident, he could probably see my name and national ID number on his lenses within seconds.[1] Before I knew it, I was surrounded by police. I didn't know where they came from, or how long they had been watching me. But they didn't look happy.

A six-foot-four man in a regular police uniform, with an officer's cap and a white button-down shirt, grabbed my phone and demanded my passport.

"Come with us," he said.

It was a frigid December day, and I was posing as a backpacker in Kashgar. I had arrived the previous morning on a two-hour flight from Urumqi, disembarking at the small, ramshackle Kashgar Airport. My tourist visa allowed me to visit this little-known frontier, a predominantly Muslim region of desert oases and freezing mountains twice the size of Texas, in China's far west on the edges of Afghanistan and Pakistan.

During the previous decade, I had carved out a niche by documenting the rise of authoritarian governments worldwide, and the increasingly sophisticated ways they deployed new technologies to surveil, control, and even murder their people. I'd covered insurgencies, dictatorships, and a genocide throughout North Korea, China, Myanmar, and Russia. But when I was detained by the authorities in Kashgar, I realized I'd never seen a surveillance state so well honed and menacing as this one.

It's likely that I'd been watched from the moment I arrived. Fellow journalists had warned me that my hotel room would be bugged and any laptops or smartphones I left in my room would be scanned. With 170 million cameras nationwide,[2] some able to identify anyone from up to nine miles away,[3] and government devices called Wi-Fi sniffers gathering data on all smartphones and computers within their range,[4] the state probably knew a great deal about me the moment I stepped off the plane.

A "public security officer," the term China uses for police who have broad powers of search and seizure, inspected my passport.

"Japan? Cambodia? Egypt?" he asked suspiciously, looking at the stamps. "What do you do for a living?"

"Business consultant," I said. "Just visiting . . . backpacking."

I was nervous. I hadn't seen a single other Western "tourist" because it was the dead of winter. I also feared that the police might discover I was wearing a hidden voice recorder disguised as a wristwatch.

The officer called someone and then gave me a stern look.

"You must delete all the photos on this phone." I had purchased the phone a few days earlier in China, and had used it for the sole purpose of snapping photos of curious-looking buildings, propaganda signs, and the police.

He watched as I did so, then handed me back the phone and my passport.

"Welcome to China," he said. "Please do not take sensitive photos. Now, you can go back to your hotel."

[ ]

When I woke up in my hotel room the next morning, my mind was racing. It was December 10, 2017, and at eight o'clock it was still dark. Distant police sirens had been blaring all night. After only three days, I was exhausted. Before arriving I'd had no appreciation of the intensity of the government surveillance, monitoring, and paranoia I would experience. I felt like I was being watched constantly. But I couldn't put my finger on where or how.

I had come with the intention of discovering how China had built the most sophisticated surveillance apparatus humanity had ever seen. I thought I could get a glimpse of how artificial intelligence and China's vast camera surveillance network operated, maybe through the occasional comment from a local, or through run-ins with the police that I could then use for my reporting. Instead, I felt overwhelmingly that the state was reporting on me.

I descended in the elevator to the lobby of the Qinibagh Hotel, the former residence of the British consul general, which had recently been renovated. Facades made to appear like rugs and wall paintings, similar to what you'd find in Afghanistan or Iran, bedecked the grounds. The hotel felt more plastic than historic, as if the owner was trying to prove something, or worse, cover something up.

As I ate a Western buffet breakfast of scrambled eggs and sausage, the restaurant TV showed a news documentary about terrorism and chaos in the Middle East, playing spooky music that sounded like *The Twilight Zone* theme. Bombs were exploding, terrorists were shooting AK-47s in dusty desert villages, and Muslims were depicted at a mosque praying for the death of innocent people. Then the Twin Towers were shown falling.

"Love the Party, Love the Country," the news announcer concluded.

Because the Chinese government mandated that Kashgar run on the same time zone as the capital city of Beijing, despite Beijing being an almost seven-hour flight east, the mornings stayed dark until ten o'clock. I left the hotel in pitch black, passing through a gate guarded by an armed security guard. I began to explore the city, walking through alleyways and markets and a plaza, where police pillboxes sat on almost every street corner and even the children wore a look of suspicion.

"Passport!" said a Chinese police officer, approaching me on the street. He pointed to my beard. "Pakistani? Afghan? Muslim?"

I shook my head.

"American," I told him in Chinese.

He checked my passport and waved me through his checkpoint with a warning.

"Don't go too far."

[ ]

I have lived in Asia and then the Middle East since 2008, which has opened my eyes to a world Americans don't ordinarily see.

In the West—an area spanning the Atlantic Ocean that consists of North America and a sliver of northwest Europe—we live under an apparatus of organized nation-states with a shared language and a set of laws and customs that stand above our loyalties to ethnic groups, political factions, and religious leaders.

From my perch in Asia I had begun to see the world differently, as a region informed by centuries of trade, conquest, and the rapid transformation of ideas and faiths that created new kingdoms, and just as quickly swallowed them up.

I'm a small-time collector of antique maps, focusing less on Europe, East Asia, and North America and more on the landmass extending from China to the Mediterranean Sea. It too tells a story. What's called Eurasia is a stretch of oases, steppes, and mountains that is messy, conflict ridden, and difficult to govern. Just look at the Balkans, Syria, Turkey, Israel and Palestine, Libya, Ukraine,

Chechnya, Iraq, Iran, Afghanistan, and Pakistan. It's a region littered with crisscrossing ethnic and religious loyalties that both precede and supersede modern governments. Most violent conflicts in the world today are happening in Eurasia. It's also rich in oil, rare earths, and mineral wealth—and rife with dictatorships, inequality, and religious fundamentalism.

I became fascinated with the history of the Silk Road, the thread of trading routes winding from Europe to Asia, over which gold and precious metals flowed east to China and silk flowed west to Europe. It was first made famous to us in the West by the travels of Marco Polo in the thirteenth century. I read the accounts of European explorers who traveled through the harsh and unforgiving Taklamakan Desert, one of the world's largest, just beyond Kashgar, the city that is the heartland of the Uyghurs.

"Quite suddenly the sky grows dark," wrote the German archaeologist Albert von Le Coq in 1928.

> The sun becomes a dark-red ball of fire seen through the fast-thickening veil of dust, a muffled howl is followed by a piercing whistle, and a moment after, the storm bursts with appalling violence upon the caravan. Enormous masses of sand, mixed with pebbles, are forcibly lifted up, whirled round, and dashed down on man and beast; the darkness increases and strange clashing noises mingle with the roar and howl of the storm . . . The whole happening is like hell let loose. . . .
>
> Any traveler overwhelmed by such a storm must, in spite of the heat, envelop himself entirely in felts to escape injury from the stones dashing around with such mad force. Men and horses must lie down and endure the rage of the hurricane, which often lasts for hours.[5]

The deadly sandstorms were called "black hurricanes," and because of them the Taklamakan could be lethal. The British consul general at Kashgar called the desert "a Land of Death." Sven Hedin, the Swedish explorer, called it "the worst and most dangerous desert in the world." The British correspondent Peter Hopkirk wrote that in the local Turkic language the word "Taklamakan" meant "go in and you won't come out."[6]

Looking at a map of China's western frontier, the desert looks like a football that stretches about six hundred miles east to west. Six oasis towns surround it, historically called the *Altishahr*, with Kashgar on the western side.[7] For centuries, explorers and traders like Marco Polo would rest in the city after an arduous trek through the mountains of what are today Iran and Afghanistan, before heading farther into dangerous terrain.[8]

When I was growing up in Chicago, Illinois, I knew Eurasia only as Iraq and Afghanistan, nations made relevant after the attacks of 9/11. I scarcely thought about Azerbaijan or Uzbekistan or Tajikistan. They were backwaters, a muddy mess of post-Soviet nations that happened to be Muslim, but were peripheral. But the longer I stayed in Asia, the more I learned that my Western-centric perspective was deeply flawed.

The story of the world was not what I read in the *New York Times* about the spread of democracy and the people's embrace of the free market, a reprieve from an ideological cold war that ended when I was a toddler. Across Eurasia, I watched as democracies failed, oil-baron oligarchs seized power, and religious and tribal leaders escalated warfare.

As I read more and more history, anthropology, and global news coverage, it began to hit home that the Midwest of the United States, where I'd grown up, was only a few hundred years old, whereas Kashgar, the relatively small city where I woke up that cold December morning, had for centuries been a Silk Road cultural and trading gateway, once a cosmopolitan resting point for travelers of the world.

[ ]

In the years after 9/11, I watched as China, whose culture had long fascinated me, began to reach westward through the region called Xinjiang. Since 2013, China had been building a $1 trillion network of roads, ports, oil pipelines, and railroads. It's called the "One Belt, One Road" initiative.[9]

China wants to move away from its overexploited coast, trying to establish global trading routes that could become an alternative to crossing the Pacific Ocean. It wants to convince companies— like Foxconn, the manufacturer of Apple's iPhone that makes devices on the southeast coast in Shenzhen, near Hong Kong—to move their manufacturing inland. The companies would then use land routes, which are becoming cheaper, to reach export markets in the European Union and Middle East. But there is a grander idea as well. China's revival of the historic Silk Road has the potential to reshape the world order.

Xinjiang means "New Dominion," and it was the starting point for the new road and pipeline networks. It quickly became China's most sensitive border, where the One Belt, One Road project would first be exposed to foreign inspection; it was where the world would first encounter China. But there was a problem: Xinjiang needed to be pacified.

From 2011 to 2014, Uyghur terrorists escalated their attacks on civilians in Xinjiang and across China. They launched two car attacks that included a bomb in Tiananmen Square;[10] stabbed and slashed commuters with knives during an assault at a train station in Kunming in southern China;[11] assassinated a prominent *imam* (a Muslim religious leader) in Kashgar;[12] and attempted but failed to hijack an airplane flying between two cities in Xinjiang—the passengers, crew, and plainclothes police overpowered the six hijackers and beat two of them to death.[13]

The attacks were the work of a radical fringe contingent of Uyghur terrorists who had trained in Afghanistan and Syria. The Turkestan Islamic Party, as they were called, announced their goal was to form a "caliphate"—an Islamic nation ruled by a religious leader who would be the successor to the prophet Mohammed— across Xinjiang and Central Asia.[14] The Chinese government seized on the attacks and turned them into an opportunity to unite the nation against a common enemy.

"All ethnic groups nationwide should cherish ethnic unity and work together to thwart the political intentions of the three forces of separatism, extremism and terrorism," Xinhua, China's state-run media and a government voice, wrote in a commentary in August 2014.[15] It was a declaration of intent.

In 2013 and 2014, China began intensifying an apartheid relationship to Xinjiang that it had been building since the end of the Cold War, openly admitting its ethnic underpinnings. The Uyghurs were a Turkic ethnic group, tracing a shared heritage with the peoples who had founded Kazakhstan, Kyrgyzstan, Azerbaijan, and three other nations. From the sixth to eleventh centuries, they had descended into Eurasia from the steppes of Siberia and Central Asia. Then, in 1453, they conquered the capital of the Eastern Roman Empire, Constantinople (today Istanbul), establishing the Ottoman Empire, which lasted 450 years until its defeat in World War I.[16]

Despite the shared heritage, the Uyghurs occupied a very distant frontier from the center of the Ottoman Empire. Various Turkic and Chinese Muslim leaders ruled independent city-states, or swore fealty to Mongol, Manchu, and Han Chinese dynasties, as distant subjects. By the mid–eighteenth century, China's Qing dynasty, created by the Manchus in a power struggle against a Mongol group that had dominated the region, had taken over what is today Xinjiang.

But Xinjiang, early on, was hardly targeted and oppressed. "The [Qing] Manchus prohibited Chinese settlement in densely Uyghur areas for fear of destabilizing them, and did not interfere with Uyghur religion, food, or dress," wrote James Millward, history professor at Georgetown University. "This culturally pluralist imperialism worked well, and despite a series of minor incursions from Central Asia into southwest Xinjiang, from the mid-18th to the mid-19th century the region was on the whole peaceful— enough so that the Uyghur population increased fivefold and the economy expanded."[17]

But the Qing dynasty fell apart in 1912, sparking thirty-eight years of nationwide rebellions and strife between military leaders and foreign-backed factions—and also a movement to reform and modernize schools and society in Xinjiang—until China was united under communism in 1949.[18] Then, the Uyghurs and other

Turkic ethnic groups became second-class citizens, relegated to a system of segregation, given short shrift when they applied for jobs, opened bank accounts, or bought new cars and homes.

Pledging an end to ethnic strife and separatism, China's leaders unveiled, over the next six years after the terrorist attacks intensified in 2013 and 2014, a vast social experiment in suppression, control, and brainwashing intended to secure total loyalty to the state. The Chinese government transformed the region into a testing laboratory for the most cutting-edge surveillance technologies of a dystopian future.

"There could be an alliance between authoritarian states and these large, data-rich IT monopolies that would bring together nascent systems of corporate surveillance with an already developed system of state-sponsored surveillance," the financier George Soros declared at the World Economic Forum in January 2018. "This may well result in a web of totalitarian control the likes of which not even Aldous Huxley or George Orwell could have imagined." He predicted that China would be among the first countries to adopt an "unholy marriage" between an authoritarian government and technology companies.[19]

In August 2017, when I began planning my trip, several foreign correspondent colleagues and diplomats who had been visiting Xinjiang warned me off.

"Wait till you get to Kashgar," a journalist in Beijing told me. "It's apocalyptic."

On August 24, 2017, just as I was preparing to board my flight from Chiang Mai, Thailand, where I was on a quick vacation, I received alarming text messages from journalists and human rights investigators.

The Cambodian government, a Chinese ally, had somehow learned about my work in western China and spun it into a conspiracy. I'm not sure how the Cambodian government knew about my proposed trip to Xinjiang. I suspect they somehow got access to my flight data from a Chinese airline, or monitored my social media posts. But I had only written one post on Facebook about the deteriorating political situation in Xinjiang, low-key enough to avoid the attention of a government or intelligence agency. Or so I thought.

"Geoffrey Cain left Cambodia on August 18 to Xinjiang province, China, the region where the Uyghur ethnic group is rebelling against Beijing's government," the article on the popular website Fresh News, which is connected to the government and cited on all of Cambodia's prime-time evening news shows and big newspapers, claimed. It accused me of fomenting unrest all over Asia—in South Korea, Cambodia, and another country it didn't name, as a spy employed by an unnamed "superpower country."[20]

The accusations, of course, were ludicrous. I hadn't even been to Xinjiang yet. But an Australian filmmaker had already been arrested in Cambodia on similar espionage charges, and was set to face trial.[21]

So I didn't go to Xinjiang. Instead, I stayed in Thailand, then retreated to Washington, DC, hoping that my one-man superpower spy scandal would blow over.

It didn't. Nine days later, Cambodia's opposition leader was arrested, accused of working with a so-called spy ring that included me.[22]

Cambodia's prime minister ordered the government to "investigate the presence of all people of American nationality suspected of conducting espionage." Then his military commanders declared their goal was "the elimination of all foreigners whose intent is to commit aggression against Cambodia" and that they'd "smash each and every person."[23]

I waited four more months for the paranoia to blow over, in which time I grew restless. I was curious to see the surveillance dystopia of the future, after covering authoritarian governments elsewhere. I stopped in Beijing for a few days, to debrief with people familiar with Xinjiang, and had dinner with an American diplomat.

"Where are you going next?" she asked me.

"Xinjiang," I said. "For a project."

"Don't go there!" she shrieked. "They'll follow and detain you. You're not going to be safe!"

CHAPTER **2**

The Panopticon

The Panopticon is a marvelous machine which,
whatever use one may wish to put it to, produces
homogenous effects on power.

—MICHEL FOUCAULT,
  Discipline and Punish: The Birth of the Prison

I flew to Kashgar the next day, where I met my guide, Mansur.
(I've changed his name for his protection.) Mansur was a warm
and well-informed character whose wife had been summoned to
hours-long patriotic classes almost every day for no clear reason
at all. He wanted to tell his story to the outside world. He told me
she had been attending the classes, where she studied and recited
government propaganda, for "a few months."

"Let me tell you about the Situation," he said.

On our first of four days together, we left Kashgar on a day trip
through the snowy, sandstone landscape of the countryside, away
from cameras and informants.

"Being a guide, that's my connection to the outside world," he
explained. "That's the only way I don't go crazy. That's how I don't
lose my mind.

"They call [the surveillance system] Sky Net." It sounded ominous, not least because that's the name of the AI controlling the
world in the dystopian future of the *Terminator* movies.

Then he began to tell me the three steps of creating the perfect police state. Mansur, who held a degree in business and was
well informed about current events, talked about these steps for

three hours of our six-hour trek up a mountain, when no one was around, and so I've condensed and often paraphrased his observations.

Step one, he said, is to identify an enemy—minorities, immigrants, Jews, or in this case Muslims—and blame them for your problems. Convince your people that these enemies are everywhere, "that they're a threat to national strength and honor."

Step two is to get control of technology to monitor your enemies. At first, technology executives will look the other way if profits are strong and collaborate if profits are weak, because they need government support.

It helps to deploy cameras and social media that can gather data on your enemies: their facial features, DNA, voice recordings, what they do on the web. "Spread fake news about your enemies on the social media [sic] and apps." The goal is to create a mood of hysteria, accusation, and paranoia.

Step two, he explained, comes with a twist. New technologies in AI and facial recognition will almost always have imperfections. Maybe new software or devices aren't as efficient or smart as you think, unable to track down criminal suspects that easily. But you can turn these technological weaknesses into strengths.

"How can you do that?" I asked.

Conceal and obfuscate the details of how your technology works. Use optimistic "newspeak" that makes your tools impenetrable to the common person.

"It's not just about making your people scared," Mansur said. "Making your people uncertain is a good way to keep them under control."

Step three is a tricky one for any government, he said. He went on to explain the idea of exploiting the post-truth paranoia you created with tech tools. With cameras, artificial intelligence, and facial and voice scanners, "you can turn your country into a panopticon."

"What's a panopticon?" I asked.

A panopticon is a prison set up in a circular format, in which a guard can see everything from a sentry post in the middle, but none of the prisoners can see the guard, Mansur replied. The panopticon is an effective tool for controlling people, since everyone thinks they are being watched but nobody knows when or where. They were pioneered by eighteenth-century British philosopher Jeremy Bentham, the man who influenced George Orwell.

"And how does this play out now," I asked, "out here in Xinjiang?"

"You've seen it already. Cameras everywhere, hacking smartphones and computers, forcing everyone to scan ID cards when they enter markets and schools, recruiting family and friends to snitch on each other. Also giving everyone a 'social ranking' for trustworthiness."

Then, he explained, "enforce your rules at random." Take your enemies away to concentration camps, even for minor infractions like having dinner with someone with a low social ranking.

"Society quickly breaks down," he went on. Blocked from facts and truth, and constantly under surveillance, most people cannot discern between enemy and friend, and don't have the information they need to challenge the government. Friends betray each other, bosses snitch on employees, teachers expose their students, and children turn on their parents. Everyone must turn to their government for protection.

Technology used this way, I realized, is no longer a liberator of our better angels. It's a prison for our darkest impulses. And, in China, people who control the technology also control the nation.

[ ]

Two days later, I was detained for taking photographs. I decided it was time to leave. My next step was Cairo, Egypt, where a Uyghur contact told me exiled Uyghurs were being hunted down and deported back to China.

As I boarded a flight for Cairo, I loaded up a list on my computer that a contact in China had sent me: "75 Behavioral Indicators of Religious Extremism." He told me police in Xinjiang were handing out the list, advising citizens to be suspicious of certain behaviors that might indicate people were terrorists. Following are some of the warning signs:

> [People who] "store large amounts of food in their homes."
> "Those who smoke and drink but quit, doing so suddenly."
> "Those who buy or store equipment such as dumbbells . . .
> boxing gloves, as well as maps, compasses, telescopes, ropes, and tents without obvious reasons."[1]

Landing in Cairo, I grabbed a taxi to a small hotel off Tahrir Square, the city center, passing by Islamic minarets and spice sellers jostling for position in the sweaty crowds.

"I found some people who want to meet you in Cairo," my Uyghur contact in Washington, DC, emailed me after I settled in.

I agreed to meet "Asman" and "Osman" in a rented study room at a kids' after-school academy, where I pretended to be teaching them English. This was the security cover we'd agree on, since the Egyptian police had been looking for them.

For six months, these two men and their families had been effectively stateless and on the run, staying in a new home each week. When Asman walked over to the window to let the smoke from his cigarette drift into the open air, his hands were trembling.

"They sold us out!" he exclaimed. "They're bowing to foreign power! We thought we'd be safe here, but we aren't safe anywhere!"

It had all started in September 2016, he said, when Egypt and China began signing a series of agreements in which China eventually promised $11.2 billion to help fund a new government capital, an electric railway, a satellite launch, and other infrastructure investments embraced by the One Belt, One Road project.[2] As part of these deals the two countries committed to exchange information on "extremist organizations."[3]

"That meant China had the right to demand information about all of us Xinjiang exiles from the Egyptian police surveillance," Osman confirmed.

On July 3, 2017, thirteen days after Egyptian and Chinese security officials agreed to exchange information, Egyptian police began raiding dorms, restaurants, and homes. They hauled away Uyghur students and residents and deported them back to China, even if they were legal residents of Egypt.[4]

"We knew this was not good," Asman said. "Our clock was ticking and they were coming for us."

In July 2017, the doorman called his apartment.

"I looked out the window and saw the Egyptian police . . . waiting outside," he told me. "So I ordered everyone, all my houseguests and my family, to go to the roof and stay quiet."

After searching through his room, the police left, but Asman knew they would return.

Osman told me he was planning an escape from Egypt but wasn't sure if he and his family would make it out, or even survive, if they were forced to return to China. In 2017, the news service Al Jazeera reported that 90 percent of the seven to eight thousand Uyghurs in Egypt had returned to China.[5]

"All this shows the power of China," Asman said ruefully. "It shows how willing governments are to do what China wants, once China gives money. It's truly terrifying."

[ ]

I spent most of 2018 in Washington, DC,[6] where I interviewed more than a hundred Uyghur refugees, among them Tahir Hamut, one of the foremost modern poets writing in Uyghur. Since the late 1990s, he'd also worked as a film director with his own film production company, making features and documentaries. His biggest hits were Uyghur pop music videos and documentaries on Uyghur culture and history. Because Hamut's movies explored Uyghur traditions, the Chinese government later censored them. In August 2017, Hamut resettled in a Virginia suburb of Washington, DC, with his wife and two daughters.

"We almost didn't make it out [of Xinjiang]," he said. "The disappearances were happening more and more. If we didn't get out then [in August 2017], I don't want to think about what would happen. Technology is supposed to serve the benefit of humankind, but some countries want to monitor, oppress, and punish people. ... This is one of the greatest tragedies of our time."

Every Uyghur I interviewed from 2017 to 2020 had at least two family members and three friends who had disappeared, hauled away, probably to a camp. They often couldn't say for certain what had happened to them, but about one-third reported that their entire families were gone, and they were the only ones who had escaped.

[ ]

In 2017, China had begun building a network of at least 260 concentration camps,[7] so-called vocational education and training centers,[8] throughout Xinjiang, and also repurposing high schools, gymnasiums, and government buildings as camps. The government claimed people went to these centers voluntarily[9] and that they could leave of their own accord. While in the camps the "visitors" learned job skills, like making footwear and clothes and speaking the Chinese language, in addition to taking "de-extremization" courses that taught them not to be terrorists.[10]

The real purpose of the camps, however, was far more sinister. China treated the camps as functioning outside the criminal justice system. No one detained there was charged with a crime. Of all the police tactics and technologies deployed in Xinjiang, what went on in the camps was the most chilling—the endgame of escalating government paranoia and control over the lives of every citizen. It wasn't enough for the government to monitor and surveil its people. It wanted to reach further still: to purge their thoughts, to "treat and cleanse the virus from their brain and restore their normal mind."[11] Medical language like this recurred in government speeches, state media reports, and leaked documents.

"Round up everyone who should be rounded up," declared Chen Quanguo, Communist Party chief of Xinjiang, in internal government documents. In February 2017, in a speech made in a town square in Urumqi, he told thousands of police officers and military troops standing in formation to prepare for a "smashing, obliterating offensive."[12]

In late 2016 and 2017, the early days of the reeducation programs, Uyghurs, Kazakhs, and other primarily Muslim ethnic minorities in Xinjiang were asked to report to police stations. Or they were visited in the night and hauled away by police officers, who put a cloth over their head and drove them to a camp in the back seat of a police car. Dozens of former detainees told me the police promised them they'd be held for ten days, or at most a few weeks, while they attended reeducation classes. Once they "graduated," they'd be released.[13]

Instead, all of them said they were required to stay for months that often extended to years, accused of harboring extremist and terrorist thoughts. Detainees were shuffled around between camps, seemingly at random. Their eventual release came because of the extreme overcrowding. Before they were allowed to leave, however, guards pressured them into signing a document stating they promised not to tell anyone about what had happened to them in Xinjiang.[14]

In 2017, Xinjiang accounted for 21 percent of all arrests in China, despite making up only 2 percent of the population. Arrests were running at eight times the level of a year before.[15] Some party officials had doubts about the effectiveness and the ethics of the sweeping campaign. One county official secretly released thousands of detainees and was imprisoned, according to leaked government documents. China's government responded with purges and the firing of officials it thought stood in the way.[16]

As prison numbers swelled, the Chinese government began building new camps with even stricter security measures and more imposing architecture, including guard towers, heavy concrete walls, and giant iron doors at the entrance, usually patrolled by police with well-trained attack dogs. The camps were completed in six months, as opposed to the many years needed to build prisons. Some camps ran their own factories where inmates were forced to toil on garments and shoes, infecting the global supply chain with slave labor. Most were big enough to hold ten thousand prisoners each, according to a BuzzFeed investigation.[17]

By October 2018, I was back in Istanbul to pursue the story. Turkey was home to tens of thousands of Uyghur and Kazakh refugees from China, as both the Uyghurs and Kazakhs were Turkic ethnic groups. The president of Turkey, Recep Erdogan, welcomed them and would later become one of the few Muslim leaders to condemn China's treatment of the Uyghurs.

Tahir Hamut introduced me to Abduweli Ayup, "Teacher Abduweli," as his disciples and acquaintances called him. A strong-willed and hot-tempered linguist and writer, Abduweli had studied at the University of Kansas, and through his blog, captivated Uyghurs with stories of life in the West. Because of his American education and contacts, and the kindergarten he ran in Xinjiang that taught the Uyghur language, the Chinese government deemed him a danger after he returned to China in June 2011, and just over two years later, detained him for a year and three months.[18]

"China tortured me. They sleep-deprived me. They wanted me to renounce it all," he told me. "It wasn't an old-style genocide with the intent of killing an entire group. They were more sophisticated. They wanted to erase my thoughts, my identity, everything—who I was and everything I had written. History and culture are where our memories lie. Erase the memory, the being, the spirit, and you can erase a people."

Abduweli managed to get out of China after he was released from the detention center, and became a refugee in Turkey in August 2015. He was remarkably well connected. An influential literary figure within the Uyghur community, he published his subversive writings online and got all kinds of accolades from his peers. After we met in Istanbul, he took me to Ankara, the capital, where he introduced me to a young Uyghur woman, Maysem, then in her late twenties.

"You need to meet her," Abduweli told me on the train. "She hasn't come out in public yet. Her story is incredible."

One evening in October 2018, we gathered for tea in her sparse, large apartment on the outskirts of the city, barely decorated because she had recently moved in. Maysem was completing her master's degree in the social sciences[19] and preparing to apply for a PhD in the United States. She had a pale complexion and long brown hair, and a delicate way of speaking and handling herself as she prepared tea. But her small and slender frame didn't fool Abduweli and me. We sensed a tough, strong personality from her way of speaking. As she moved between small talk about her favorite teas and life in Ankara, she dropped in literary references and bold statements about the state of the world.

"People say a woman shouldn't be educated," she said. "I say education for women will change the world." She dashed around from the kitchen to the living room, preparing food one moment and pulling out books from her library the next.

In Xinjiang, the Chinese government was targeting fellow Uyghurs, hiring them as agents and informants, and having them call exiles to pressure them into betraying friends and neighbors they knew overseas. Dozens of Uyghurs in Turkey told me that on these calls Uyghur agents would send them photos and videos of family members held in Chinese detention centers. The agents promised the exiles they would be allowed to talk with their long-lost siblings, parents, and children back home, and would ensure their families' well-being—if they sent information on the whereabouts and activities of other Uyghur exiles in their neighborhoods.[20]

Maysem wasn't sure at first whether to tell me her story. She was ashamed that she had left her family behind. Many of them were missing, almost certainly in concentration camps.

"My burden is heavy. My family is gone and I am a pawn in a new world order," she said. "But I will tell you how we got here."

CHAPTER **3**

Sky Net Has Found You

Show absolutely no mercy.

—XI JINPING

"In Xinjiang when I was growing up," Maysem began, "the party cared for everyone, and everyone had their path set from a young age. Men usually became police officers and women became schoolteachers."[1]

Maysem was a rare exception. She was born into a respected family, graduated at the top of her class in secondary school, then gained entrance to an elite Chinese university and was on track for a job in the diplomatic corps, unusual accomplishments for a young woman from an ethnic minority.

The change in the way the state treated its citizens in Xinjiang was so gradual that at first Maysem didn't notice what was happening around her. Like tiny cracks in an eggshell, it came in increments. It started in July 2009 when, after ethnic riots against the government in Urumqi, the police began rounding up young men suspected of whipping up unrest.[2]

From 2009 until 2014, disaffected men traveled to Afghanistan and Syria to learn the ways of jihad.[3] Some hoped to return to China. Others wanted to settle under ISIS permanently, believing they would find community and belonging. The Chinese government responded to terrorist attacks with brute force, arresting and executing the suspects.[4]

Then, from 2014 onward, the government extended its authoritarian hand to the population at large, unable to distinguish who was a terrorist and who was an innocent bystander. First, in August 2014, public displays of religion, including beards for men and veils for women, were banned on public busses during a sporting event.[5] Soon, these bans were extended to beards and veils in any public places.[6] That summer, Maysem had to show her ID card to enter the shopping mall and the gas station, where guards surrounded the gas station as she pumped her car with gas. That year she heard announcements from the government that it was going to create a "Safe City" in her hometown of Kashgar.[7]

Then surveillance cameras started to appear in larger numbers. More and more, until there were thousands, everywhere you looked.

"The police told us they were doing these things to fight crime and stop terrorism and keep an eye on foreigners and Muslims who could have extremist views," she said. "Too many people agreed at first. Too many people went along with it."

By 2016, Maysem was a graduate student, kicking back at her family home during her summer vacation, one year away from completing her master's degree in the social sciences in Ankara. One day in June 2016, she was summoned to the local police office in Kashgar. After checking her identification papers, the guards held up a smartphone that scanned her face and confirmed her identity. Then there were mandatory medical checks. An officer took her DNA by swabbing her mouth, then drew her blood and checked it in the government database. Then her voice was identified by recognition software. Sky Net had found her. And Sky Net knew her.

"Name: Maysem _____" flashed the guard's computer screen, which Maysem saw.

"Social ranking: Untrustworthy."

Because of her time overseas, the police ordered her to take weekly propaganda classes in civics and government. After that she intended to return to Ankara, complete her master's degree, join the diplomatic service, and make her family proud.

But one day, a local neighborhood watch official, appointed by the Chinese government, knocked on Maysem's apartment door, handing her papers directing her to report to the nearby police office once again. When she checked in at the front desk, three

Chinese men in suits approached and hustled her into the back seat of a black four-by-four SUV. They went off together for an hour-long drive. When they reached their destination, the guards there told her it was a "reeducation center" where she would begin more intensive daily civics classes. The classes would begin at 8 A.M. and she could go home at 6 P.M.

But within minutes she was relocated to a second, higher-security compound that the guard called a "detention center," which she would not be allowed to leave. She was escorted to the courtyard of a building that looked like a remodeled home, with a sign posted in front:

"Love President Xi Jinping."

"You will go inside," the guard told her. They shut the doors behind her and Maysem found herself standing alone at the beginning of a long cement hallway. Cameras were pointed at her every few dozen yards.

"The walls were covered in paintings with propaganda slogans," Maysem said. "On one side of the wall, a painting showed Muslim women wearing veils, who seemed sad and repressed. And on the other side of the wall, they had women in high heels and modern clothing, enjoying the city life. On one side, they showed crying children being taught by a Muslim Uyghur teacher. On the other side, they showed happy children being taught by a Han Chinese teacher."

Maysem was escorted to a courtyard and told to wait. She stood there, numb and bewildered. Ten guards surrounded her.

"Do you know why you're here?"

"It's a mistake," she said. "I shouldn't be here. I've done nothing wrong. I come from a good family."

"Let's show this bitch who's boss," one of the guards shouted.

Two of the men pushed her on the ground, pulled off her shoes, and dragged her by her feet outside and into a smaller courtyard where there were several other angry- and unhappy-looking men and women, clearly also there against their will.

"Slut!" the guards shouted. "Bitch!" "Whore!"

Maysem thrashed her arms and legs, struggling to escape. After a few minutes, the guards backed away, laughing.

By then it was around noon. A boiling August sun stood high in the sky. The guards picked Maysem up and dragged her to an iron chair fitted with cuffs and restraints. They secured the cuffs around her arms and legs.

"The discomfort was extreme," she told me. "It was the tiger chair. We'd all heard of it. That's how they made an example of you, torturing you by contorting your body."

The other prisoners watched.

"But they were like patients who'd recovered from the head trauma of a car crash and lost their personalities," she said. "They didn't seem able to think, ask questions, show emotion, or speak. They just watched me with an empty stare, and then they were herded away back into the building."

The guards left Maysem in the sun for eight hours, until her skin reddened and burned.

"As I was sitting there in the heat of the day, I imagined waking up from this nightmare and being home with my mother. I felt the hugs, the kissing of both cheeks, the stories of life and adventure and travel overseas, and the never-ending conversations about the latest books I was reading."

The pain from her scalded skin jolted her back to reality. And for the following hours, Maysem swung back and forth between unconsciousness and fever dreams of her life at home.

How did I get here? she kept asking herself.

[ ]

For the past two decades, Maysem's world in Xinjiang had been on a slow descent, culminating in a sudden collapse into despair and distrust. Her homeland had once been a place she remembered fondly. She never imagined she would end up in something as terrifying as a concentration camp.

During the 1990s, Maysem enjoyed a quiet, fairly rural upbringing with her parents.

"My life at home was close to nature," she recalled. "We woke up early and had simple corn soups and fruits for breakfast. No television, not in the morning. I liked books anyway."

She would walk out to her family's little allotment just outside Kashgar and pick fruits and vegetables. No adult in the family was allowed to sleep during the day; that would be a sign of laziness.

"Every Friday, we made a donation to the poor. We brought boxes of food, money, and clothes to poor women from around the city. My mom didn't want them to feel like they were only taking money, though. She would call them and ask for little favors, like helping around the house or driving the kids to school, and gave them small salaries for their help.

"Friday is important for Muslims, a day for doing something good," she said. "Many other families did this too."

During her calm childhood, Maysem's creativity and imagination flourished.

As a seven-year-old, she was driven by her family along dusty riverbeds to a desolate shrine in the desert. She peered out the car window at the vast expanse around her.

"I was scared of the Taklamakan Desert," Maysem recalled.

She was taken aback by what seemed like a haunted, wretched sight: "the skull of an animal, and so many white flags" bound together with bundles of sticks or placed on top of bricks.

These were tombs where a saint might lie, or sometimes a memorial to a historical figure who had become a character in Uyghur myths or epics. When people visited one of these shrines during a festival, the shrine's guardian, a storyteller versed in poetry, would stand before the crowds, reciting stories of the people who rested there, or telling tales of legendary kings and heroes and spirits.[8]

"My homeland was a magical place," Maysem said. "We listened to traveling storytellers recite their epics outside the bazaars. Heroes, gods, adventurers, conquerors, battles, quests. The audience swayed and shouted with the movements of the poetry. We believed in spirits in the trees and the mountains, and demons and genies in the desert. We heard stories of lost civilizations, ancient treasure, roving caravans, and the sandstorms that killed them off. We embraced the beauty of being at the center of the world, the crossroads of empires."

At that age, Maysem would wander with her parents into the bazaars of Kashgar, with their alleyways of carpet sellers, vegetable markets, and kebab spinners. They'd merge into the crowds on the main thoroughfares, standing around a roving poet telling a story. Her parents would throw the storyteller a few coins and join the audience. These tellers of myths passed along orally through the generations, drawn from written stories called the *Tazkirah*, would ask their audience to join them in the storytelling. She was enthralled as the listeners wept, shrieked, cheered, and cajoled their favorite fictional protagonists.

> They will strike off this guiltless head of mine,
> And lay my diadem in my heart's blood.
> For me no bier, shroud, grave, or weeping people,
> But like a stranger I shall lie in dust,
> A trunk beheaded by the scimitar.
> —*Siyavush*, the story of a Persian hero[9]

When Maysem went to school she was in a different world altogether. Every Monday morning to begin the week and Friday afternoon to end the week, the class stood before the national flag and sang the Chinese national anthem, the "March of the Volunteers."

> Arise, ye who refuse to be slaves!
> Let us amount our flesh and blood towards our new Great Wall!
> The Chinese nation faces its greatest peril,
> The thundering roar of our peoples will be heard![10]

"The song became a part of my childhood," said Maysem.

When she wasn't studying literature or math, she read comic books handed out by her teachers, which showed Americans as beer-bellied, blond-haired men with giant protruding noses, wearing soldiers' uniforms. "They pointed their military rifles at poor women and children and basically terrorized everyone."

Maysem and her friends passed the books around and giggled.

"From a young age, I didn't really see myself as Uyghur. For me, communism and China and being Uyghur were all one. I was so proud."

On weekends, Maysem would visit her maternal grandfather at his country home. A retired local community party chief, he would sit in his living room, his head buried in book after book, until he'd look up to talk about the news of the day.

"He must have had more than a thousand books," Maysem recalled. "Some of them were very old. Practically antiques."

Maysem could make out the shimmer of the opulent old Persian and Arabic script.

"I'd steal the books for myself and read them. One day I'd read about history. The next day I'd be reading about the science of earthquakes. I'd get lost in them."

The love of reading was inherited from her mother's side of the family.

Her mother, she said, was an elegant, quick-witted woman who wore stunning opulent dresses, and knew exactly what to say at the right moment, drawing on an encyclopedia of personal knowledge gleaned through her love of literature.

"Mom wanted me to study and succeed," Maysem said. "She was [just] a schoolteacher, and she didn't even have a university degree."

After the others had left the table, her mother would stay behind, reading newspapers, magazines, and books, sometimes out loud.

"Did you hear about the new party chief?" she'd ask no one in particular.

"George Bush is visiting China," she remarked on another occasion.

But book learning had not proved to be a gateway to freedom for Maysem's mother. She had shared with her daughter the painful story of her marriage, showing her faded photographs of herself as an ornate stylish bride, dressed "like a true lady."

The day of the wedding, her mother had waited alone at the altar for her groom. Hours passed and he didn't arrive. Night fell.

"Your father showed up the next day at my house. I figured out he had another woman. She was a beautiful dancer in our town."

Maysem was shocked, but remained quiet as her mother went on to explain why despite her humiliation she had gone ahead with the marriage.

"Your grandfather basically forced me to marry that man, even though he wasn't honest or smart, because he was a Communist Party cadre."

"I was in the Cultural Revolution," he'd tell Maysem's mother repeatedly, referring to the decade of political mayhem from 1966 to 1976, when communist youth leagues roamed the country, purging and executing the educated, the affluent, and anyone they considered opposed to communism and class struggle. Somewhere between 1.5 and 2 million people are thought to have died, though no official count has ever been released.[11]

And as a devout communist himself, Maysem's father and mobs of his fellow students had denounced and beaten up elementary-school teachers. His party loyalty earned him admiration and credits, and he was promoted through the bureaucratic ranks to become the head of a local administrative office.

"What then," he asked Maysem, "is the point of education? Be a simple girl. You're going to finish school and then you'll become a schoolteacher."

Maysem saw the irony: her dad had led student mobs against their teachers yet wanted her to become a teacher now. "In Xinjiang, you didn't need a college education to become a teacher," she told me. "Our society saw it as a job for good girls and good women who finished high school and got married. That's how my dad thought about it."

Maysem's parents argued over her future. Changes were afoot for young people of the millennial generation in the 1990s and 2000s. Her mother began to sit beside her every evening, guiding her through essay writing and homework, recommending new poems and books.

"She taught me how to study, to do well and succeed at school."

Her father's view was exactly the opposite.

"Books are dangerous," he said. "Reading will only get you in trouble." But he stayed out of the way because he frequently went on work trips, and wasn't at home to see what Maysem was reading.

Maysem's family had prospered by building political connections.

"My mom's side of the family was actually influenced by the Soviet Union. Her parents spoke fluent Russian." In the 1930s and early 1940s, the Soviet Union supported Uyghur and Chinese Muslim military commanders in Xinjiang with money and weapons. The commanders and warlords were fighting China in a campaign to break away and create an independent Uyghur nation, one the Soviet Union hoped would become a communist satellite in its geopolitical struggle with China.[12]

China didn't have a communist government then—Mao Zedong's communist troops would seize control of the country in 1949—and nationalist leaders and communist ideologues were embroiled in a civil war.[13]

"When the Soviets came here, my grandparents [on my mom's side] were so influenced by them. They became the first cadres, the first communist leaders in their village back then.

"Even though my grandpa was an academic, he became politically powerful with the help of his Soviet education, and since he knew a lot of influential people as a professor. And so he had an easier time getting land grants and buying up properties. He was a landowner. That's where our wealth came from."

By the turn of the millennium, as Maysem was coming of age, communism, as originally defined by Karl Marx and then developed by Vladimir Lenin and Mao Zedong and the cultural revolutionaries, was losing its hold in China. A hybrid form of capitalism and conspicuous consumption, guided by state planning, had begun to replace it.[14]

In her first year at a small high school in the early 2000s, there was only a single computer connected to the internet. Still, intrigued, Maysem sat down with her friends and began clicking away.

"I was curious," she told me. "I never saw the internet before high school. Now, with this machine, I could download articles and books and read them. The internet was censored, so I couldn't read everything. But it really showed us a new world out there.

"I saw the wisdom of the day. People were saying that China would soon be the center of gravity for the world's technologies and economy. We had more than a billion people, and they were all getting so interested in the internet and turning China into something greater after a tough century."[15]

It was a chance to reverse the "century of humiliation," as the Communist Party called it, referring to the long period when China was exploited, abused, and weakened by foreign powers.[16]

At the same time, a different sort of cultural awakening was taking hold in Xinjiang.

"It was a powerful mixture of ethnic nationalism, religious influences from Islam, Chinese communist thinking, and Western liberal thought," Eset Sulayman, a Uyghur intellectual historian based in Washington, DC, told me. "Since it couldn't actually be all four there was conflict, and struggle and factionalism."

The existentialist Uyghur writer Perhat Tursun, influenced by the French author Albert Camus, published his controversial novel, *The Art of Suicide*, in 1999. It had descriptions of suicide—shocking content for a society that had been closed under communism and was now under the influence of Sunni Islamic clerics. The editors at state-run presses were supposed to act as censors. Tursun received death threats, and became a symbol of liberal thought in a newly thriving literary scene.[17]

"He challenged the taboos head-on," his friend, the poet Tahir Hamut, told me. "The conservative writers and the Islamists were deeply upset."

One school in southern Xinjiang staged a book burning of *The Art of Suicide*. Turson's wife left him, unwilling to put up with the mob that threatened their family.[18] Hamut, Tursun, and others began forgoing traditional journals and magazines, which went through state censors, and started publishing their work on a thriving collection of indie Uyghur-language websites that somehow evaded official scrutiny.

"Don't get us wrong. There was still repression in China," Abduweli, one of these online writers, told me. "People went to prison for sedition charges. But we truly thought things were getting better, that we were in an age of globalization and that any kind of heavy-handed rule could not continue forever."

"It was an exciting, hopeful time," Maysem recalled, as we sat drinking tea so many years later in a different country altogether. "But there was a problem. We had a blind spot. The same forces that lifted us up could also tear us down."

CHAPTER **4**

China Rises

There is no force that can shake the
foundation of this great nation.

—XI JINPING

As China asserted its newfound importance in the world through trade, economic growth, and technology, Maysem found herself swept up in a torrent of patriotic pride: "As I got older, I knew I wanted to be a diplomat. I wanted to serve my country, and do something distinguished, that matters."

When she sat for the national exam on June 15, 2007, Maysem spent a grueling six hours a day, over two days, answering multiple choice questions on math, literature, and history.

"I was nervous about the results," she said. "Then, the envelope arrived in the mail." Maysem and her parents held their breath as she opened it.

"I scored among the highest in all of Xinjiang. That meant everything to me. I was going to Beijing, to the capital. But I was scared. I'd never lived away from home before."

Three months later, in September 2007, Maysem traveled with her father to Beijing to begin her major in the social sciences.

"I saw this small, harmless-looking girl and we introduced ourselves to each other," remembered a medical student who, though a few years older, would become a good friend to Maysem. "She was in the cafeteria with her father as they got ready to say goodbye. She was crying."

But Maysem was excited too: "I said goodbye to my dad and set out for class in the capital. Beijing was scary. It was also glamorous."

[ ]

I had first visited China as a college student on a summer exchange trip in 2007. I was part of a group of university students. We were allowed to speak with the CEO of a new tech company, who described the exuberance felt in China as it began to realize new opportunities.

"When I was growing up, all we knew about Americans was the 'big nose,'" he joked, referring to the same cartoon stereotypes of Caucasian Americans Maysem had laughed at in her comic books.

"Now we are the manufacturing center of the world," he said. "And we're moving up the value chain. We're starting to make our own computers and software too."

The mood, indeed, was buoyant. A group of us paid a visit to a street in Beijing called Zhongguancun ("Electronics Street"). There, we heard from a Chinese Microsoft employee: "Microsoft, you can say, has become the central pillar of new technologies in China. It's difficult to express in words how far we've come."

Seven years earlier, Bill Gates, then the CEO of Microsoft, had dispatched his senior advisor Craig Mundie to China. His mission was to create a new business arrangement to help the government of a country keen to adopt technology—a country of one billion people with an estimated 120 million PCs, meaning 120 million potential Windows users.[1]

Chinese users had been buying pirated versions of Microsoft Windows on the street for a few dollars and Microsoft had responded by aggressively suing in Chinese courts, losing many cases.[2] The Chinese government, meanwhile, was concerned that Windows contained malware installed by the US government that could be used to spy on China.

"I remember going back to Redmond," the location of Microsoft's headquarters in Washington, "and saying, 'Our business is just broken in China,'" Mundie told *Fortune*. "But where we were most broken was that our business practices and our engagement did not reflect the importance of having a collaborative approach with the government."

"As a result, in 2003 the company offered China and 59 other countries the right to look at the fundamental source code for its Windows operating system and to substitute certain portions with their own software—something Microsoft had never allowed in the past," *Fortune* reported.[3]

Listening to Mundie's advice, Gates had realized that Microsoft was at fault. Flat pricing for Windows all over the world, whether in rich or poor countries like China, wasn't viable. It made piracy inevitable.[4]

As a goodwill gesture, Gates built a research and development laboratory in Beijing, called Microsoft Research China, later re-named Microsoft Research Asia (MRA). The lab was constructed in an emerging stretch of city blocks, Zhongguancun. This was a place where until recently farmers had roamed the area with ox carts and "men in cheap suits hawked power strips and printer ink from street-side kiosks, where pirated software was so common that the street got the name 'Crook Street,'" wrote the journalist Mara Hvistendahl.[5]

But Zhongguancun was being turned into a science park that eventually came under the direct supervision of the government.

Gates entrusted a rising star named Kai-Fu Lee, a citizen of Taiwan, to set up MRA.[6] Lee had made a name for himself in the fields of voice recognition and artificial intelligence. As a PhD candidate in computer science at Carnegie Mellon in the 1980s, he developed the first AI program that could defeat the world champion of the relatively simple eight-by-eight board game Oth-ello, a major feat at the time.[7] Then he joined Apple as a software executive, and in the early 1990s created the company's first voice recognition technology, called Casper.[8]

Based in California, Kai-Fu Lee had fallen into a career slump when Microsoft approached him to build MRA. Its mandate was to snatch up China's best minds and develop breakthrough tech-nologies five to fifteen years in advance of the market.[9]

"[Microsoft Research Asia] went on to train over five thousand AI researchers," Lee wrote in his book *AI Superpowers*, "including top executives at Baidu, Alibaba, Tencent, Lenovo, and Huawei," five of China's biggest and most valuable technology companies.[10]

Until now, American corporate giants—Microsoft, Apple, Yahoo!, and IBM—had called the shots all over the world. But with MRA, China was laying the groundwork for an ecosystem that could stand on its own.

That emerging ecosystem was cutthroat. Companies rose and fell on what seemed like a weekly basis. Entrepreneurs copied each other's products and websites, rather than innovating on their own. They got their start in garage-like conditions, developing a system of innovation with which they could swiftly tweak their hardware and software. This allowed them to expeditiously copy and mimic Western and Japanese technologies, and sell them cheaply to the insatiable Chinese consumer market.[11]

"The messy markets and dirty tricks of China's 'copycat' era produced some questionable companies," Kai-Fu Lee wrote, "but they also incubated a generation of the world's most nimble, savvy, and nose-to-the-grindstone entrepreneurs."[12]

That would change as the government became more involved.

The Chinese government saw the potential of the internet to power the economy of the future that it so desired, to allow for the easy exchange of goods and academic research, and to realize its vision of Chinese technology attaining a global reach. But the prospect of citizens organizing protests online, or accessing subversive websites, was deeply opposed by those in the government who believed China had to remain a one-party authoritarian state.[13]

So from 2000 onward, the government began enacting regulations that required internet service providers to make sure the information sent through their services adhered to policies of the state.

In 2002, China blocked Google for the first time, and established four principles for internet "self-discipline": patriotic observance of the law, equitableness, trustworthiness, and honesty. It meant that when in China, internet companies would be expected to conform to China's rules, no matter how heavy-handed or authoritarian.[14]

Yahoo!, the US search engine, was one company that signed the pledge. Two years later in April 2004, Yahoo! notified the government that the Chinese journalist Shi Tao had leaked a Communist

Party document instructing the media on how to cover the anniversary of the 1989 Tiananmen Square massacre to a website in New York. Shi Tao was sentenced to ten years in prison.[15] The following year, in 2005, Microsoft signed the pledge. Google signed on in 2006.[16]

The "Great Firewall" became the nickname of China's system of internet censorship, one that blocked websites based outside China. It was developed by computer scientist Fang Binxing. Fang became hated nationwide for his role in censoring the internet, pelted with shoes and eggs by one angry man in 2011. But the policy took hold, and China developed a related second system called the Golden Shield that allowed the government to inspect any data being received or sent, and to block domain names within China.[17]

The US government was beginning to notice the fledgling and fast-growing Chinese tech firms, and worried that China's technological modernization could pose a threat to American military interests and national security.

In 2005, the US Air Force commissioned the RAND Corporation, the prominent Cold War–era think tank, to write the first comprehensive report on the future of Chinese military capabilities. The report would come to define the conversation about Chinese technology, and whether or not it could bolster authoritarianism and make military conflict more likely. This kicked off talk of a second cold war.

"The Chinese military is in the midst of a C4 ISR (command, control, communications, computers, and intelligence) [and surveillance, and reconnaissance] revolution," the authors of the report wrote, "characterized by the wholesale shift to digital, secure communications via fiber-optic cable, satellite, microwave, and encrypted high-frequency radio."

The RAND researchers called China's emerging system a "digital triangle" that consisted of "booming commercial information-technology companies" like Huawei, "the state R&D institute and funding infrastructure," and "the military."[18]

What the report claimed, in other words, was that China was building a novel military-industrial complex, reconfigured for the needs of the future.

[ ]

In reality, however, in 2005 Chinese technology still lagged far behind the suspicions and fears of the Pentagon. The Chinese Academy of Sciences, a government-run body, lamented that year that Chinese technology firms were short-sighted and not very innovative.[19] The government knew it had to catch up if it wanted to sustain its dream of an economic miracle.

"The Chinese internet is unusable," a Chinese writer in Beijing told me in 2014. "And there's a huge problem. The government has been censoring its own people so heavily that I really don't think it knows what's going on in the country."

I concurred. I'd recently finished a project as a consultant to the World Health Organization (WHO) in Beijing, where I designed a curriculum for Chinese journalists on how to report on the innocuous topic of road traffic safety.

Almost half of the forty-person audience at my training session turned out to be police officers, the WHO representative told me. They'd been invited to attend to build "goodwill" between the press and the police, but I suspected it was really an effort to keep the government involved, to allow the police to keep check on what reporters were saying and maybe even intimidate them.

"If you don't know the topic," argued a policeman in the audience, standing up, "then you shouldn't write about it."

The problem was that few of these reporters had access to reliable data. They couldn't report authoritatively on the epidemic of fatal road crashes and haphazard law enforcement on China's lawless streets.

Foreign Policy's James Palmer later lamented the near total absence of reliable data in the article "Nobody Knows Anything about China":

We don't know the real figures for GDP growth . . . We don't know the true size of China's population . . . We don't know *anything* about China's high-level politics . . . We don't know what people really think . . . We don't know the real defense budget . . . We don't know how good Chinese schools really are.[20]

[ ]

The Chinese state was almost as much in the dark about the lives of its citizens as foreign China-watchers. So it set about trying to design ways to track its citizens. Among the Uyghurs and Kazakhs who once worked for the Chinese government was Irfan. He was a technology worker in his thirties who came from Urumqi, the regional capital and commercial hub in northern Xinjiang, where he implemented mass surveillance projects until he left his job in 2015. He fled Xinjiang in 2018 and settled in Turkey.

Irfan had originally experienced trouble finding a job in the poor Urumqi region. Many of the top jobs went to Han Chinese migrants who sidelined the local Uyghurs.

"But I had a friend who had some access to the mayor of Urumqi," Irfan explained. "He put in a call for me. And then the telecom company contacted me in 2007 with an offer. They needed an IT manager who could help set up one of the first surveillance systems there. You should understand how important this was to me," he said. "Uyghurs can rarely work these jobs. And yet I got into a position that offered me the government's protection and good money."

In his new job, Irfan was granted access to two key locations: the local public security office, where he helped manage the company surveillance network, and the telecom company's network itself.

"My access," he said, "was pretty deep. China had set up Sky Net two years earlier. Our mandate was to scour the city and plant cameras everywhere we could. My supervisors said the government wanted us to fight crime. I accepted that. I thought it was an honorable mission."

With a small team, Irfan searched street corners, alleyways, streets where cars tended to speed, and pockets known for robberies and purse snatchings, as documented in municipal data. Then his team would connect cameras to optic cables that went back to the public security buildings, where police operatives would survey the city from a control room.

"When I saw the right place for a camera, it was like a lightbulb in my head. 'That's the spot!' I told my colleagues. Over time, it became an art."

In the parts of the city that still weren't electrified, they installed battery-powered cameras good for eight hours at a time.

A technician would arrive with a camera branded with the logo of a government agency called the Zhongdian Haikang Group, which owned a 40 percent stake in a rising surveillance-camera giant called Hikvision.[21] Irfan would watch as the technician mounted the camera on a pole or building, and then plug the device into the government's surveillance system. Huawei, another big Chinese firm, provided the switching system that helped power the cameras.[22]

Irfan described how, throughout the late 2000s, a number of Chinese tech companies came together to build an early surveillance system consisting of what were called internet protocol (IP) cameras. These cameras sent video over a network, making obsolete the old network of closed-circuit television (CCTV) that needed a local recording device, like a videotape recorder. It was a relatively new and more efficient technology that China quickly mastered, tapping into the potential of the internet to send data from cameras to control centers.[23]

Irfan knew that something important was beginning. Until now, American, European, Japanese, and Taiwanese companies had pretty much dominated the market for surveillance cameras. But most of these giants were stuck in analog, selling CCTV cameras. They were put off by the expensive price of a single IP camera that was otherwise vastly more efficient when linked up to a Wi-Fi or data network, able to process a feed at a much higher quality and without the need for a tape or laser disc to record anything.

In the United States and elsewhere, part of the reason for the disconnect was that people tended to be slow technology adopters. Surveillance camera manufacturers like the American firm Cisco and the Swedish company Axis sold their products through two US distributors that resisted the shift to digital; they simply lacked the expertise to install early digital surveillance cameras. The camera firms were instead focused on outsourcing their manufacturing to China, hoping to cut costs.[24]

Emerging in their place were the "Big Two," Hikvision and Dahua. They would eventually dominate one-third of the video surveillance industry worldwide, helping power the new police state.[25]

"The state surveillance system, with that broad term Sky Net to describe all of the systems, ran right through our telecom company," Irfan said, drawing a picture of how the surveillance cameras sent back video feeds to the public security bureau. "There wasn't much of a division between business and government at all. Mosques, places of worship, were our big targets early on."

After installing the latest in what quickly became a vast network of cameras, Irfan would return to his control room in a nondescript concrete building, where he and other information technology workers sat in front of large wall-mounted video screens. The seven floors were filled with server hardware and the computer coders managing them, trying to find ways to position cameras toward the capture of lawbreakers, gangsters, and other criminal suspects.[26]

But robberies happened fast, and the perpetrators zipped off before they could be apprehended.

"The pressing question was how to identify them faster," Irfan said, "with the help of their Unix operating system, also designed by Dahua and Hikvision, that could power and control the hardware." (Unix, an open-source and highly customizable operating system, allowed any company to design its own version of Unix for its own purposes.)

The answer? Artificial intelligence.

Throughout 2010 and 2011, Irfan and his colleagues became increasingly aware of how they could train AI algorithms to recognize faces and behaviors, match them up with a national database of citizens, and help police find perpetrators.

Irfan watched as new equipment with a focus on AI arrived at the center. His manager announced that Irfan's team would attend a training in 2011. The name of the training was "Safe Cities."

"The getaway [in China] was supposed to be for learning how to use the Safe Cities systems. But actually, it was fifteen days of drinking and karaoke. And the organizers hired twenty pretty girls to tag along with us. They were basically escorts. So we didn't learn anything. We worked under high pressure catching criminals. This was our rest and relaxation."

[ ]

On day fifteen of the training, Irfan got his "certificate of completion" and returned to the office. It was time to fight crime, to see what the new Safe Cities system was capable of. "Since I hadn't really learned anything at the training, I didn't know why I thought I could fight crime now," he joked.

Armed with the latest AI technologies, Irfan sat down in the control room. He was in shock as he witnessed someone murder a restaurant owner not far from his office. He typed in commands to get close-up photos of the killer as he was making his escape.

"This was my moment," he told me. "We were putting our entire system to the test. We were guessing who he was, with our facial recognition technology. But the technology wasn't good enough yet to match his face for certain. We forwarded the photographs to the police."

And to his great surprise, the police filed a report—but then did nothing. The killer got away. He was never punished for his crime.

"Another time, someone broke my car window and stole my computer inside. We had the video footage but the police still couldn't find him and press charges."

With many other similar cases, early AI was considered a failure. Police complacency made it worse.

"We learned that you can't just rely on computer software to get things done. You still need the human hand. And why did the police do nothing?" he said. "I later figured out what their priorities were."

One day, outside Irfan's office, a Uyghur independence advocate unveiled the blue Uyghur flag with its crescent, a symbol of the occasionally passionate independence movement that had emerged in the region since the end of the Cold War.

"Of course the police showed up right away." Alerted by the nearby cameras, the police arrested the dissident, hauled him away, and took down the flag.

Irfan's job was to keep building the system, and he knew how to enhance it.

"We had the hardware, we had the cameras, we had almost everything we needed to make this work," he said. "But we realized that we were missing the key ingredient: *we needed more data.*

"Otherwise, the facial recognition technology was useless. The AI needed data, in the form of either facial images, social media, criminal records, credit card swipes, or whatever other data resulted from some kind of activity or transaction. Then the system could plough through all the information we fed it and find correlations that humans couldn't, in a fraction of the time."

"Why was there so little data?" I asked him.

"State secrecy," Irfan replied. "The government didn't have good information on its own country and its people. And so we didn't have the quality data that we needed to feed into the AI software. Without a good database on all our citizens, we couldn't match up people's faces or criminal records that easily. We couldn't use AI to catch criminals. It was a terrible system."

Irfan's team scoured other company offices and the government for data. They came up empty-handed.

"The solution didn't come from the government," Irfan confirmed. "It came from the corporations."

[ ]

In October 2010, a small team at Tencent, a technology company set up in 1998 and staffed by alumni of Microsoft Research Asia, began toiling away on a project in the southern city of Guangzhou. Few took notice. After all, the app they were developing, called Weixin ("Micro-message"), didn't seem especially groundbreaking or innovative. Anyone could already send messages on their computers using Tencent's other successful PC application, the instant messenger QQ, or using its QZone social network, similar to Facebook. QQ had nearly 780 million active users.

Tencent released the new mobile app on January 21, 2011, about three months later. It offered basic services like text messaging and the ability to send other people voice recordings and photos. The dominant American-made app of the era, WhatsApp, which would later be acquired by Facebook, had been released the previous year.[27]

So what could this new, obscure messaging app possibly offer in an already crowded market?

"At the time," Irfan explained, "all the telecoms companies had their own messaging apps that were pretty popular. WeChat united them on a single platform. And that was our solution."

Weixin, rebranded now as WeChat, quickly took off. Within a year it had 100 million users,[28] and 300 million users within two years.[29] Facebook had taken four years and Twitter five years to reach that number.[30]

As time went on, part of WeChat's success rested on clever marketing and thorough functionality that enabled users to live their entire lives on their phones. The app released features that allowed them to book a doctor's appointment, call a taxi, pay at the local 7-11, hire a house cleaner, match with a potential date, and manage investments—novel functions at the time when WhatsApp was still relatively minimalist, and before the age of Tinder and Uber.[31]

Other functions were quirky but attractive to users looking for their next burst of dopamine. For example, if they wanted to connect with a stranger from around the world, they could shake their phones to connect with anyone else who also activated the "shake" feature.

It also helped that the competition, Facebook and Twitter, were blocked in China.[32]

WeChat dominated lives in China, especially among the young. Crucially, it meant that everything WeChat users did was gathered and could be monitored. "People were becoming surveillance experiments," Irfan recalled, as WeChat provided "a massive online database of human experiences, of purchases and likes and break-ups and text messages. The ecosystem was coming together. We were building the large amount of data that we needed for mass surveillance."

Then in April 2013, Irfan said, "I got an assignment from my managers, who took their own orders from the government." Xinjiang's regional government had been dealing with a series of terrorist attacks in the region, and wanted to gather intelligence on terrorist suspects.

"I was in charge of installing about four thousand servers in Xinjiang. The servers were going to store all QQ and WeChat metadata and phone numbers [of people in Xinjiang]."

The Safe Cities project, now expanded to mass data gathering from people's smartphones, had begun to make Irfan feel uncomfortable.

"Some people in our office were unhappy," he told me. "Does the government really need a database of everyone's WeChat metadata to fight crime?"

"The public security bureau was able to scoop up metadata from WeChat. We gave the government access to our [telecommunications] servers as part of the project, and so the public security bureaus could store the metadata in Xinjiang . . . It was all secret. They didn't tell people they were reading their metadata."[33]

How did Irfan's office obtain WeChat's metadata in the first place?

"In China, we didn't need to ask for permission. If [the] Ministry of Public Security requests the metadata, at least in Xinjiang, every Chinese app developer will turn it over."

Metadata is generally the simplified data that describes or identifies other parts of data, like the phone numbers you called, but not the phone conversations themselves. Irfan said the government didn't have the capability to store actual phone conversations on the new Xinjiang servers, unless particular calls were targeted and intercepted by public security officers or their intelligence-gathering counterparts, state security officers.

That didn't matter yet. Metadata was enough. The state security bureau in Xinjiang could map out anyone's relationship with pretty much anyone else they messaged or called through WeChat. That web of connections meant they knew which friends and contacts and family members to reach if they had to question or detain someone.[34]

As Irfan wound down his project, the mood in his office was continuing to change. There were only a few Uyghurs working there. Pretty much everyone was Han Chinese. And more and more, the Han Chinese managers were suspicious of Irfan, a Uyghur, whom they saw as a second-class citizen who shouldn't be trusted with sensitive state secrets.

Irfan continued working at his office despite the mood of distrust around him, but he feared China was figuring out how to build an apartheid society based on technology. It had gathered the data it needed from the WeChat messaging app and from Irfan's telecommunications network that monitored phone calls and data transfers.

Could China take the surveillance any further? Irfan wondered. He believed the state could.

CHAPTER 5

Deep Neural Network

Do Not Panic, Believe in Science, Do Not Spread Rumors
—CHINESE PROPAGANDA BANNER

Despite all these advancements, there was still a problem. China's tech businesses were essentially pushing "me too" products: apps and services inspired by their American and European counterparts, and then adjusted for the Chinese market.

Chinese corporations, backed by the state, had a practice of using what businesspeople called "forced intellectual property transfer" when dealing with foreign partnerships. Foreign companies typically had to partner with a Chinese company to enter China's closed market. And one informal requirement was that the foreign partner transfer its sensitive technologies—in semiconductors, medical equipment, and oil and gas—to the Chinese firm.

The practice was illegal under World Trade Organization rules, but American businesses begrudgingly gave up their trade secrets anyway, eager for access to China's 1.4 billion potential customers.[1]

Once China started to amass data on all its people, netting information on their use of apps and services like WeChat, the country's nascent technology businesses were especially interested in becoming leaders in the growing, lucrative field of artificial intelligence. China's burgeoning pool of AI researchers was paying close attention to breakthroughs being made in the United States, the world's AI leader. Chinese companies hoped to unlock AI's secrets by scouting out talented Chinese AI developers who had studied overseas and worked at Microsoft and Amazon, luring them home with remunerative pay packages and appeals to their patriotism.[2] By the early 2010s, China's computer scientists were getting closer to building a deep neural network, the holy grail of the surveillance state, a system that could learn to find patterns between millions of images and data points.

For years, AI researchers had relied on what's called the "rules based" system of programming. The researchers would program a computer to recognize a cat by telling it: "Look for a circle with two triangles on top." The approach made sense since computers lacked the processing power to do much more. But this method also limited what AI could accomplish; not all images of cats are a perfect circle with two triangles on top, nor are all circles with triangles on top actually cats.[3]

The newer technology, deep neural nets, had all kinds of benefits. Humans no longer needed to go through the monotonous, time-consuming work of manually categorizing images and data, and then writing all the rules for an AI system. Instead, the software could connect the dots on its own when looking at vast datasets, and then learn from that data. The software could then improve its algorithm for the task its creators built it for.[4] With fewer humans supervising and limiting the software, businesses could deploy AI for far broader uses. Deep neural nets could control self-driving cars, help physicians diagnose patients, and detect credit card fraud.[5]

Until 2012, the idea of creating a deep neural network that could impact the market was dismissed as quackery. No matter how many times they tried, the computer scientists at Microsoft Research Asia, and other emerging companies, were hitting a wall.

AI developers in China and Silicon Valley told me in 2012 that building a neural network would be a gold mine for Microsoft. Microsoft had acquired Skype, the popular visual calling and conferencing software used worldwide, for $8.5 billion in May 2011—its largest acquisition up to that time.[6] If Skype or Microsoft Windows could secure the ability to recognize speech and faces, it would be a breakthrough. It would form the basis for real-time translation abilities and cybersecurity that depended on facial recognition.

In 2011, I had met a group of young Chinese researchers in Beijing who, enduring late nights and weekends, toiled away at a gnawing set of problems. Their big questions were, How can a computer system learn to "see" and "perceive" a person? How can it hear and identify their voice? Can AI learn to speak?

"The timing is right," one of them told me at dinner, after work. "The internet and social media can be a source of data that can power AI. We can gather information on people's clicks, purchases, preferences."

The Chinese, he said, had less than 10 percent of their population linked up to the internet in 2005, but had rapidly become the world's most enthusiastic users of social media, mobile apps, and mobile payments.[7] In 2011, almost 40 percent of the population, or about 513 million people, had their own internet connections.[8] All those internet users were producing the data, through their purchases and clicks, that could train the neural networks to solve myriad tasks, including surveilling the users.

The same year, in 2011, a pair of research assistants working for the famed AI researcher Geoffrey Hinton, a computer science professor at the University of Toronto and Google AI researcher, made a hardware breakthrough that made these advances possible. The researchers realized they could repurpose graphics processing units (GPUs), the components installed in devices that allowed for advances in computer game graphics, to improve the processing speeds of a deep neural net.[9] With GPUs, AI developers could utilize the same techniques for displaying shapes and images on a computer screen, and use them to train a neural network in finding patterns.

Building a neural net had once been prohibitively expensive. But the GPU breakthrough was important because it slashed the costs of the key hardware that would power the software. For years, GPUs had been getting cheaper and more commoditized, even as the industry elevated their memory and processing power.[10]

With better hardware and a growing number of datasets, the timing was perfect to build a deep neural network that could process that data.

Through trial and error, a Microsoft team led by Dr. Sun Jian set out to build more "layers" in a neural network that would allow the AI system to constantly update its knowledge and learn from the data that flowed through it. Neural net layers are like a collection of neurons that receive inputs of data, process them, and pass them on to more layers, for more processing, so the AI can learn about the subject it is analyzing.

The more layers, the more sophisticated the intelligent machine, in theory. Success proved much harder in practice. One challenge was that signals disappeared as they passed through each layer. The Microsoft researchers were hindered from training the system.

In 2012, the team trained a system with eight neural layers to recognize images. By 2014, the system had thirty layers. By adding more layers, the team had instigated a breakthrough in a computer's ability to intelligently recognize objects in videos and images.

"We didn't even believe this single idea could be so significant," Dr. Sun said.[11]

The Chinese technological ecosystem began attracting the attention of venture capitalists, no longer centered only in the traditional finance and technology hubs of Silicon Valley and New York. These venture capitalists wanted an early start in two industries with huge potential for the surveillance ecosystem: facial recognition technology and voice recognition technology.

The first big investment was in facial recognition technology.

In 2013, Sinovation Ventures, the AI-focused venture capital firm set up by Kai-fu Lee, backed the growing facial recognition platform Megvii ("Mega Vision") with an undisclosed sum.[12] Then SenseTime (Megvii's competitor, founded in Hong Kong in 2014) released the first algorithm that under certain conditions could detect people more accurately than the human eye—and claimed it beat Facebook, a landmark in the AI industry.[13]

"Public security" applications, SenseTime's product development head and Microsoft alumnus Yang Fan admitted, were a lucrative market.

"There's a strong, hard demand driven by smart cities and surveillance," he told *Forbes Asia*.[14]

But facial recognition software needed cutting-edge semiconductors that could power the AI. Where would they come from?

SenseTime and other Chinese AI companies turned to US companies for the semiconductors to power their software. And American companies, it turned out, were interested in the applications of Chinese software technologies for mobile apps and law enforcement. US telecommunications company Qualcomm set up a relationship with Megvii: it supplied semiconductors to Megvii and could in turn use Megvii's artificial intelligence software for its own devices.[15]

"We see explosive demand in China," Li Xu, cofounder and CEO of SenseTime, said at a business conference in June 2016, on the stage with Jeff Herbst, vice president for business development of Nvidia's venture investment arm.[16]

Founded in 1993, Nvidia emerged in the 1990s and 2000s as the leading manufacturer of GPUs. Now, it was poised to cash in on the emerging AI boom.[17]

Nvidia soon began inking high-profile deals with Chinese facial recognition firms. Chips made by Nvidia and its major competitor, Intel, were used to build some of the world's most powerful surveillance computers at the Urumqi Cloud Computing Center, which opened in 2016. These computers watched more surveillance footage in a day than humans could in a year.[18]

"When I'm in China, every lightpost has a camera," Herbst said. "It feels like everything is being watched. But the problem is you got all this video coming in and there's a guy sitting in a control room looking for something to happen. It all needs to be automated, right?"[19]

Li Xu recognized that public security was interesting to the Chinese government, but also that "the existing surveillance system is severely handicapped by the lack of a smart engine, especially in terms of video processing."[20]

He set out to offer an alternative.

Li Xu knew that Nvidia's chip technology, repurposed from similar technologies in graphic processing, was "fundamental" to its work, and that Nvidia was using fourteen thousand of them in servers across Asia to power its facial recognition technology.

"I feel like we're going to have a long relationship with you guys," Nvidia's Herbst told Li Xu at the business conference.[21] He may not have intended his words to sound ominous, but they were.

By 2015, the building blocks of a surveillance ecosystem were falling into place. It consisted of software that could recognize faces, scan text messages and emails, and pick up the patterns in speech and human interactions.

Now the investors were putting money in another pillar: voice recognition, or software with the capability to understand and process the human voice.

Back in the late 1990s, a promising young researcher named Liu Qingfeng had turned down an internship offer at Microsoft Research Asia and instead dedicated his career to his start-up, iFlyTek, with a mission to develop cutting-edge voice recognition technology.

"I told him that he was a great young researcher but China lagged too far behind American speech-recognition giants like Nuance, and there were fewer customers in China for this technology," Kai-fu Lee wrote. "To his credit, Liu ignored that advice and poured himself into building iFlyTek."[22]

In 2010, iFlyTek set up a laboratory in Xinjiang to develop speech recognition technology for translating the Uyghur language to Mandarin Chinese,[23] technology that would soon be used to track and monitor Uyghur populations.[24] By 2016, iFlyTek was the supplier of twenty-five "voiceprint" systems in Kashgar that captured the unique signatures of a person's voice in order to help identify and track people.[25]

"All these companies were coming to Xinjiang," Irfan recalled. "I saw all of them. Their equipment, their software." Dozens of Uyghurs who fled Xinjiang in the years after 2014 remembered seeing the company logos on equipment. And the presence of these companies in Xinjiang is shown in online government tender documents, official corporate reports, human rights reports and US sanctions documents, and Chinese state media reports. "But so many people saw it as harmless. The feeling was 'we're just fighting crime.'"

Finally, Huawei, a national symbol of Chinese technology, stepped up its presence in the Xinjiang market from 2010 to 2015, after working with local police to build cloud-computing services.[26]

Huawei (roughly meaning "China Shows Promise") was started with $3,000 by former military engineer Ren Zhengfei.[27] It began by developing telephone switchboards in the 1980s, which it reverse engineered from foreign examples.[28] An early supporter of the government's acceleration of technological development, Huawei became known at home and abroad for its surveillance and network equipment, and was building its presence in the smartphone market.

Ren, whom former employees talk about as though he were an almost mystical figure, one who speaks in parables of streams and mountains, had big plans for a global expansion. Plans his company could only accomplish by reassuring Western democracies that Huawei was not connected to the Chinese Communist Party (CCP) and would not use its technology to spy on them. At the same time, Huawei executives were eager to sell network equipment to the government in Xinjiang, seeing "public security" as a lucrative business.[29]

"We were at a team-building event in 2015," William Plummer, a former American diplomat who became Huawei's vice president for external affairs in Washington, DC, told me. "Somebody put a slide up. The slide said, 'What's Huawei's identity?' And the first bullet says, 'For domestic audiences, Huawei is a Chinese company that supports the Communist Party of China.' Then the second bullet said, 'For overseas audiences, Huawei is an independent company that follows internationally accepted corporate practices.'

"What they were actually saying was that in China you follow the regulations, and in other countries you follow their regulations. . . . But to put that on a slide, that slide alone was damning."

By 2015, the last piece needed to complete the surveillance ecosystem was coming tantalizingly within reach: cheaper surveillance camera technology. Cheap enough that it could be made commercially at scale. Hikvision, based in China and the world's largest manufacturer of surveillance cameras, joined the market in Xinjiang. It supplied millions of cameras that enabled the authorities to surveil the population—cameras so advanced they could identify people from nine miles away[30]—and use the AI software developed by iFlyTek, SenseTime, and others to analyze people's faces and voices.

Sky Net, the government's radical and thorough surveillance system unveiled conceptually a decade earlier in 2005, was finally realizable.

[ ]

All this technological advancement and the somewhat sinister combination of various elements to create an AI state had not occurred entirely unnoticed. As early as 2010, China's biggest foreign adversary, the United States, was getting nervous.

American policy makers had started to suspect Huawei and its peers were fronts that enabled the People's Liberation Army (PLA) of China to plant "backdoors" in servers and software, allowing it easy access for cyber spying.

"We assess with high confidence that the increasing role of international companies and foreign individuals in US information technology supply chains and services will increase the potential for persistent, stealthy subversions," the US National Security Agency (NSA), charged with intercepting communications around the world, wrote in a 2010 slide leaked by the whistleblower Edward Snowden.[31]

Edward Snowden's leaked documents also revealed that the NSA was tracking twenty Chinese hacker teams attempting to break into US government networks and companies like Google. Huawei was also laying undersea cables that the NSA hoped to intercept, so it could read the communications of Huawei customers that happened to be "high-priority targets," like Cuba, Iran, Afghanistan, and Pakistan.[32]

The NSA hacked Huawei's headquarters, monitored the communications of its top executives, and ran an operation called Shotgiant aimed at finding a link between Huawei and the People's Liberation Army. The NSA then took it a step further, looking to exploit Huawei's technology, so that when other countries and businesses bought its products, the NSA could surveil Huawei-made servers and phone networks, and launch cyber attacks on those countries. The NSA was able to accomplish all this with the vast hacking capabilities and backdoors it had created with the cooperation of American telecommunications firms, thus circumventing the usual technological barriers to engaging in mass spying on foreign citizens.[33]

Talk of a cold war was brewing between the United States and China, even though the two nations were joined at the hip through trade and technology. In 2012, a congressional panel released the results of a year-long investigation, claiming it had obtained documents from former Huawei employees that showed Huawei supplied services to a cyber-warfare unit in the Chinese army.[34]

The US government began taking aim at CEO Ren's daughter, Meng Wanzhou, who went by the English nickname "Cathy." As Huawei's globe-trotting socialite, Cathy hosted business events that had Q&As with Alan Greenspan and others.[35] Behind the scenes, the FBI and Department of Homeland Security were monitoring the business activities of Cathy and Huawei. It suspected that she oversaw a front company in Iran called Skycom that broke US trade sanctions by doing business with Iranian telecommunications companies.

"We had made representations to the US government about Huawei in Iran, and about Skycom, and how it was just an independent company even though she [Cathy Meng] sat on the board for two years," Plummer admitted to me. "We made those representations because that's what we were told, and that's what we believed was in good faith. None of that was true. The employees in Iran for Skycom were wandering around with Huawei business cards."

Plummer said he got a frantic call from his Huawei bosses one day in 2013. After one of her glamorous business galas, Department of Homeland Security agents had pulled Meng into secondary questioning as she prepared to board her flight at New York's JFK airport.

"They had her PC, her tablet, and both of her phones for four hours," Plummer said. "Those things were cloned by the US government." Meng was released. Huawei executives prepared for the legal fight to come, shutting down Skycom's office in Iran's capital of Tehran, and distancing Huawei from Skycom.

And while the United States slung mud at Huawei and China, accusing them of planting the alleged backdoors that allowed for state-sponsored hacking, and of running a front company, the NSA was caught planting its own backdoors in American network products being shipped to China.

Der Spiegel, the German newspaper, obtained a fifty-page catalog created by an NSA unit called the Advanced Network Technology (ANT) Division, charged with intercepting difficult-to-access networks.[36] The NSA intercepted shipments from the US server company Cisco headed for China, and secretly installed surveillance devices. Cisco claimed it had no knowledge of this hack by its own government.[37]

Another NSA product, HALLUXWATER, was labeled a "backdoor implant." It hijacked Huawei's firewall, allowing the NSA to plant malware and rewrite memory.[38]

"This monitoring behavior of the United States is within expectations," Ren Zhengfei told reporters in London. "It has just been proved."[39]

China soon showed its own hand in the emerging geopolitical rivalry. The country mined 93 percent of the world's rare earth minerals like lithium and cobalt, exported and used to improve the batteries and displays in iPhones and TVs worldwide. In September 2010, a Chinese fishing trawler collided with two Japanese coast guard boats nearby the disputed Senkaku Islands. Japan arrested the fishing trawler captain on suspicion of violating Japan's fishing rights in an area Japan controlled, but that China had long claimed.[40]

China retaliated. It blocked rare earth exports to Japan, jeopardizing the production of the hugely popular Toyota Prius, which needed at least two pounds of rare earth elements in each of its engines.[41]

More than two weeks later, Japan released the crew members, without charges.[42]

"China and Japan are important neighbors with important responsibilities in the international community," declared Prime Minister Naoto Kan emolliently in New York City at the UN General Assembly.[43]

But as Cold War II heated up, a distinction between the American and Chinese technology strategies became apparent.

China was attempting to steal US technology, including commercial trade secrets and intellectual property, and then hand those technologies to private Chinese companies, which wanted an edge over Silicon Valley.

The United States, on the other hand, wanted to infiltrate Chinese companies like Huawei. The point wasn't to steal Chinese technology, still inferior at that point, and pass it on to private companies like Amazon and Google. Rather, the goal was to gather information on possible military links and national security threats from China and its companies.[44]

[ ]

While on a reporting trip in June 2014, as I wandered the streets of Beijing, Shanghai, and China's tech hub, Shenzhen, I felt a palpable, self-styled nationalism growing, especially among young people in China. The talk of another cold war seemed to be unsettling people, a development made worse by government propaganda.

A Chinese technology executive tried to explain China's new self-confidence to me. "You know that Google exited China," he said with pride.

After four years in the Chinese market, Google had shut down its Chinese search engine in 2010, in the midst of a dispute over a hack of the company and censored search results.[45] "That doesn't matter," he explained. "We have our own search engine, Baidu. We have our own companies now. The world is changing, and I hope that Silicon Valley and the NSA will not dominate forever."

"But don't you think if China wants to get to the level of Silicon Valley, it'll have to open up the internet," I asked him, "so researchers can get the information they need to make good technology?"

"That doesn't matter, either," he said. "In China, our technology is connected to the future of our country. We don't have strong separation of powers like in the US. Our only goal is to make China great. We want to stand as equals with the Americans, so that no one will look down on us again."

CHAPTER 6

Do You Think I Am an Automaton?

Many People, United By One Heart

—CHINESE PROPAGANDA BANNER

Maysem had entered college in Beijing proud and enthusiastic about China's rise, but she quickly found that her country's patriotism came with an underbelly of racism and xenophobia. The Han Chinese ran the country. In the capital city, Uyghurs were looked down on as backward, blindly religious, and a bit dumb.[1]

College was hard for Maysem, an experience mirrored by other students from ethnic minorities in China. Despite stellar grades and hard work, her professors routinely passed over her when she raised her hand in class.

"You're a foreigner," one professor told her, pointing out her pale skin and the fact that she was from the Uyghur ethnic group.

"I'm Chinese," she responded, but Maysem's entreaties fell on dumb ears. "The university was, to say the least, a lonely experience."

Nevertheless, with her small group of friends, she scoured both the physical and online libraries, pulling out classic books at random and discussing them.

"It was then that we discovered Jane Austin," she said. "*Pride and Prejudice* was my favorite."

Pride and Prejudice is the story of a woman, Elizabeth Bennet, who rejects a marriage proposal from a wealthy man whose character she misjudges. Then she must overcome interference from her family as she figures out her true feelings for him. It was ironical and witty at the time it was written in England, almost two hundred years earlier.

From the broader perspective she was gaining, Maysem was beginning to embrace the complexity and uncertainty of life, an ambiguity her strict communist education hadn't afforded her. The heroes didn't always win.

"Sometimes, people choose money. They choose comfort. They choose the convenient life given to them by the system, even if that means giving up what they believe in."

But Maysem was consoled by one line in another favorite book, *Jane Eyre*, when Jane addresses Mr. Rochester, who has tried to make Jane jealous by pretending he wants to marry another woman:

Do you think I am an automaton?—a machine without feelings? . . . It is my spirit that addresses your spirit; just as if both had passed through the grave, and we stood at God's feet, equal—as we are![2]

The academic resources of the university proved fruitful for Maysem, who began building her own collection. It included not only Jane Austen and Charlotte Brontë, but writers like Joseph Nye, the political thinker who developed the concepts of "hard power," "soft power," and "smart power" embraced by both the Clinton and Obama administrations. Those books were supplemented by old Persian and Greek epics, bought from local bookstores.

"I wanted to be like my grandfather," she said. "I wanted to be a true scholar, a woman of learning."

At summertime, Maysem brought a portion of her small library back home, reading material she could plough through for the next three months. But this wasn't welcomed by her father.

Fearful and still remembering his days in the Cultural Revolution, he built a pit of rocks in their yard, piled the books inside it, doused them in gasoline, and tossed in a burning match.

"Books," he said, "will only get you in trouble."

[ ]

During her college years in Beijing, Maysem felt like the world resisted her imagination, her ideas, her identity. Her father frowned upon the literary life, the university treated her like a hick, and she realized the same prejudice would probably result in her government rejecting her ambition to become a diplomat, no matter how hard she worked or how talented she was.

Maysem wasn't the only one to feel her dreams were being thwarted. A sense of skepticism and frustration was increasing across Xinjiang, where growing demands for autonomy and freedom, and the feeling that local people were being denied justice at the hands of the country's ethnic majority, were actively rebuffed by the state.

The frustration exploded on July 5, 2009, when protests and riots erupted in the regional capital of Urumqi. This was more than a week after two migrant Uyghur workers were killed in a four-hour racially charged melee outside a toy factory in the southeast city of Shaoguan. The fighting was sparked by an anonymous online blog post claiming six Uyghur workers had raped two Han Chinese women. But city officials said the rape never happened.[3]

"I looked outside my office and I saw people gathering in the city center," Tahir Imin, a Uyghur businessman who witnessed the events, told me.

The Uyghur protesters gathered near key Communist Party buildings to protest the police handling of the Shaoguan incident. A crowd also formed at the grand bazaar in the city center.

Within a few hours, the angry crowds morphed into about a thousand full-scale rioters.[4] Angry young men—and most of the rioters were men, as shown in news footage—roamed the thoroughfares, standing in front of cars and busses in the streets, ordering them to stop, pulling out the drivers, turning busses on their side and setting them on fire.[5] Homes and stores were looted, windows were shattered, crowds shouted, "Down with China!" and "Down with the Communist Party!" according to a dozen witnesses I interviewed later.

One woman who was there told me she saw a pregnant woman lying unconscious on the road with her belly cut up.

"It was a scary day," a local Uyghur told me. "There were bodies on Dawan North Road. The local police didn't come to protect us until much later."

Riot police showed up and attempted to disperse the crowds, who retaliated by throwing stones. The government said that 197 people died during the riots, which flared for several days.[6]

For China, the riots signaled it was time to act. On July 6, 2009, the government shut down the internet, attempting to stem information on ethnic riots from reaching the outside world.[7] China wanted to convince its people and the world that it was not home to racial tensions, that its citizens enjoyed ethnic unity and harmony. But once the authorities had isolated Xinjiang, they moved in on the population.

"Chinese law enforcement agencies carried out a massive campaign of unlawful arrests in the Uyghur areas of Urumqi," reported Human Rights Watch, "many of which resulted in 'disappearances' of the detainees."[8] Uyghur protesters told me later that plainclothes police in unmarked cars kidnapped them, took them to desolate neighborhoods outside the cities, tied them to trees, and beat them with batons and rifle butts.

"I turned on the TV after the riots were over," said Tahir Imin, "and I saw the governor of the region [Xinjiang] lowering his head and calling the protestors terrorists. All the other TV feeds were cut."

In 2009, the Chinese government was reactive to events in Xinjiang. It still lacked the ability to preempt social unrest. But as it gained technological expertise in the years to come, all that would change. China was determined not to permit Xinjiang to continue as a restive, rebellious province. It was the obvious target for the surveillance state.

[ ]

Maysem, luckily, was far off from the Urumqi riots, at her university in the comfortable capital city of Beijing. In May 2009, Maysem and her friends heard that Ilham Tohti, a prominent economics professor and a respected Uyghur intellectual, was holding an open course at the Minzu University of China every Saturday. When she entered the large lecture room, it was packed with students jostling to find a seat.

Professor Tohti sauntered in, carrying books, his hair slightly frazzled, and from the look on his face, his mind restless.

Tohti didn't have the majestic physical figure Maysem and the friend she was with had imagined for a man so admired. He was "short and a little fat," Maysem's friend remarked, "and it's not like he had a handsome face or anything."

But when Tohti spoke, he was blunt and powerful.

"I don't care whether you are a policeman, a spy, or you love the Communist Party. I really don't care," he began. "We built this nation together. You are in my class to learn that."

In January 2011, Ilham Tohti had written: "I love this land which has nurtured me. But I worry about my homeland and my country falling into turmoil and division. I hope that China, having endured many misfortunes, will become a great nation of harmonious inter-ethnic coexistence and develop a splendid civilization."[9]

Born in 1969 to a prosperous family in western China, Tohti grew up in an apartment block for government employees, where the local Muslim Uyghurs lived together with the dominant ethnic group, the Han Chinese. His father, a military veteran, "died tragically during the Cultural Revolution" in 1971 at the age of twenty-eight. He wrote. "The older generation has kept silent about the past . . . As a result, while we were proud of our father, I don't really know what kind of a person he was and how he died."

Many of Tohti's family members, including his second brother, sister-in-law, and nephews and niece, held respectable ranks in the ministry of public security, the powerful government organ that acts as the chief law enforcement body.

After graduating college in 1991 with a degree in geography, Tohti taught development economics and studied overseas in South Korea and Pakistan. He learned on his own how to speak English, Korean, Japanese, Urdu (the language of Pakistan), and Russian. A businessman on the side, he made a small fortune on the Chinese stock market, investing small amounts of money and profiting from China's economic boom.

Tohti almost decided to start his own business. But the state of his country troubled him.

"Having witnessed a great number of cases of ethnic conflict and killing, political unrest and failed social transformation during my extensive travels . . . my desire grew stronger and stronger to completely devote my energies to researching Xinjiang and Central Asian issues, so that tragedies abroad won't take place in China."

Tohti built a name as a social critic, and began to be harassed by the authorities. In 1999, he was forbidden to publish articles. Then he was barred for four years from teaching at his alma mater and employer, the prestigious Minzu University.[10]

"Once he started getting involved in social issues, we became distant," his daughter, Jewher Ilham, who resides in a Washington, DC, suburb, told me. She was a teenager living in Beijing at the time, and had been close to her father.

"I was really frustrated. I wanted love from my parents. But his nose was tied to his computer. I began to have a bad attitude. Sometimes [when] he wanted to show me something related to his work, I closed the door and walked out."

Seeing that he stood in a unique position to advance a cause from among an ethnic group where "not many people . . . have enjoyed a quality education," Tohti joined the chorus of those taking to the nascent internet to voice their views. In 2005, he set up a popular website called Uyghur Online, inviting Han Chinese and Uyghur intellectuals to discuss sensitive topics on his web forum, even if their perspectives and opinions clashed.

"They [my relatives] have often bitterly entreated me in the hope that I will speak out less," Tohti complained. "They wanted me to mind my own business, and focus on making money."

Tohti urged a moderate, reasoned, tolerant approach. The explosive economic growth of the past two decades had brought with it the uprooting of family and community social structures, mass migrations to cities in search of affluence and opportunity, and the resulting "theft, pickpocketing, drug trafficking, drug abuse and prostitution."

People, it seemed, no longer trusted each other.[11]

Tohti watched as the Han Chinese members of the *bingtuan* (called the Xinjiang Production and Construction Corporation in English) built new suburbs and farms and ran its own paramilitary organization. The bingtuan thought of itself as a civilizing force over the frontier. But the organization, with 2.7 million members, consisted of mostly Han Chinese settlers who devised policies that pushed the Uyghurs off their native lands.

Uyghurs told me that the term "bingtuan" aroused their frustration and anger. The Chinese Communist Party had founded the organization in 1954 as a paramilitary force consisting of decommissioned soldiers, with the goal of building schools, hospitals, and roads.[12] It also wanted to rewrite history to cast China as a benevolent power that, it falsely claimed, had controlled Xinjiang for more than two thousand years.[13] In reality, the lands we know as Xinjiang today were ruled by Turkic, Mongol, and Manchu empires, by a Soviet-supported warlord, and were independent at times, before the Han-dominated Chinese Communist Party took control.[14]

The CCP had taken power in Xinjiang in 1950 and sought to pacify the region. For forty-eight years, the bingtuan reported to the regional government, expanding and consolidating large landholdings and strategic waterways that gave it political power over the local population. Then, in 1999, the national government elevated the bingtuan to the same bureaucratic status as the regional government, turning it into a "state within a state" with political authority separate from the regional government of Xinjiang.[15]

With the help of the bingtuan, Han Chinese migrants poured into China's Wild West throughout the 1990s and 2000s, offloading from trains and setting up residence at flashy new high-rise apartment blocks. Meanwhile, the government slated Xinjiang's stunning old cities for "redevelopment," meaning they were bulldozed under the claim they had poor sanitation and wobbly structural foundations. Both sides were increasingly suspicious of and hostile toward each other. Han Chinese migrants saw the Uyghurs as backward religious fundamentalists, while Uyghurs looked at the Han as money-grubbing opportunists pushing them off their historical homeland.[16]

Ilham Tohti emerged as a vocal critic of the bingtuan, a precarious position since he was challenging a powerful organization. He called the bingtuan "a throwback to six decades of centralized economic planning, a redundant bureaucracy propped up by vested interests and extolled by political propagandists."[17]

"The atmosphere around it [the bingtuan] is both plain strange and also terrifying," Tohti wrote in the another essay on January 17, 2011. "The situation is getting gradually worse, fewer and fewer people dare to speak out."[18]

Tohti, for all his public challenges to a potentially dangerous paramilitary force, announced that he didn't want to be seen as a political leader. He just wanted, as an academic, to contribute good thinking about moderation, reason, and reconciliation.[19]

"He wanted to be seen as moderate, as a peaceful figure who could reach across the divide," Tahir Hamut, who knew him personally, told me. "He did not agitate for fighting or independence. He knew that to get things done, to build a nation, you had to work together, even with the people you disagreed with."

"He represented the best in thinking, the most enlightened," said my Uyghur translator and assistant, Abduweli Ayup, who also knew Tohti personally. "He didn't let his passions get the best of him. He knew he had to keep an even temper. He inspired others to be optimistic."

Every Saturday, Maysem and her friends attended Professor Tohti's wide-ranging lectures on global economics and politics, which covered everything from the effects of steel tariffs to comparisons between the Chinese Communist Party and the US electoral system.

"The problem," he told the class in May 2009, according to Maysem, "is that our government looks to the worst-case scenarios. They're building a policy towards minorities based on fear and suspicion. But what about the best-case scenarios? What about the countries where minorities have been integrated and have become a part of these societies?"

He told stories about Nelson Mandela and Abraham Lincoln to make his point.

"He treated his students like he was a parent," Jewher told me. "We always had students coming to our house. Dining with us. Cooking with us. My father even gave part of his salary to his students as money for the Eid holidays." (Eid is the Islamic holiday that marks the end of Ramadan, when parents and elders are expected to give a little cash to younger people.)

"He loved to sing and loved to laugh," she said. "He loved making silly jokes. He thought he was funny but actually he wasn't."

"That was Ilham Tohti," Eset Sulayman confirmed to me. "He was from the modernizing camp. There were three camps: the Islamists, the modernists, and the traditionalists. He believed that to get somewhere with your cause, you had to work with the real world."

"This man, we thought, was going to become our leader," Maysem's friend told me.

But Tohti insisted that he didn't want to become a political leader. He only wanted to be seen as a scholar.[20]

"I'm sure my father wouldn't want to be the leader," Jewher confirmed. "He always wanted to be a simple man. But this was a time when people want[ed] someone to lead them."

CHAPTER 7

The Great Rejuvenation

The great rejuvenation of the Chinese nation is no walk
in the park or mere drum beating and gong clanging.

—XI JINPING

Ilham Tohti was correct when he said that China was showing a new, less tolerant, more authoritarian face. A changing of the guard was underway that would redefine how China saw its leaders and how those leaders cracked down on their enemies.

In 2012, at the same time Tohti was lecturing about reconciliation, I landed in Chongqing, an industrial port city in southwestern China. I was looking into the revival of old-school Maoism, a nostalgia spurred by a star Communist Party leader named Bo Xilai, who ran the city like a mayor.[1]

At this time, Bo was the defendant in a massive trial generating headlines all over the world. Yet just two years earlier in 2010, because of his governance model, *Time* magazine had named him one of the hundred most influential people in the world.[2] Bo bucked the trend of runaway economic growth and favored anti-corruption drives, mafia busting, and a reinvigoration of the spirit of Chairman Mao. That spirit represented a return to heavy state intervention in the economy and business, and circumventing the law to detain criminal suspects and seize their assets.[3]

But his wife, a successful lawyer named Gu Kailai, sealed Bo's downfall. She stood accused, and was later convicted, of murdering a former family friend, the high-rolling British citizen Neil Heywood. She had introduced Heywood to influential allies who wanted him to work as a fixer for a real estate project in Chongqing, luring in British investors. After the project fell through, Heywood asked Gu for a portion of his promised commission, and pursued the money from her wealthy son in London, igniting a feud between Heywood and Gu.

In her court confession, Gu said Heywood attempted to blackmail her family and threatened her son. Outraged, she hatched the plot for his murder. Gu met Heywood in a hotel room where, after drinking whiskey together, he got drunk and began vomiting into the toilet. Afterward, Gu held him down on the bed, and from a soy sauce container dripped the deadly toxin potassium cyanide mixed with green tea into his mouth, killing him.[4] In August 2012, Gu was convicted and sentenced to death for Heywood's murder, though the sentence was ultimately commuted to life imprisonment.[5]

In September 2013, Bo himself was also sentenced to life in prison for taking bribes, embezzlement, and abuse of power. The court found that he took bribes worth more than $3.3 million, which included a villa in Cannes in the south of France, and that he abused his power by firing the police chief in an attempt to stop the investigation into his wife's murder of Heywood.[6]

And with that, China had purged one of its most powerful and revered political families, transforming them into a symbol of the corruption and excess that had beset the new China, which needed fixing with a national rejuvenation.

In the gray and gritty streets of Chongqing, the legacy of Bo Xilai was clear.

"China was growing and people were getting rich," one gruff middle-aged man, slurping noodles at a street stall, told me, "but my job as a construction worker was always tough and my family had a hard time putting food on the table.

"The new China should not be just about making money. That's what causes corruption. The new China needs to be about being strong and united."

"Even though he said he was going after corrupt officials, [Bo] became a symbol of everything that was wrong with the new China. There was crime, corruption, the idea that we should leave behind who we are. People wanted to grab the spoils," a Chinese friend told me who, like others, didn't want to be named for fear of angering the government. "You could say he was a kind of scapegoat."

The runaway growth of the previous two decades had lifted hundreds of millions of people out of gut-wrenching poverty. But economic growth came with soaring inequalities, corruption, and crime. China, a growing chorus of leaders believed, had lost its way.

[ ]

Until his disgrace, Bo Xilai was rumored to be a favorite to be appointed the chairman of the People's Republic of China,[7] the equivalent of president, at the coming Communist Party Congress in November 2012.

Once Bo was dislodged from political power, the man who rose in his place was a bureaucrat named Xi Jinping. His father, a former vice premier, had been a leading figure. At fifteen, Xi was sent to work on an agricultural commune, common practice at the time, and embraced communism. His worldview was shaped, like that of many party cadres, by having suffered through the Cultural Revolution as a teenager, an experience that taught him the hardships of life and toughened up the shy teenager who loved classical poetry.

"I always had a stubborn streak and wouldn't put up with being bullied," he said in an interview in 2000. "I riled the radicals, and they blamed me for everything that went wrong."

In May 1966, four years after his father was purged from the Communist Party for supporting a novel Chairman Mao opposed, and sent to work in a factory, Xi Jinping's high school classes were halted.

Chairman Mao had declared the "cultural revolution" that whipped up the masses and purged his enemies for total control, forging a personality cult. Chaos swept across the nation and student mobs began denouncing their teachers and parents. Red Guards patrolled the streets, beating up people who wore bourgeois clothes. Businesses, schools, and other symbols of capitalist excess were looted and abandoned. As a result, China was submerged in a decade of hunger, destitution, and violence.

The revolutionaries looted Xi's family home. His father, the former party cadre, was paraded in the streets in humiliation. His own wife denounced him.[8]

But Xi didn't blame the Communist Party for his suffering. Rather, like other leaders of the first generation to lead China under Mao, he saw himself as a legitimate heir to the communist legacy of his parents' generation. He learned to be suspicious of the populists and rabble-rousers, such as the young cultural revolutionaries who upended hierarchy and order, instigating chaos. For Xi, the desirable status quo was a kind of obedient patriotism. A pragmatist, he chose to survive hardship in China by becoming "redder than red," according to one leaked US diplomatic cable based on a discussion with a well-connected embassy contact.[9]

Xi moved to a small village where he lived in a cave and worked as a local government administrator. His sister killed herself on an unknown date during this time. Xi was rejected from party membership seven times, being admitted finally in 1974, but only after befriending a party official.[10]

Like other party bureaucrats, Xi studied engineering in college, though he never worked as an engineer. He graduated in the late 1970s and began rising steadily through the party ranks, just as China was beginning its market reforms and opening up to the world.[11] Xi's political career began as old-fashioned Maoist communism entered its twilight years. The generation that grew up with the totalitarian system of Chairman Mao was fading in favor of a more collectivized, bureaucratic leadership system.

For some, including Xi, China was losing its soul. The party "had become corrupted and devoid of an ideological center," wrote political scientist Elizabeth Economy in *The Third Revolution: Xi Jinping and the New Chinese State*. "In the eyes of Xi, nothing less than dramatic, revolutionary change could save the party and the state and propel China forward to realize its full potential as a great power."[12]

In 2012, Xi Jinping was elected by elite cadres as the new chairman of the Communist Party. He succeeded Chairman Hu Jintao, a soft-spoken and methodical bureaucrat. Hu was a type common among leaders of his generation, a man without an outsized personality or charisma. The rise of Chairman Xi represented a departure from Hu's softer style of leadership. Xi wasn't afraid to bust corrupt officials, shake up the system, or make enemies.

Xi believed his mandate was to remake the system. China was about to undergo a patriotic rejuvenation, away from the corrupting market forces of the past and back to national unity and discipline. Xi wanted to lead the movement.[13]

Exuding a natural charisma, Xi fashioned himself as a Renaissance man, who nonetheless projected the comfortable presence of a member of the red elite. More simplicity and less indulgence was his trademark calling.

"He radiates incredible strength," a European diplomat told the French journalist François Bougon.[14]

He was also an intellectual.

Xi liked to list the names of the national authors he'd read, in every major country he visited. When he traveled to the United States and met with President Barack Obama, Xi claimed in a speech to have read Hemingway, Whitman, Thoreau, and Thomas Paine's "Common Sense." When he visited Russia, the list was Krylova, Pushkin, Gogol, Lermontov, Turgenev, Dostoyevsky, Nekrasov, Chernyshevsky, Tolstoy, and Chekhov.

Whatever the country, Xi droned on and on.[15]

"It's totally ridiculous," a Chinese friend told me in Beijing. "You could write an *SNL* skit about this stuff. Except it'd get censored and you'd end up in jail."

Xi was also proud of his military knowledge, having served as the assistant to the defense minister in the 1980s. Military might, he believed, was an expression of national power.[16]

"He has experienced much, and gone through many a difficult period," said the Singaporean prime minister after meeting Xi in 2007. "I would put him in Nelson Mandela's class of people. A person with enormous emotional stability who does not allow his personal misfortunes or sufferings to affect his judgment."[17]

Xi had a powerful sense of history, and used it to frame his view of China's future.

"The five thousand years of Chinese civilization are an intellectual strength," Xi said. He promised his people they'd live out the

"Chinese Dream," restoring China to the position it held when it was a major power that collected tribute from around the world.[18] "The superiority of our system," he declared in November 2012, "will be fully demonstrated through a brighter future."[19]

Part of that future included the rediscovery of China's western frontier of Xinjiang and Central Asia.

"The Silk Road, which ran through the western part of Eurasia, was once an important bridge for communication between eastern and western civilizations, as well as for commercial activities," wrote Wang Jisi, an influential geopolitical strategist and professor at the elite Peking University, on October 17, 2012.

Momentum was building for what Wang called a "March West," a new strategy that would pivot China toward its barren, western frontier, since the United States, Japan, and South Korea dominated China's eastern border, the Pacific Ocean.[20]

"As a Kazakh proverb goes, 'The history of a land is the history of its people,'" Xi said in a landmark speech at Nazaybayev University in neighboring Kazakhstan, on September 7, 2013:

> Over 2,100 years ago, during China's Han dynasty, a Chinese envoy Zhang Qiang was sent to Central Asia twice with a mission of peace and friendship. His journeys opened the door to friendly contacts between China and Central Asian countries as well as the Silk Road linking east and west . . . Shaanxi, my home province, is right at the starting point of the ancient Silk Road. Today, as I stand here and look back at that episode of history, I could almost hear the camel bells echoing in the mountains and see the wisps of smoke rising from the desert. It has brought me close to the place I am visiting. . . . We should take an innovative approach and jointly build an economic belt along the Silk Road. This will be a great undertaking benefiting the people of all countries along the route.[21]

So began the One Belt, One Road initiative, the planned $1 trillion network that harkened back to the history Xi had studied carefully.

At the beginning of the sixteenth century, when European explorers were first arriving in the New World, Eurasia generated 89 percent of the world's gross domestic product.[22] Europe at the time was emerging from an era of seemingly endless plague, famine, and warfare. Europeans were seen throughout Eurasia as primitive Christian barbarians who harassed their lands with ragtag crusading armies.

In the meantime, Asian and Middle Eastern empires had developed biology, paper, movable type, gunpowder, and algebra. China's Ming dynasty was a regional hegemon sending its seafaring explorer Zheng He to India and Africa.[23] But China's strength didn't mean that it dominated Eurasia. A mosaic of kingdoms, empires, and tribes had populated the Silk Road for thousands of years.[24]

The Oxford University historian Peter Frankopan writes that Europeans shifted their share of the global economy and political power away from the East when they began massacring indigenous peoples of the New World, and looting the Americas' wealth. Global trading and military power transferred from the land to the sea, and the creation of modern European navies helped kick-start the industrial revolution in the eighteenth century.[25]

While Europe mechanized its forces and built powerful, modern nation-states, China's leaders were dismissive of modern technologies and weaponry. They clung to the idea that their emperor was the son of heaven with no equal, who had an uninterrupted heritage predating the lineages of neighboring powers like Japan and Korea. Gifts given to the emperor by an envoy from King George III were treated as tributes rather than gifts presented to an equal sovereign.[26]

By the middle of the nineteenth century, China's feudal kingdom was becoming increasingly outdated, corrupt, and ineffective in a changing world. The ruling class, hooked on opium, had fallen into debt, addiction, and crime. China attempted to halt the British opium trade, but Britain sent gunboats to Hong Kong to keep the market open, in what became known as the First Opium War. In the Chinese Communist Party's history writings later on, this marked the beginning of the "century of national humiliation" at the hands of Western powers, a shocking reversal of China's role in the world. The emperor was effectively placed at the feet of the most powerful seafaring empire the world had ever seen.[27]

And once prosperous Eurasia too fell into war, religious bigotry, and disrepair. This was the result of pilfering conquest by European colonials and the corruption of the tribal governments bought off by them.[28] After years of Maoism and economic brutalism, in 1973, as China was about to inch toward market reforms, it accounted for only 5 percent of the global economy.[29]

The lesson for China's government? Modernize. Stand strong, stand tall. Embrace technology. Xi Jinping was explicit about it in passages from two speeches he delivered in July and August 2013:

> Advanced technology is the sharp weapon of the modern state. An important reason that Western countries were able to hold sway over the world in modern times was that they held the advanced technology. You cannot buy the truly core technologies. It's been aptly put that "The sharpest weapon of a state should not be revealed."

And

> Our technology still generally lags that of developed countries, and we must adopt an asymmetrical strategy of catching up and overtaking, bringing our own advantages to bear. In core technological fields where it would be impossible for us to catch up by 2050, we must research asymmetrical steps to catch up and overtake. Internationally, if you don't have the advantage of core technologies, you don't have the political momentum. We must make a big effort in key fields and areas where there is a stranglehold. The same applies to the military.[30]

Xi never clarified what he meant by an "asymmetrical strategy" in technology. He might have been obliquely referring to copying and imitating Western technologies to catch up to them, as Japan and South Korea did in previous decades.

Gradually, Xi began to oversee China's expansion into a "supercontinent" by exerting its influence across Eurasia. The United States had done something similar with its destruction of Native American lands and rights in its relentless march to the Pacific Coast; and with its double-dealing to achieve the construction of the Panama Canal, which allowed it to move ships quickly between the Atlantic and Pacific Oceans, giving it enormous geopolitical power. The British did the same with the Suez Canal in the Middle East, speeding the trade route between London and its most valuable colony, India.[31]

"Eurasia is by far the world's largest and most central supercontinent, with well over a third of the Earth's entire land area," noted the political scientist Kent E. Alder. "Beneath its soil lies nearly two-thirds of the world's oil and over 80 percent of conventional gas reserves . . . Eurasia's constituent nations hold almost 85 percent of world foreign exchange reserves, while generating close to 70 percent of global GDP in PPP [purchasing power parity] terms, not to mention nearly half of the world's manufactured goods."[32]

A supercontinent connected through trade networks and roads was exactly what China needed and wanted. With its economic growth losing momentum by 2013,[33] China could move its workers and infrastructure projects to the underdeveloped west, and through the plateaus, mountain ranges, and deserts of Central Asia and the Middle East.

But China's leaders had other worries that went beyond the slowing economy, according to internal party documents leaked to me and other journalists. Two years earlier, in June 2011, the United States had begun gradually withdrawing forces from neighboring Afghanistan, leaving behind a potential vacuum from which extremists and terrorists could launch attacks on their other "godless" enemy next door: communist China.[34]

"He [Chairman Xi] is a strong, bright man," then vice president Joe Biden told students at the University of Pennsylvania in May 2013, after he visited China. "But he has the look of a man who is not at all sure all is going to end well."[35]

[ ]

On a chilly overcast day in October 2013, Tiananmen Square, the symbol of national greatness and the famous site of the violent antidemocracy crackdown more than two decades earlier, was its usual self: crowded, congested, and smoggy.

That morning, witnesses heard a car honking in the distance. An SUV appeared, racing down a thoroughfare. It ploughed into the crowd and crashed into a bridge rail. It exploded, just steps away from the portrait of Chairman Mao that stood prominently in the square. When the smoke cleared, two people lay dead on the ground, along with three suicide terrorists in the burnt-out vehicle.[36]

Police in the crowd began forcing onlookers to delete the photos from their cameras. A BBC crew attempting to record footage was briefly detained, and online news reports were censored in China. But authorities soon released the BBC crew, and the news hit the outside world.[37]

It was an incredible strike at the heart of China. Heads were going to roll. In its wake, the top military commander in Xinjiang was removed from his position.[38]

Chinese authorities, in fact, had created their own terrorist problem, radicalizing part of the population after years of relentless arrests, repression, and forced disappearances of Uyghur suspects. Starting in 2009, and picking up in 2013, thousands of Uyghurs flew to Afghanistan and Turkey and then hopped in cars and busses to Syria, an exodus of people who saw themselves as the victims of government injustice and wanted to train themselves to use weapons and mount an insurgency.[39] "Then we hoped we could return to China," a jihadist who fought in Syria in 2013 and later returned to Turkey told me. Back in China he had been a doctor, and only embraced religious piety after arriving in Syria. "We didn't care about the Syrian civil war, or who would win. We just wanted to fight the Communist Party [of China]."

The October Tiananmen Square attack was the most dramatic indication of the campaign of terrorism that had developed in China. Five months later, on March 1, 2014, a group of eight terrorists, dressed in black and armed with long knives, raced into a train station in China's southwest and started stabbing and slashing people. A SWAT team stormed the station and found 172 victims bloody and wounded. More than two dozen died. The only member of the four-person SWAT team with an automatic rifle shot and killed four of the terrorists. Police arrested one, and the remaining three were apprehended two days later.[40] The authorities identified the suspects as violent Uyghur separatists. China's state media began calling the attack "China's 9/11."[41]

"A nationwide outrage has been stirred," wrote a commentator in Xinhua, China's state news outlet. "Justice needs to be done and terrorists should be punished with iron fists."[42]

"Today," Rebiya Kadeer, president of the World Uyghur Congress, a peaceful advocacy group for Uyghur rights, had said the day after the October 2013 Tiananmen Square attack, "I fear for the future of East Turkestan and the Uyghur people more than I ever have."[43]

[ ]

Maysem was in a WeChat group with her friends when one of them sent news of the Tiananmen Square car bomb. Chinese authorities said terrorist propaganda was found in what they claimed was the suicide car, including the blue flag of Uyghur independence, according to the reports her friend was reading. Maysem knew these reports weren't always reliable.

"I can't believe it," said her friend. "It seems so extreme."

Maysem was immediately worried about the reputation of the Uyghurs, that people all over China were turning on them. As she discussed the situation, at home with her friends, she felt a heaviness was settling on the land she had grown up in.

"People began calling their families overseas and said, 'Don't come back here.'"

Chairman Xi was on his first and only visit to Xinjiang in April 2014, when two Uyghur militants bombed a train station in Urumqi, injuring seventy-nine people and killing one. The two suicide bombers were killed in the explosion.[44]

Then, less than a month after Xi's visit, more Uyghur militants tossed grenades and explosives into a vegetable market in Urumqi.

At least forty-three people died, including four of the assailants, and more than ninety were wounded.[45]

Xi Jinping called a series of emergency sessions with his top cadres and advisors.

"In recent years," he said in one meeting, according to leaked documents, "Xinjiang has grown very quickly and the standard of living has consistently risen, but ethnic separatism and terrorist violence have still been on the rise. This goes to show that economic development does not automatically bring lasting order and security."

Xi was revising the state's view of liberalism that had characterized the national strategy for the previous three decades. China was no longer opening its borders in search of new ideas. It was closing them and returning to more totalitarian ways.

"After the United States pulls troops out of Afghanistan, terrorist organizations positioned on the frontiers of Afghanistan and Pakistan may quickly infiltrate into Central Asia," Xi said. "East Turkestan's [another name for Xinjiang] terrorists who have received real-war training in Syria and Afghanistan could at any time launch terrorist attacks in Xinjiang."

Xi compared religious extremism to a drug: "You lose your sense, go crazy and will do anything."

Xi had come of age during the collapse of the Soviet Union, and came to the conclusion that to preserve China it was time for muscle, weaponry, and strength—and also for a sweeping campaign against the Uyghur and Kazakh minorities. He called for the use of new technology, and told his cadres to study how Americans had responded to the September 11 attacks.

"We Communists should be naturals at fighting a people's war," he said, pointing out that China should use the public to infiltrate and spy on each other. "We're the best at organizing for a task."[46]

With that, Xinjiang's future was determined.

CHAPTER 8

China's War on Terror

We Must Solemnly Reject Religion

—CHINESE PROPAGANDA BANNER IN KASHGAR

China had already been organizing for counterterrorism since 9/11. At that time the Chinese ambassador to the United States declared at an embassy reception that China would stand "side by side with the US in the war against terror."[1] China also began hunting down terrorist suspects in Afghanistan, Central Asia, and the Middle East. But in accordance with Chairman Xi's remarks in 2014, the country began deploying more aggressive intelligence agents around the world, hoping to gather information on terrorist suspects.

These spies had a mandate to protect China from terrorist plots, with intelligence officials under pressure to find the enemy wherever they could, and report their successes back to their government leaders. The leaders then paraded these "successes" in state news outlets. China's spies were caught in a vicious cycle: in countries like Turkey, they were forced to blur the boundary between violent jihadists and peaceful Uyghur residents. (Although peaceful residents were usually critical of the Chinese government.) [2]

"The more enemies they can find," Abduweli Ayup said, "the more they can unify the country."

Abduweli had tracked down a Chinese spy preparing to defect. He had gone into hiding in an obscure seaside town in Turkey, where few fellow Uyghurs lived. Here, the spy believed there was little chance he would be betrayed by another Uyghur reporting in secret to the Chinese government. Abduweli offered to introduce me to him.

Because Abduweli was well known among Uyghurs and foreign journalists around the world, since he posted articles and commentaries on his popular website, he frequently received tips and letters of interest from people who wanted to connect with correspondents through his network.

The spy was one such person who wanted to tell his story before he defected. Being in the media's eye offered him some protection should the Chinese government target him. And it allowed him to get some of his past deeds off his chest. So he was willing to meet an American journalist.

Abduweli and I boarded a bus for the long ride to the seaside. "Meet me at the seafood restaurant on the main road," the spy wrote to us on Signal, the encrypted messaging app.

At six o'clock that evening, Yusuf Amet, who allowed us to use his name, walked in, dressed in camouflage pants and a puffy white jacket. He admitted to being on his fifth beer. Quickly, he filled us in about his family life before he had gone into hiding.

Yusuf came from a broken family whose father had deserted his mother and siblings. He said that growing up he had sought a kind of masculine prestige, absent of a father to guide his maturing into manhood. He thought being macho would win him the love and admiration of his single mother and other women in his life.

"If my wife misbehaved," he bragged, "I beat her. Eventually, she left me." In 2010, having dropped out of high school, Yusuf decided his calling was to take up arms as a fighter in Afghanistan, where he would train for an independence war against the Chinese government in Xinjiang.

"I wanted to make my mother proud. My mother was my life. I loved her so much," he said.

"My mom and I went to the airport. She was about to send me off on the flight," he went on, "when suddenly the police raced in and arrested us. They'd been tracking us. They knew what we were up to."

Yusuf spent two years in a Chinese prison, interrogated by intelligence officers who put him in the same tiger chair Maysem had endured in the boiling courtyard of the detention center.

"In the cell next to me, they tortured my mother. I heard her screams. They wanted me to hear her. It was then that I met a chief of intelligence. A powerful local chief in a town in western China," he said. That man called himself "Abdulshukur."

"Neither of us want to see you in prison for the rest of your youth. And think about your mother. We'll release her if you help us," the intelligence official told him.

Then he laid his cards on the table. Instead of prison, Yusuf—young, healthy, and strong—could spend three years spying on his family in China. Then, having proven his loyalty, he would travel around the world posing as a young man interested in joining terrorist groups. He would infiltrate so-called cells and report back to his new boss.

"They saw in me that I was a bit crazy. They played on my need for recognition."

After a year on parole starting in 2013, reporting to the police every few days on his weekly activities, Yusuf did as he was ordered, and reported to the intelligence services on the harmless activities of his siblings and cousin. They were sent to detention centers as a result, he said.

Then, in 2016, the Chinese intelligence official explained that terrorist cells had infiltrated the entire Middle East and were plotting imminent attacks against China. He wouldn't say who the terrorists were except that they were crazed, violent, troubled young men preparing a "jihad." Yusuf was given a diplomatic passport.

"They sent me to Pakistan. I arrived at the airport and met our mole in the Pakistani government." This was a former Pakistani military commander who'd been paid off to smuggle foreign spies across the border into Afghanistan.

"After a flight over the mountains, I arrived at my target. It was a village in southern Afghanistan where I was supposed to join a local militia that was connected to the Taliban."

The Chinese government had already infiltrated the Taliban, and the group welcomed Yusuf as a new fighter, not knowing he was reporting their movements to his handler back home.

"My mission was to monitor Chinese citizens," meaning Uyghurs and other Muslim groups fighting in Afghanistan, "who were joining terrorist groups. China did not want terrorists spill-ing over into its border."

But the mission was much less exciting than he'd imagined. "We had the occasional shootout," he said. "Little skirmishes with the Afghan government troops. Didn't see any Americans."

After six months, he was bored and restless. He had experienced none of the battlefield glory he'd envisioned for himself as an as-piring independence fighter, before being recruited as a spy. Yusuf messaged his handler on WhatsApp to tell him he wanted out.

"We always used WhatsApp. We thought it was secure," he said. "We didn't use WeChat. Even Chinese intelligence was concerned that they were being monitored, since the government could or-der WeChat to turn over its data."

Yusuf showed me his WhatsApp messages from his handler, with whom he was still in contact. "He is a master manipulator," Yusuf said. "He knows the art of manipulating people."

The handler immediately got back to him with a new assign-ment.

"You'll stay a little while longer," he said. "You're a talented young man. You have a big future ahead of you. Soon, we'll send you to the Middle East."

China was building hundreds of oil pipelines, rigs, highways, and other infrastructure projects that it would later place under the umbrella of One Belt, One Road. To protect China's invest-ments, Chinese intelligence agencies needed spies who could go around the world, infiltrate Uyghur communities, and convince local authorities to send Uyghurs back home to China, where they'd be imprisoned.

According to Yusuf, Chinese intelligence services were con-vinced overseas Uyghur communities were plotting to blow up Chinese bridges and oil and gas pipelines, to impede the belt and road projects. Governments might be reluctant to work with China if their cooperation invited terrorist attacks.

Under enormous pressure to stop the alleged plots, China's in-telligence work became sloppy. The intelligence services decided on a dragnet strategy: treat every overseas Uyghur as an enemy, and monitor them until they could prove their innocence. Once this strategy was in place, the Chinese spies lost their focus on the real targets: the actual terrorists fighting in Syria and recruiting extremists in Turkey. It wasn't an effective way of conducting intelligence, Yusuf confirmed.

In 2017, he crossed the border back to Pakistan. He then boarded a flight to Istanbul in Turkey, the country that hosted the most Uyghur refugees, and had a larger Uyghur population than any nation other than China. He was "supposed to meet Uyghur businessmen and convince them to let me join their business associations."

Yusuf walked into a local restaurant, met an elderly target, and made his pitch.

"I'm looking for a job," he said. "I have all kinds of skills, but I just arrived here poor. Can you help?"

No job offer followed, but Yusuf kept setting up meetings, trying to pry his way in. The further his infiltration, the more ominous the orders from his handler became.

"He told me that there was a real purpose behind my business meetings," Yusuf said. "He said I was actually meeting with terrorists. They were connected to a violent group in Syria called the Turkistan Islamic Party (TIP). He said I was supposed to get a regular job at some local business, so I could then get into the TIP, so they could ship me to Syria and then I'd be hunting down terrorists."

Although Yusuf had assumed he wanted an adventure, the growing paranoia of his handler unsettled him. The business association he was monitoring consisted of relaxed, elderly men who seemed rather moderate in their religious beliefs. They had little reason to risk being arrested and ruining their businesses. They seemed very unlikely sponsors of terrorists in Syria.

Yusuf found himself wondering if his intelligence supervisors, starved of the enemy they needed, were beginning to see adversaries everywhere. And his supervisors still hadn't released his mother, as they'd promised four years earlier, in exchange for his spying missions.

[ ]

I'd met members of the TIP in Turkey, where they were coordi-
nating their military operations in Syria, fighting against the government forces of dictator Bashar al-Assad. I'd heard from military
sources in Syrian Kurdistan, a place of heavy conflict, that Uyghur
fighters were suffering heavy casualties, and many key jihadis had
been captured. The idea that terrorists, hardened by battle against
Assad's forces, would then return to Xinjiang to form a caliphate in
China's west seemed far-fetched. But it was a narrative that suited
the Chinese state, and the government cultivated it regularly.

[ ]

The story of Uyghur terrorists went back to 9/11. Through
heavy-handed repression and paranoia, China helped bolster their
ranks, legitimacy, and recruitment among young men who felt
persecuted by the Communist Party.

Among these men was a group of twenty-two Uyghurs who
were captured in Afghanistan and flown to Guantanamo Bay in
Cuba. They had been members of a loose coalition at camps in Afghanistan and Pakistan, where they had received weapons training they could use in the future against China, if the opportunity
arose.

Their detention was legitimized by an alleged political maneu-
ver in 2002. At the United Nations, Chinese diplomats protested
America's proposed invasion of Iraq. Hoping China might drop its
opposition, lawyers defending the Uyghur terrorist suspects believed that the George W. Bush administration designated the Uyghur independence group, the East Turkestan Islamic Movement
(ETIM), a terrorist organization. China continued to oppose war
in Iraq despite the alleged favor, but didn't vote to block the Iraq
invasion at the UN Security Council.[3]

All of the Uyghur detainees said they hadn't heard about al-
Qaeda until after they were sent to Guantanamo Bay.[4] But as far
as the United States was concerned, they were not disgruntled
dissidents fleeing persecution in China and passing through Afghanistan, as they claimed, but militant jihadists waging a war on

liberal democracy itself.[5] Even if the liberal democracy in question was Chinese.

"I'd never heard of the ETIM before," Sean Roberts, an expert on the Uyghurs and professor of international relations at George Washington University, told me. "None of the experts had heard of it."[6]

Suddenly, with America's blessing, China had what it needed: a terrorist bogeyman.

Chinese intelligence operatives were allowed to visit Guantanamo and interrogate the twenty-two captives, a red-carpet treatment. China was the only foreign country whose representatives were allowed to enter the camp and photograph the Uyghur suspects.

But the Uyghurs refused to cooperate and answer the Chinese intelligence agents' questions. They'd been tortured in China, after all, and their families back home were in danger.

After the Chinese agents interrogated each Uyghur suspect for up to eight hours, sometimes every day for three to four days, a team of Pentagon interrogators allowed the Chinese agents to take their photos. US soldiers held at least one Uyghur in a chokehold as the Chinese visitors took their photos. The US government then handed over the Uyghurs' classified files to the Chinese agents, despite earlier promises to the Uyghur detainees that their files would remain secret, free from Chinese eyes.

"I was disappointed in my country," their military translator, Rushan Abbas, told me. By October 2002, the Pentagon's interrogators had begun to conclude that some of the Uyghur prisoners were not jihadi terrorists, but separatist fighters training for an independence movement against China.[7]

Oops.

"Many of them were wonderful, sweet people. They clearly weren't terrorists who had some vendetta against the US," Abbas told me.

Another month passed, but still the Uyghurs were held in their cells. The US government wasn't sure what to do with them. Since they were held extra-judicially under the Defense Department's improvised label of "enemy combatant," their detention had no grounding in any American law or the Geneva Conventions. Consequently, no legal procedure existed to determine where and how to release them.[8]

The legal limbo continued as, behind the scenes, American diplomats tried to arrange deals with other countries to grant the Uyghurs asylum as refugees. They weren't welcome in America, where members of Congress didn't want Guantanamo "terrorists" to be resettled in their districts.

In May 2006, after five of the twenty-two men had been imprisoned in Guantanamo for three years, those five were resettled in Albania, the only country that would take them in.

"The five people accepted by Albania are by no means refugees, but terrorist suspects of the East Turkestan Islamic Movement," declared a Chinese government spokesman four days after the release. "It has a close relationship to Al Qaeda and the Taliban."[9]

The Communist Party had a hot-list of threats to China, on which were the "five poisons": democracy agitators, Taiwan supporters, Tibetans, the Falun Gong spiritual group, and Muslim Uyghur terrorists.[10]

Meanwhile, seventeen Uyghurs languished in Guantanamo's highest-security compound, Camp 6, nicknamed the "Tomb." It was a place so dark and dank that its inmates clamored and applauded when the sun came over the prison's single rooftop window.[11]

Finally, in 2009, after seven years in American captivity, six of the seventeen remaining Uyghurs were resettled in Palau, a tiny Pacific island, while the remaining captives were resettled in Slovakia, El Salvador, Bermuda, and elsewhere. These were the only places that would take them, but only after the United States promised to pay $93,333 per man, to help cover each Uyghur's housing and living expenses.[12] Feeling unwelcome and not at all at home, most of them gave up their newly appointed abodes and later moved to Turkey.[13]

But China had what it needed. The decision to lock up the Uyghurs at Guantanamo Bay, with no evidence of a terrorist plot, helped China justify its treatment of the Uyghurs. It painted them as a terrorist time bomb that needed to be defused through heavy-handed measures.

Fifteen years after 9/11, Yusuf had become part of that defusion operation in Afghanistan, Pakistan, and Turkey: locate a terrorist hidden in every home, street corner, school, and food truck. No one from the Uyghur ethnic group was to be trusted.

[ ]

Even Yusuf, loyal to his country's cause, grew skeptical and tired of the propaganda over time. Every one of his missions ended in failure, since he couldn't find the terrorists his supervisors insisted were everywhere.

"I sent back WhatsApp messages telling my boss about what local businessmen were doing," he said. "They really were just businessmen, going about their days. But the intelligence people got more and more paranoid. They were under pressure from the top to find the villains. They became convinced that I should trust no one."

The final straw came when the government asked Yusuf to spy on an esteemed and charitable community leader.

"We suspect he's a terrorist," Yusuf's handler told him. "We have strong evidence." They never shared the intelligence, citing the national security threat; they just dropped dark hints.

"Why else would a Muslim man invest so much money into becoming a philanthropist? Clearly this must be a front for recruiting terrorists."[14]

But Yusuf had hung around the man, attending his events and speeches, and found no evidence that he was up to no good. So Yusuf abandoned his mission to infiltrate the extremists of Turkey and Syria.

"I wasn't with my wife and kids. I was all alone. A young guy in the Middle East, drinking too much and smoking too much. I began to realize what a horrible thing I'd done. I thought I was going to fight terrorists, but instead I was turning on my people. So I ran off to where I am now, and became a gas station attendant to be anonymous. I wanted to disappear." He was devastated that the intelligence operatives broke their promise and never released his mother.

Abduweli and I visited the small number of other Uyghurs in the town, and asked around about Yusuf.

"He's quiet," said one. "We don't really know much about him at all."

Abduweli and I had interviewed Yusuf every evening for four days, after he finished his gas station shift. And we'd been attracting attention from some of the locals. A restaurant manager, a group of teenagers, and other passers-by wanted to know why an American "tourist" would visit this ramshackle, insignificant seaside industrial town of Zonguldak, which even local tourists skipped over.

The threat from Chinese spies wasn't our only concern. Turkey was becoming an increasingly authoritarian state, with political purges of the military and universities. I'd heard from many Turkish professors and former policy makers that intelligence operatives were monitoring people.

"Be careful," Yusuf warned us. "The intelligence services are always recruiting spies, and you might be a target for their surveillance." Yusuf then accepted the possibility that as an ex-spy speaking to journalists, the Chinese intelligence services might retaliate against him. He said he just wanted closure.

A foreign correspondent traveling with a Uyghur refugee like Abduweli was conspicuous and odd to locals. Before we gained any more attention, we decided it was time to leave. We returned to Istanbul and, after a brief hiatus from our interviews, went back to Ankara and to Maysem.

CHAPTER 9

The Three Evils: Terrorism, Extremism, and Separatism

The struggle against terror and to safeguard stability
is a protracted war, and also a war of offense.

—CHEN QUANGUO, XINJIANG COMMUNIST PARTY CHIEF

By 2013, back in Kashgar, Maysem's father had been instructed by the increasingly paranoid local government to travel the countryside and give patriotic speeches to the farmers.

"We stand united with China," he proclaimed. "We stand against the terrorists. Long live Chairman Xi Jinping, our glorious leader!"

"Dad was so proud," Maysem recalled. "He came home at the end of the day and talked about how great his speeches were, and how it reminded him of the Cultural Revolution."

"Let's stand against the three evils: terrorism, extremism, and separatism!" he would say to them. He told her the farmers all applauded, though Maysem couldn't tell from her father's accounts whether they really meant it.

One day, Maysem's mother came home with shocking news.

"A group of boys beat up a girl for wearing a veil at the school," she said. "I caught them and brought them to the principal's office.

"The principal looked at the case and decided not to discipline the boys. He never gave a reason. But there was a nervousness in his eyes." A fear, her mother believed, that by punishing the perpetrators, he'd get on the wrong side of government authorities, with their increasingly belligerent talk of a "Muslim terrorist" threat.

"They shouldn't wear a veil," Maysem's father said emphatically.

[ ]

When, after four years of intense study, Maysem graduated from her Beijing university with a degree in social sciences in 2013, she applied to a graduate school in Turkey.

"I want to see the world," she said. "Turkey was a good choice, since it accepted so many Uyghurs as residents.

"Plus, Beijing made me lonely. I wanted to be a part of something. I began turning to religion," she said, even though she'd grown up relatively secular. "I decided that I was, in my heart, Muslim, because China kept pushing me away, as some kind of 'other.'"

After passing the exams, she elected to do a master's course in social sciences in Ankara. The Beijing professor she was most sorry to bid farewell to was the one she most admired, Professor Tohti.

Maysem's mother was proud. Her father seemed unsatisfied, but admitted he would miss her.

"It was time for our goodbyes. So I set off in the fall of 2013. But home was never going to be the same after this. I just didn't realize it."

Quick-witted and intelligent, Maysem didn't have trouble excelling in graduate school, where she continued her favorite pastime of devouring books and writing fluent essays and analyses.

It also helped that she got on well with a new group of friends who understood her and her growing religious faith. At the Ankara university, she met a PhD student in her department named Arman, who'd previously been a journalist. He was an older, divorced man, a kind of eccentric loner lost in the medieval texts he studied for his dissertation.

"Now that I was out of China, we could use Facebook. It opened up a world of communications for us." Facebook, censored in China, was important for their relationship because they could always be in touch while they attended classes and side jobs in Turkey.

"When I saw her in person," Arman told me over tea in her apartment, "I knew I had found a special woman. We had the same interests." During the evenings, Arman serenaded her with

poetry on Facebook Messenger.[1] Some of the poems were taken
from centuries-old texts. One from the fifteenth century became
their favorite:

> True lovers are rare; has a true lover set foot on the path
> And not found his beloved at the first step?—that cannot be
>
> O Nevai, show respect, bring wine to the house of the heart
> For where wine is brought, in that house never will there
>   sorrow be[2]

"We quickly fell in love," she said.

But Maysem had planned to return home to Xinjiang for the
summer, so she and Arman promised to stay in touch whenever
they could, though not on Facebook, which was blocked in China.

She returned to "a changing place. Xinjiang wasn't the same as
I remembered it."

In Kashgar, Maysem was riding the bus to visit family when it
stopped at a police checkpoint. The police ordered everyone off,
specifically checked the Uyghurs' IDs, and scanned them with
their smartphones.

"Why are you going to that town?" the police asked each pas-
senger. They checked and double-checked all the luggage. Maysem
didn't think much of it at first. This was part of the government's
police campaign, called Strike Hard, to ferret out criminal suspects who supposedly abided by the three evils of terrorism, separatism, and extremism. Sure, the mood in Xinjiang was different
now, she thought. But campaigns with slogans like "Strike Hard"
had come and gone for almost two decades since 1996, the first
time the government instituted a Strike Hard campaign to clear
out drug smugglers and criminal gangs. She assumed this latest
campaign, despite her discomfort, would pass too.[3]

"I didn't have any bad run-ins with the police. They checked
me briefly and just whisked me through the checkpoints. It helped
to be from a respected family."

But over time, the mere act of going for a drive or a walk became
psychologically burdensome. Maysem was stopped at checkpoint

after checkpoint. Within a month, she was feeling mentally worn down.

"In this kind of world," she remembered, "you become more and more defensive, like you don't want to talk to anyone, you don't want to go out and meet people, and you trust no one."

City streets slowly emptied out, since no one wanted to risk going outside and being harassed by the police. That year "essential travel" to school, work, the grocery store, or to visit family soon became the only justifiable reasons to be outdoors. Xinjiang was in a kind of coronavirus-style lockdown, except the virus was excessive state control.

One day, Maysem drove with her parents to the gas station. Armed guards stood outside and watched them as they disembarked, looking for any sudden moves or suspicious behavior, though it was never clear what behavior might be deemed suspicious. Maysem's mom scanned her ID card. To Maysem, it seemed like the government had been rolling out a crude, early ranking system for Xinjiang residents that assessed their trustworthiness, based on whether they were from the Uyghur ethnicity, were unemployed, or had a family member in another country. Maysem lived in Turkey, which could negatively impact her family's trustworthiness ranking.[4]

If they scanned their IDs and then the system ranked Maysem or her family members untrustworthy, they would be denied the right to buy gas. The police also had the latitude to make this determination themselves. "It was tiring," Maysem said.

As Maysem met with relatives and friends at local hangouts, police appeared, checked everyone's IDs, eyed them suspiciously, then left without ever providing a reason for the interruption. It was intrusive surveillance, a low-level but persistent intimidation.

By the middle of the summer, even Maysem's mother, always the more liberal parent, counseled her daughter against meeting with friends too often or too late in the evening.

"Stay at home," she told her. "The authorities don't trust us."

But Maysem wasn't willing to withdraw into seclusion. When she went to a friend's wedding one day in August 2014, she wore the Islamic veil she'd adopted during her years in Beijing. A security guard stopped her at the door to the hall where her friend was to be married.

"Take off that veil," he said. "Are you crazy?"

"You can't dress like that," her father told her when he heard about it that night. "You're only going to attract the wrong attention."

The family instigated a new rule: when they went outside, they would avoid wearing traditional clothing that might provoke the police. Instead, Maysem was urged to wear unnaturally bright reds and pinks that didn't fit her style, but that were urbane, feminine, and made her look like a "refined lady." Her parents also expected her to smile for the police officers, almost always men. A smile and a bright, tight red dress were a sure way to stay out of trouble.

"People told me I looked beautiful," Maysem said. But as she ran errands around town, visiting the grocery store and the pharmacy for her parents, she thought, *This is not who I am. I am not myself.*

As police surveillance increased at the end of the summer, in August 2014, people had no choice but to wear disguises. At a medical clinic, at the bank, at the gas station, there were often two lines: an expedited one for the majority Han Chinese and a slower, more bureaucratic one for Uyghurs and other minorities. The Uyghurs had to smile and behave, or else they might be denied service. Maysem observed with displeasure how quickly people put on artificial qualities in the presence of power, toadying to state and corporate bureaucrats.

State television presented a certain image of Uyghur culture. "Every time I saw a Han Chinese TV show about the silk roads or about the Uyghurs, it was false and unbelievable," Maysem said. "We were the minority that was always singing and dancing. To the TV producers, our culture only consisted of the surface things, like our foods and marriage customs. We were exotic. We were becoming like a museum piece for everyone to look at." Maysem finally retreated. "I just wanted to stay at home and read books all day long." She was becoming distant and unrelatable to her family and friends.

"You came here from Turkey?" one acquaintance said to her that summer. "Are you some kind of religious person now?" Chinese officials began placing signs and paintings on the walls of government offices that showed the police and military, depicted as heroes, arresting and defeating Uyghur terrorists, portrayed as backward, rural Afghanis. *You're either with us, or against us.* The mood pervaded Xinjiang, and almost all of Maysem's acquaintances made clear, everywhere they went, that they were on the side of the government.

One day, Maysem's mom was jolted awake by what seemed like the sound of men shouting outside her house. She peered out the window at the public security bureau across the street, the local headquarters of the officers who watched over the population and arrested people. In China, the public security bureau is a symbol of state power. A group of seven men dressed in white robes, the traditional Islamic way of dressing a corpse, had charged the police station.

"The men were calling out someone's name," Maysem said.

Her mother wasn't sure what was going on. The men didn't look like they were armed. But then she heard gunfire from within the public security bureau and backed away from the window.

"We assumed those men were shot," Maysem said. "But we didn't know what they were doing, since Mom couldn't see guns or knives in their hands. White robes are a way of saying, 'I am prepared to die.'"

Maysem's mother checked the online news the next morning, and again the morning after, but there wasn't a word about what had happened that night. "I thought it was some sort of terrorist attack, but it was censored in the newspapers." Friends and passers-by on the street acted like nothing had happened.

Not long after, the family woke up again to what sounded like distant gunfire, bombs, and grenades. The next day, when Maysem's mother walked to the grocery store on the main thoroughfare, there was blood splattered on the street. Black-clad SWAT teams had closed off the market. Once more, no explanation was offered for what had happened.

[ ]

In 2013 and 2014, an estimated 592 Uyghurs were tried on security charges, though there is no way of knowing how many of those accusations were legitimate. China also held twelve thousand trials for people accused of hurting the social order,[5] but those in the Uyghur refugee community, who knew some of these defendants, told me the defendants had merely joined peaceful protests, challenged government bans on religious observance, or distributed banned information.

In 2014, the government began recalling Uyghurs living in Urumqi (and, according to Maysem, other parts of China), ordering them to return home to their country villages, under the guise of having to renew their ID cards. When they returned, the police took at least one of them away for what they called "reeducation," for reasons not entirely clear. Others were restricted from moving between villages without the approval of the government.[6] Whispers lit up around Kashgar about disappearances.

"It was as if Xinjiang was creeping towards war, in which no one trusted anyone," Maysem said. "The population itself was the enemy."

[ ]

Maysem heard that the police were harassing her old professor, Ilham Tohti, "with what seemed like an arrest every week."

Tohti had always been freed after detainment, accompanied by warnings not to agitate with his students.

The pattern gathered momentum in 2012, with a ten-hour interrogation after he published an online essay that accused China's military of monitoring Uyghurs during the Ramadan holiday. Two months later, he was briefly held under house arrest and released.[7]

At three o'clock on the morning of February 2, 2013, Tohti and his daughter, Jewher, left their home for Beijing's Capital airport, to board a stopover flight to Chicago's O'Hare airport. Tohti was

set to begin a research fellowship at Indiana University Blooming-
ton in the United States. Their flight was scheduled to depart at
10 A.M., but Tohti thought the authorities would be less likely to
monitor them if they left in the middle of the night.

At the airport, security agents pulled them aside and inspected
their passports.[8]

"We were at the airport about to leave," Jewher told me. "I was
going to stay for about a month and he was going to stay for a year.
The police were prepared to let me leave the country, but not my
father. I asked him what I should do, not wanting to leave him
behind."

Tohti was clear in his advice: "I think you should take this
chance and leave." He pushed his daughter away, afraid she would
refuse to leave and place herself in danger too. "Go, just go," he
said.

Jewher crossed through airport security for her stopover flight
to Chicago, unsure when she would see him again.

[ ]

"There is a lot of tension around here," Tohti, speaking from
China on July 24, 2013, told a reporter from Radio Free Asia, a
nonprofit exile news service in Washington, DC.

> In the past few days, I have been under constant surveillance
> by police vehicles and national security police officers. . . .
>
> I have realized that I don't have too many good days ahead
> of me and have a feeling that they [the Chinese government]
> may not have the best intentions in dealing with my situation.
> Therefore, I feel that it is necessary for me to leave a few words
> behind before I no longer have the ability to do so. . . .
>
> If I do pass away in the near future, know that it is not be-
> cause of natural illness and it certainly will not be suicide. . . .
>
> If I say anything that deviates from my morals after my ar-
> rest, know that those are not my words. . . .
>
> Regardless of the interrogation strategy or the torture
> method, regardless of what body parts I am about to lose,

know that I will never speak words that will work against the interest of Uyghurs, nor will I ever betray the Uyghurs. . . .

I have relied only on pen and paper to diplomatically request the human rights, legal rights, and autonomous regional rights for the Uyghurs. . . .

However, I have never pursued a violent route and I have never joined a group that utilized violence.[9]

After Jewher settled in Indiana, she began talking with her father on Skype every day. Sometimes three times or more a day.

"One day, all of a sudden, he asked me to write down the names and phone numbers of journalists and American diplomats he knew," she said.

"Why are you doing this?" Jewher asked, worried.

"I have a bad feeling," he said. "You study hard. You need to get into college as soon as possible. Start creating your social media accounts. If I'm gone, remember that I have a lot of friends over there in America."

Tohti knew influential journalists, activists, and diplomats whom he hoped would help Jewher if something terrible happened to him. "You haven't met them. But they're going to help you. You'll need to reach out to them. And remember that social media is important to get your voice out for Dad."

Jewher enrolled in an English-language program, hoping to gain entry to Indiana University as an undergraduate. Her plan was to begin her undergraduate classes in September 2015.

On November 4, 2013, an unmarked police car rammed into Ilham Tohti's vehicle while he was traveling with his wife and other kids. Luckily, there were no serious injuries, but no one believed it was an accident.[10]

In January 2014, police raided Ilham Tohti's home, taking away smartphones and PCs and arresting Tohti. The next day, Jewher was in her dorm room taking a nap when she was woken by a loud banging on her door. It was Elliot Sperling, a friend of her father's and a preeminent scholar of Tibet, but also an activist working to help minority groups in China.

He brought grim news: "Your dad was arrested."

"Elliot took me under his wing," Jewher told me. "He took care of me for a few years, like a father."

A prolific speaker who wasn't afraid to criticize either the Dalai Lama or the Chinese Communist Party, Sperling began traveling with Jewher, making impassioned speeches and generally alerting the world to the cause of Ilham Tohti—and warning of what was likely to come in Xinjiang.

Tohti had been detained on unspecified criminal charges. A public security office soon accused him of "inciting ethnic hatred" on its government blog. One Chinese search engine began censoring his name.[11]

[ ]

One day in September 2014, Maysem opened her chat group of friends on WeChat. There was a message: Ilham Tohti, their mentor and professor, had been sentenced to life in prison.

His crime?

"Separatism," largely for what he'd taught in class and posted on his website. Authorities alleged Tohti had formed a secessionist group that included seven of his students, who were also detained and would face trial.[12]

People in the WeChat group suspected the government was monitoring their smartphones. "I love the Communist Party," everyone wrote carefully, trying to avoid arrest. It was the most bizarre show of loyalty Maysem had ever seen.

The life imprisonment of Tohti was deeply disturbing to Maysem and her friends who were also Tohti's students. She needed time to get away.

[ ]

Now that she was back in China in the early fall of 2014, before her return to Turkey she and her family took a week-long trip to their country vacation home. A traditional house with a center courtyard, it was painted light blue. Maysem and her mother lounged for hours at a time in the living room, resting on pillows on the floor in the Uyghur tradition, as they sipped tea and ate rounds of sweets and samosas.

Here was a place for calm reflection. But Maysem's sense of peace was quickly interrupted by a knock on the door. It was a local party official.

"We've received reports from the neighbors that your interior is painted light blue," the man said.

Blue, a traditional color, was also the color associated with the Uyghur independence movement, and was the color of the independence flag. But Maysem and her family didn't associate with the independence movement, didn't own a Uyghur flag, and had decorated their home many years before the independence movement grew.

"We're giving you an order to paint your interior red," he said, handing them papers.

Red, the color of the Communist Party, was a trustworthy color.

Maysem's mother protested.

"This is a beautiful old home! We can't damage it!"

But the local official persisted, and the family was forced to paint their home themselves, doing the best they could do with simple brushes. The blue was erased.

Upset and disillusioned, Maysem went to a local mosque near her family's country house, looking for solitude and contemplation. It was closed, and there was no indication when it would reopen.

"Do not let them pray," read a threatening graffito on the door.

[ ]

The closed mosque was a sign of a widespread destruction and desecration of Uyghur culture that would greatly accelerate within two years. Starting in 2016, the government, as part of a project euphemistically called the Mosque Rectification Program, would demolish many mosques and damage others. It removed the mosques' Islamic features, such as minarets, and justified its actions under the claim of structurally unsafe construction. One investigation found that the government destroyed as many as five thousand mosques in Kashgar over a three-month period.

The head of Kashgar's Ethnic and Religious Affairs Committee, the body charged with overseeing the demolition of mosques and cemeteries, told Radio Free Asia that, in 2016, 70 percent of Kashgar's mosques had been demolished "because there were more than enough mosques and some were unnecessary."[13]

[ ]

A few days later, Maysem felt the urge to travel to the Id Kah, the historic main mosque that stood over Kashgar's town square, a symbol of Uyghur history.

The Id Kah, meaning "place of festival worship" in Persian, was a majestic and historic Islamic mosque, more than five hundred years old. According to my guide the interior, with its courtyard of pear trees and apricots, was designed according to Uyghur tradition to reflect a mixture of indigenous and Islamic beliefs in the structure of the heavens. Beyond that was the prayer hall, adorned with ornate carpets and green pillars.

For Maysem, stepping inside the Id Kah gave her a consoling sense of an unbreakable connection to the mosque's long history. Ever since the tenth century, this site had been a cemetery,[14] later turned into a prayer hall by Saqsiz Mirza, the ruler of Kashgar, in 1492.[15]

The Id Kah survived invasions, new dynasties, and new governments. It was a cultural and political center, expanding through the centuries, with an enormous gateway that once led outside to a bustling market, home to political gatherings and protests. During China's Cultural Revolution, the decade of communist unrest from 1966 to 1976, the mosque was under its greatest threat, and suffered severe structural damage.[16]

Yet it had survived China's unforgiving politics. Maysem believed it was the only place that couldn't be demolished, even as the government destroyed other traditional buildings around

Kashgar, transforming old neighborhoods into high-rise apartment blocs. Ten thousand worshippers flocked there every Friday.

She stood in the town square. Then she took a deep breath and began her approach.

"In the Central Asian tradition, women weren't allowed to enter," Maysem explained.

Maysem paid the entry fee at a ticket booth. She managed to get through because her ID card said she lived in "Beijing," a designation that had not changed since her time at the university, so the man at the entrance didn't realize she was a local.

Maysem paced through the courtyard wearing her veil. A few men there gave her odd looks. Inside the prayer room she kneeled on the ornate carpet, bent down, and touched her forehead on it.

"I pray to you for the longevity of my parents, and my own longevity," she said softly, "so that we may see your justice."

"What are you doing?!" shouted an imam, a senior priest, who rushed toward her. State officials were also present and raced toward Maysem.

"Women can't pray here!"

"Look at all these women in our mosque," Maysem retorted, pointing to the tourists snapping photos everywhere. "You have nothing to say to them. They're not even wearing head scarves."

"What's wrong with you?! What did your parents teach you?"

"A mosque is a place for prayer. I want to pray. That's all."

Maysem was escorted out and given a warning.

"But I was content," she said. "I made a stand. And in doing so, I kept a part of myself alive."

When she went home and recounted what she had experienced, even her tolerant mother warned her daughter to never defy the authorities again.

CHAPTER 10

People as Data

Tencent has a big user database, from which you can
help disclose the most objective and accurate analysis
and provide us a channel to hear the public voice.

—XI JINPING, SPEECH MADE DURING VISIT
TO TENCENT, DECEMBER 7, 2014

Maysem was far from certain whether the authorities noticed her subversive mosque visit, or had the wherewithal to care. Didn't they have more pressing security problems?

In 2014, Irfan, the Uyghur technology employee, admitted China lacked "that one thing we needed: enough data to get the surveillance truly working."

That year the Chinese government rolled out pilot projects all over the country, through private companies, for a system that would monitor purchases and web browsing habits, and rank all citizens by their trustworthiness. The goal was to have the system fully operational in six years.[1]

For Chinese companies, the ability to control massive digital payment platforms—Chinese consumers didn't use credit cards, preferring to pay with their mobile apps—naturally led to the urge to expand into credit rankings, making use of all that data on hundreds of millions of people who were making payments every day. What if they could additionally be ranked in categories like "trustworthiness," based on their online shopping and payment activity? It was like a credit score but more all-encompassing.

In rapidly developing countries like China, millions of people had never had access to traditional credit and hadn't established a credit score. By gathering mass data on everyone, China could leapfrog the credit hurdle and empower people across the country, giving them access to loans.[2]

But social credit was sinister too. Li Yingyun, an executive at one credit service, Sesame Credit, told the Chinese magazine *Caixin* that "someone who plays video games for 10 hours a day, for example, would be considered an idle person, and someone who frequently buys diapers would be considered as probably a parent, who on balance is more likely to have a sense of responsibility."[3]

People all over China with better social credit scores would qualify for harmless benefits: VIP bookings at hotels and car rentals, and more prominent profiles on dating websites. Those who fell too low on the system could be denied bank loans and apartment rentals.[4]

But China's social credit system was far from centralized into an Orwellian panopticon that documented everything.[5] China's impenetrable bureaucracies and office politics stood in the way. A Tencent employee admitted to me that "each division in the company was reluctant to share the data being gathered from each platform we owned like QQ and WeChat. The affiliates and the offices inside those companies all competed with each other."

Irfan and other technology employees told me they saw their biggest fears confirmed in July 2015. Irfan opened his smartphone to a news article stating that China's legislature had passed the first in a series of game-changing national security laws, with 154 votes in favor, zero against, and one abstention.[6] The law permitted the government to make use, for law enforcement, of data it had accumulated by various forms of surveillance.

The law's wording was vague and replete with euphemisms and double-speak. It laid down the ultimate power of the Chinese Communist Party as a "centralized, efficient and authoritative national security leadership system."

"All citizens of the People's Republic of China, state authorities, armed forces, political parties, people's groups, enterprises, public institutions, and other social organizations shall have the responsibility and obligation to maintain national security," it stated.[7]

The *New York Times* suggested the law was a call to mobilization, a vague collection of principles exalting security as the national priority.[8]

Three months later, Microsoft hit a landmark in the development of facial recognition technology, which could be deployed for surveillance and policing. Led by Dr. Sun Jian, whose research team had spent the previous four years perfecting AI software by adding more and more neural nets, Microsoft Research Asia now had ResNet: a new AI-powered facial recognition system with a deep neural network of 152 layers. ResNet eclipsed Google and other companies at an industry competition held in September 2015, showing its software to be far more accurate in identifying faces than anything else on the market.[9]

Then Dr. Sun, like many of his former colleagues at MRA, jumped ship. He joined an old friend from the Microsoft research office who four years earlier had founded the facial recognition start-up Megvii. Megvii made the facial recognition software Face++, used by the Chinese government and private corporations interested in harvesting the demographics of their customers.[10]

The emergent ecosystem, of which Face++ was just a part, was building the technology to do everything: watch people with cameras, draw connections between faces and voices, give police the smartphones and apps they needed to monitor the population, and link all that up to a massive surveillance network processed by AI.[11]

Now, by 2015, Megvii and its competitor SenseTime, the other big facial recognition developer, were getting more attention from around the world.

SenseTime partnered with Infinova, a security camera manufacturer in New Jersey, to provide surveillance technologies in Xinjiang.

"In China, Infinova is also among the first batch of recommended brands by the Xinjiang Ministry of Public Security, and has made an integral contribution to the construction of Xinjiang's safe city projects," the company wrote in a 2015 press release.

"In 2014, it won the IP operation and maintenance project for safe city security in the entire Xinjiang autonomous region."[12]

"We use their facial recognition software but our own surveillance camera devices," Fred Zhang, former Infinova manager, told BuzzFeedabout a project in Shanghai. "We detect the face and store the picture, but we work with SenseTime to compare the pictures in the database."[13]

By 2015, seeing new breakthroughs from Microsoft, Megvii, and SenseTime, the Chinese government wanted a piece of the action, hoping to turn these start-ups into national champions for technology. It launched a $6.5 billion venture fund for start-ups,[14] with much of the new funding coming from private sources. Private venture capital, previously not a feature of the state-run communist system, increased to greater numbers than ever before. The *Financial Times* reported in January 2015 that China's private equity and hedge fund industries had ballooned, with thirty-one hundred hedge funds overseeing almost $56 billion, and another twenty-five hundred private equity managers overseeing total funds of $172.5 billion.[15]

China was putting on a new face: technologically sophisticated, benevolent, and eager to show its growing national strength to its people and its companies.

[ ]

Meanwhile, Xi Jinping turned to America and put on a different face, promising a thaw in the emerging technology wars.

In September 2015, President Barack Obama and Chairman Xi announced they'd reached an agreement to limit cyber-espionage between their two countries. President Obama told Xi that Chinese cyber-attacks that stole commercial trade secrets "ha[d] to stop."

"We've agreed that neither the U.S. nor the Chinese government will conduct or knowingly support cyber related theft of intellectual property including trade secrets or other confidential business information for commercial advantage," Obama announced on the White House lawn.[16]

And with that, the campaign of Chinese cyber-hacking, with the intent of stealing American corporate technologies, quieted down,[17] though numerous former US government officials told me regular intelligence hacking did not stop. It was a temporary understanding. A pause.

[ ]

In October 2015, one month after the US cyber-security deal, Irfan was in his office near the surveillance control room when a confidential government order came in, justified under the national security law. "All WeChat messages in Xinjiang had to be stored on our servers for two years," he said.[18]

Before, from April 2013 to August 2015, Irfan's office had been scooping up metadata from WeChat—the usernames of people who sent messages to each other, the durations of phone calls, and the times and dates of those messages. It tracked the origin and recipient of each message, but not its contents. From the metadata, it could extrapolate a great amount of information about people's social networks. But now Irfan's office had orders to take its data gathering further, delving into the WeChat messages themselves.

"The AI software was scanning everything," he said. "It found correlations we couldn't see. It even looked for messages that included words like 'bomb' and 'gun.' Humans didn't have the time to do this, but the AI software could."

The surveillance machinery once plagued with inefficiencies seemed to come to life. It emerged with what seemed like, to Irfan, an ability to think, to see, to perceive and understand, even though in reality the technology wasn't anywhere near advanced enough to be sentient. It couldn't exhibit general intelligence and it didn't have the ability to perform in more than one programmed area. It could only carry out one task: analyzing what people wrote in their WeChat messages by drawing correlations between the use of key words, like "Koran," "terrorist," and anything that seemed related to religion or violence.

The evolving surveillance system, with the help of AI, would send back random personal information to the surveillance workers in the control room.

A young woman enjoyed going to the movies. A young father maybe had a drinking problem. One man showed the hallmark signs of a thief through the mysterious use of his text messages. Others were possible terrorists.

"We didn't understand how the AI came to its conclusions," Irfan admitted. "A lot of it was random and worrisome. I had no idea whether the suspicious people named by the AI were actually suspicious.

"Once we saw the merging of big data and the AI, that's when everything changed. I got an order from my manager to move to another department. The other guys didn't want me there. They were Han Chinese and I was one of the [few] Uyghurs in the office. And I didn't feel comfortable. The Han employees maybe thought I would leak the information to help my fellow Uyghurs."

By the fall of 2015, around the time of the passage of the national security law, whenever Irfan tried to greet old coworkers, or talk during company meetings, he started to get the cold shoulder. People avoided eye contact and didn't want to be seen with him.

"Then they started blocking me from going into sensitive rooms. They told me to wait outside."

And so Irfan was removed from his position and found a minor role as a lowly propagandist at a TV station. "My job was broadcasting videos on state television about how Uyghurs were living a happy life. My bosses even wanted to distribute their propaganda movies around the world, but it never happened."

Even though Irfan no longer had access to the sensitive workings of the surveillance program, he had little reason to believe the government would stop its mass data-gathering project. How else could the government monitor, surveil, and separate its minorities from the majority? Inevitably, they would try to find ways that went beyond social media and messaging apps alone.

CHAPTER 11

How to Rank Everyone on Their Trustworthiness

For politics is not like the nursery; in politics
obedience and support are the same.

—HANNAH ARENDT,

    Eichmann in Jerusalem: A Report on the Banality of Evil

Maysem had returned to Turkey in 2015 and in 2016 to focus on her master's degree in social science, which had been drawn out beyond the usual two years because she was working part time. She failed to pay much attention to developments back home, except for the occasional gossip that made its way to her from friends on WeChat.

She went back to Kashgar for summer vacation in June 2016. Stuck at home with a stomach flu, Maysem heard a knock at her door one morning. She opened the door. Standing outside was the woman she called Ms. Ger.

"The neighbors had something to report about you," Ms. Ger announced.

Maysem knew that being "reported," as Ms. Ger called it, was not a good thing.

"The neighbors said you didn't go out for your walk today at 9 A.M.," she added. "Any reason for the change in your behavior?" Ms. Ger seemed concerned that Maysem had been behaving erratically lately: not leaving her house at the usual hour, not following a daily routine, not doing things as they were meant to be done.

"I have the flu. I'm staying at home."

"Can you offer documentation of your flu?"

"I have a fever." Maysem knew she needed paper documentation from a doctor. She begrudgingly agreed to get a certificate to Ms. Ger, went to the doctor that day, and delivered a doctor's note to the representative of the police.

In Xinjiang, households were organized into groups of ten homes whose residents were responsible for monitoring each other, keeping track of visitors who came and went, and of the daily activities of friends and family members. It drew on the *baojia* system of feudal China, when housing collectives were charged with enforcing laws and collecting taxes.[1]

Ms. Ger was the newly appointed chief of her ten-household unit, a polite woman who knocked on the door every evening. She asked the family to report on their daily activities and whether they had noticed anything unusual about their neighbors' activities.

Ms. Ger's questions were an intrusion, but Maysem's family reasoned she was only doing her job.

After asking her daily questions, Ms. Ger wrote down the answers and reported them back to the authorities. A few weeks later, in early July 2016, she began scanning a QR code (a type of barcode) containing the family's personal information, hoisted to the outside of the apartment door, to signify she had checked the apartment and all appeared fine. Then she went next door, continuing the process until she had checked all ten households and reported to the local authorities. From 2014 to 2018, the government would send 200,000 party cadres like Ms. Ger to Xinjiang to surveil the population and hand them political propaganda.[2]

"It was really effective for policing the community," Maysem said. "Everyone was turned into a watcher. If you didn't report something unusual that day to Ms. Ger, but your neighbor reported it, the government would rank you as less trustworthy. They would consider you suspicious."

The neighborhood watch system helped the authorities gather data on every resident. Soon they would place each resident in one of three categories of social ranking: trustworthy, average, or untrustworthy. Untrustworthy people could be detained by the police, or have trouble finding jobs and getting into universities.[3]

[ ]

A few days later, the ever attentive Ms. Ger knocked on the door and explained that Maysem's family was required to install a government camera in their living room.

"I apologize for the inconvenience," Mrs. Ger said politely. "But the decision is out of my control. I've received a notice from the local police that something suspicious may be happening in your home."

Ms. Ger handed over a piece of paper that explained how to install a surveillance camera, with the assistance of the authorities. Maysem and her family were sure of the reason for the intrusion: since Maysem was studying overseas, and in a Muslim country, she was "suspect." Sometime in 2015, the authorities had placed Turkey on an official list of "26 sensitive countries" that also included Afghanistan, Syria, and Iraq.[4]

"I feared that I wasn't trustworthy anymore, that the government didn't trust me," Maysem said. "The government knew I was traveling in and out of Turkey. Of course they didn't see me as trustworthy anymore."

Her instinct was correct. Ms. Ger informed her that Maysem appeared not to meet the government's criteria of "trustworthy," and she should show her trustworthiness by installing the camera.

"We had no choice," Maysem reflected. "What were we supposed to do, resist the authorities and get arrested? Everyone was watching, everyone was snitching, and you could really trust no one. We went out to the local electronics shops and looked for the right camera."

Many of the electronics markets, it turned out, were out of inventory—the police had become major customers. Finding the right camera was not easy, but the family finally located one.

An engineer showed up and installed the camera inside a transparent plastic casing built into the wall, so the family couldn't fiddle with it or try to disable it. The camera overlooked both the living room and a large swathe of the small apartment. It also recorded audio.

"This was devastating for Mom and me," Maysem said. "The home was always the place where all of us could do whatever we wanted to do. A personal place, a place of privacy. I could read and talk and speak my mind."

Maysem and her mother kept using the living room. But they didn't dare lay out their usual books or hold their candid discussions on literature or the state of the world.

"We sat there, empty-handed, sipping at tea, trying hard not to say anything meaningful."

For Maysem, the absence of conversation was unbearable. Her fertile and colorful mind, filled with words and ideas, felt like a withering flower that could no longer get water.

"I couldn't wait to get out of China again," she said. She resisted the urge to call or text her boyfriend, Arman, since the government might scrutinize her even more for calling a number in Turkey.

One month later, Ms. Ger showed up at her door with another government notice in hand: Maysem and her family were to report to the local police office for a "checkup." The so-called check-up was mandatory for the entire family, since their household was marked as suspicious.

Authorities would soon name the program Physicals for All. "You're going to get a physical, and they're going to draw blood, record your voice and face, and take your DNA sample. It's for the safety of the community. The police need a DNA database of everyone. If you want to continue traveling overseas, it's a requirement. Otherwise you won't be eligible for a new passport."[5]

When Maysem arrived at the police office, a few dozen people sat in the hectic waiting room. Babies cried and their mothers looked nervous. Police, not healthcare workers, were going to administer the physical exam.

After a long wait, someone called out Maysem's name. A police officer led her into an examination room full of "patients," without a hint of medical privacy.

First, they took her height and weight, and tested her eyesight. Then Maysem was asked if she consented to having her blood drawn, not that she could realistically refuse.

She knew she had no choice. She knew her DNA was going to be handed over to the police for some kind of biometric database, though that was not public knowledge yet.

The police officers, aided by a healthcare worker, tried to find a vein but missed. Instead, they pricked her finger and drained her blood into a small medical tube. The DNA sampling equipment came from Thermo Fisher Scientific, the American medical technology company that sold it directly in the region of Xinjiang.[6]

Then a male police officer ushered her into another room, where she underwent a series of procedures. First, Maysem was asked to stand in front of a camera. She was told to make a series of facial expressions that would be recorded for the police database: smile, frown, turn your head left and right for profile shots, along with eight other angles. Then, for the final recording, she had to read aloud a text about "national security":

"The three evils are terrorism, separatism, and religious extremism," Maysem dutifully declaimed. She had given the police her voiceprint.

Maysem saw the police take blood from the heads and feet of infants. She finished the testing after about ten minutes and waited for her family. Then they went home, exhausted and afraid, but unable to talk openly about their experiences at home, fearful of the camera watching them from the living room.

It turned out that Maysem, as a suspicious person, was one of the first people to have her DNA forcibly extracted as part of the medical campaign. That September the government began rolling out medical exams en masse,[7] eventually totaling 36 million people examined, the state news agency Xinhua reported.[8] The program, at that point, was limited to Xinjiang.

The Office of Population Service and Management and Real Name Registration Work Leadership Committee, a mysterious government body that Human Rights Watch believes reported to the police, oversaw the biometric data collection. Authorities said in government announcements that Physicals for All was meant to help them with "scientific decision-making" over poverty alleviation, "social stability," and management. They claimed the project would create better and more efficient health delivery, help identify major diseases, and establish health records for every resident of Xinjiang.

According to an official online document found by Human Rights Watch, officials had "to ensure that [information from] every household in every village, every person in every household, every item for every person" would be collected.

According to the government, the blood type information of every tested person was sent to the police. The "blood cards for DNA collection will be sent to the county police bureaus for profiling," said one online announcement found by Human Rights Watch. All the information was stored and linked to each person's national identification number, so it could be easily pulled up if authorities needed it.

I found online government announcements and tender documents that explained the workings of Physicals for All, which were later taken down from the internet.

"County Health and Family Planning Commission will organize local medical units to collect blood information and DNA blood cards for the citizen-required health examination purpose," read one online document from a county government website. "Blood information will be sent to bureaus of Public Security in the county; DNA blood cards will be tested there."

"Public Security bureaus will be responsible for collecting human pictures, fingerprints, iris scans and other biological characteristics information of those between the age of 12 and 65," read another.[9]

Everywhere I went among the Uyghurs, tales of forced medical data gathering were commonplace.

"No one could refuse to give consent. In that environment, consent is simply impossible," Tahir Hamut, who underwent similar tests with his family at a police station in May 2017, told me.

"They measured everything they could get, and put it in their database," said Tahir Imin, a prominent Uyghur businessman I interviewed. "It was a sweeping campaign of DNA collection for monitor and control."

Some of the technology, it turned out, came from America.

[ ]

China was gathering mass data for a profiling process using what geneticists call "short tandem repeat" (STR) markers. Each individual has a unique STR profile, which geneticists can analyze by examining their blood, that can be used to identify that person.[10]

If DNA is found at a crime scene, it can be matched up to a suspect using a massive database, as police agencies do all over the world. But this was a grander project. China wanted to gather the genetic profiles of every Uyghur, Kazakh, and ethnic minority in Xinjiang between the ages of twelve and sixty-five. It could then not only build a database to use for law enforcement investigations, but also to distinguish those minorities from the Han majority.[11]

"They're [China] enacting what can be called a myth of total security, the idea that through technological developments they can have this perfect security system that will prevent all terrorism," Mark Munsterhjelm, a sociologist at the University of Windsor in Canada, told me, "They're trying to get a profile of every Uyghur, Kazakh, and ethnic minority."

Previously, Munsterhjelm had studied how indigenous peoples in South America, the Pacific islands, and Taiwanese aborigines were used in forensic genetic research.[12]

China was also gathering another mass genetic dataset with a second marker, called single nucleotide polymorphisms (SNP), Munsterhjelm said. Used for analyzing traits like facial structure, skin color, and the potential for genetic diseases, researchers have long been attempting to perfect it to reconstruct faces and profile a population.

Coming out of those eerie government projects were technologies called "next generation sequencing."

"Concepts and categories of race were largely discredited during the 1970s and 1980s," Munsterhjelm told me. "But it came back in the 1990s with the rise of forensic genetics."

For fifteen years, Munsterhjelm had followed the work of one researcher, Kenneth Kidd, a genetics professor at the Yale School of Medicine.

"After 9/11, there was something called the President's DNA Initiative. It identified genetic research on ethnicity, phenotype and ancestry. The idea was to distinguish friend from enemy, or the airplane hijackers from the victims." Kidd emerged as a global leader in the field of using ancestry markers to figure out the ancestral origins of a person's genetic sample. He ran a genetic database at Yale, and was on the initiative's Kinship and Data Analysis Panel.[13]

"I noticed some of the genetic research that was going on in China," Munsterhjelm told me. "And then I started getting clued in. In 2017, I saw reports in Nature and Human Rights Watch about the sale of Thermo Fisher sequencers to the police in Xinjiang, for the mass genetic profiling of the population."

Munsterhjelm found, through online peer-reviewed papers co-published with Chinese state scientists, that Kidd was involved in the study of SNP markers that the police could use to identify a DNA sample's ancestry, whether Uyghur or another ethnic group, for an investigation. Munsterhjelm contacted Human Rights Watch and then worked with the New York Times. He wrote that the DNA campaign was "part of [the] most comprehensive and intrusive system of biometric surveillance ever implemented."[14]

Kenneth Kidd's interest in China had been kindled in the 1980s, when he first visited the country. He gained prominence in the field of genetics for his research on the role geography plays in human genetic variation. He even discovered a gene that's been connected to exploratory behavior and novelty seeking.

Few outside researchers had the opportunity to independently map out the genetic makeup of ethnic groups in China. They were required to collaborate with Chinese researchers, who were often beholden to the government in some way.

In 2010, Kidd received an invitation from the Chinese ministry of public security to travel to China. It sounded like a normal request, since Kidd worked with law enforcement around the world to apply forensics to solving crimes.[15]

There, he was approached by the chief forensic scientist at the ministry of public security's Institute of Forensic Science, Li Caixia. She was interested in his ancestry research and asked to spend eleven months as a visiting researcher in his laboratory at Yale. Kidd told NPR (National Public Radio) he had no concerns "at the outset."

As a scientist employed by law enforcement, Li Caixia had valuable access to the DNA records of ethnic minorities in China, the Uyghurs, Kazakhs, and Kyrgyz peoples.

"She [Li Caixia] says that the samples were collected with signed, informed consent," Kidd told NPR. "On what basis would I question it?"[16]

The two spent a productive year together. Kidd included the Uyghur DNA in his global database. Then they wrote an innocuous-sounding paper, published in the July 2016 issue of the prestigious journal *Forensic Science International: Genetics*: "A Panel of 74 AISNPs: Improved Ancestry Inference within Eastern Asia."[17]

Munsterhjelm and other experts believed Kidd was playing into China's national strategy to document the genes of its ethnic minorities. Since the 1990s, China had made genetic documentation a priority, since it needed to build the mythology for its people that they were part of one genetic family with a shared bloodline.[18]

"The Thermo Fisher sequencers are there for routine police use all over the world now. But in China, they're taking all that technology, and trying to simplify to as few markers as possible, to be able to differentiate between Han Chinese and Uyghurs," Munsterhjelm told me.

After their collaboration ended, Kidd says he asked the Chinese ministry of public security to stop using the genetic samples he had provided to them.

"I've gotten no reply," he admitted.

In June 2020, after the controversy calmed down, I loaded the online genetic database at Yale to check whether the questionable Uyghur phenotype had been removed. Kidd had indeed taken out the samples provided to him by the Chinese ministry of public security. Yale University, however, had many other Uyghur samples not obtained by Kidd.

"This sample of Uyghur individuals were [sic] collected from Xinjiang Uyghur Autonomous Region," read one entry. "All volunteers resided in Xinjiang Uyghur Autonomous Region for more than three generations and signed informed consents before involved [sic] in the study. This study was approved by the Institutional Ethics Committee, Xinjiang Medical University, China."[19]

"This sample consists of Uyghur individuals in Kuqa County of Aksu Prefecture from Xinjiang Uygur [sic] Autonomous Region," read another entry. "This sample was collected with informed consent."[20]

Maysem and dozens of other Uyghurs told me that if anyone refused to give their "informed consent," they'd be harassed or arrested by the government. Withholding informed consent was not an option.

"The DNA system has been set up, and the damage has been done," Abduweli, who also had his DNA, fingerprints, and footprints taken in a Chinese detention center, confirmed. Maysem agreed: "It's a terrible story of complacency. How could you not know what China might do?"

But some scientists, in fact, traveled to China, where they actively partook in genetics conferences.

In 2015, Kidd and another geneticist, Bruce Budowle from the University of North Texas, spoke at a genetics conference in China. Thermo Fisher Scientific, the American company that made the DNA sequencing equipment and sold it in Xinjiang, underwrote the conference, the *New York Times* reported.[21]

Thermo Fisher is a major corporate force in science worldwide, formed through a merger of Thermo Electron and Fisher Scientific. In 2018, it had seventy thousand employees, net revenues of $24 billion, and a net profit of $3 billion.[22]

And it has a long-running relationship with China, which delivered 10 percent of its revenues in 2017.[23]

China's ministry of public security wrote in patent filings that it used Thermo Fisher's equipment to map the genes of its people. The *New York Times* also reported that Thermo Fisher sold its equipment directly to the authorities in Xinjiang. Procurement documents said that at least some of the equipment was intended for use by the police.[24]

Human Rights Watch wrote to the company in June 2017 and August 2017 for a response to its findings. Head of global corporate communications, Karen A. Kirkwood, replied:

"Thermo Fisher Scientific does not share information about our customers or their purchases. Given the global nature of our operations, it is not possible for us to monitor the use or application of all products we manufacture."[25]

But reports in Chinese state media quoted Thermo Fisher executives enthusiastically welcoming business opportunities in China.

"We are encouraged by President Xi Jinping's speech . . . and very grateful to the Chinese government's support of global trade liberalization and opening-up," Tony Acciarito, president of Thermo Fisher Scientific China, was quoted saying in state media outlet *China Daily* in November 2018. "We are also glad to learn that President Xi holds fully optimistic [sic] attitude toward China's economic development."[26]

Munsterhjelm looked back on the situation with a mixture of disgust and exasperation. "He [Kidd] doesn't come off looking very good at all," he told me. "But he's retired, and he has so much currency anyway, that I don't think anyone can touch him."

Maysem and other Uyghurs were aghast at the American complacency around the insidious social experiment conducted against the Uyghurs in China.

CHAPTER 12

The All-Seeing Eye

*Practice has proven that the party's strategy for governing
Xinjiang in the new era is completely correct.*

—XI JINPING

Maysem told me that a few days after her DNA was collected,
Ms. Ger showed up once again on the doorstep.

"The local police office found suspicious activity," she announced.

"What do you mean by 'suspicious'?" Maysem snapped back.
"You know I'm just a student."

"I have nothing more to tell you. You have to report to the local
police station."

The police were equally unhelpful. As Maysem sat at a desk
with a security bureaucrat, he sifted through papers and looked at
her medical data and life history on his computer screen.

"You've been overseas," the officer said. "You've been studying.
What exactly do you study again?"

"Social science."

Maysem was asked to fill out a form.

"It asked about my religious practices, my travels, when and
how I got my passport, and whether I've been to one of twenty-six
sensitive countries." It was "a kind of invasive census."[1]

The security officer told Maysem she would be sent "to a civics
class. You'll have to report there twice a week. If you miss it, we're
going to have to check in on you. Just understand that if you focus
and study hard, you'll be fine and then you can go back to Turkey
for your graduate school."

"I'm already doing a master's degree," Maysem shot back. "Why would anyone need to take some stupid propaganda class?"

Once again, she had no choice. Every Friday, Maysem checked in at her civics class at a nearby government building. Each classroom had four cameras, one in each corner of the room.

"Love the Party! President Xi Jinping is our great chairman!" she'd be forced to write in her notebook, over and over.

"What are the three evils of Xinjiang?" an instructor would ask.

"Terrorism, separatism, and religious extremism!" the students would respond in unison.

Every Monday, police interrogated her for three hours on her ideology.

"Why did you choose to travel to the Middle East?" an interrogator asked her. Typically, three officers sat at a desk in the room, asking questions and punching her answers into their computers.

"I'm doing a master's degree," she explained. "It's for my education."

"Education, I see," said the interrogator. "What kind of education do you seek?"

"It's just social science."

"What would you do with social science? What sort of separatist views are you harboring?"

Another interrogator chimed in: "People who know you say you like to read books. You've been a reader since a young age. Why would a woman like you read so many books?"

Week after week, the interrogations and classes continued. They asked the same questions over and over, worded differently, until Maysem was exhausted from all the psychological mind games.

"I told you I'm a student."

"What sort of extremists have you had contact with in the Middle East?"

"None!"

But the police, Maysem later learned, were in fact gathering as much data as they could on her from her interrogations and classes in order to predict her future behavior. She and dozens of other Uyghurs told the same story.

"The medical exams, the interrogations, the visits from Ms. Ger—the authorities were gathering as much data as they could for their AI systems. Then the software could predict who was going to commit a crime, supposedly," said Maysem.

Predictive policing was being carried out through a new program called the Integrated Joint Operations Platform (IJOP). The IJOP was revealed in public procurement notices posted by the Xinjiang ministry of public security, beginning in August 2016.

I was able to find out from these online public procurement notices and from Human Rights Watch that these notices reveal

> that the IJOP gathers information from multiple sources or machine "sensors." One source is CCTV cameras, some of which have facial recognition or infrared capabilities (giving them "night vision"). Some cameras are positioned in locations police consider sensitive: entertainment venues, supermarkets, schools, and homes of religious figures. Another source is "wifi sniffers," which collect the unique identifying addresses of computers, smartphones, and other networked devices. The IJOP system also receives information such as license plate numbers and citizen ID card numbers from some of the region's countless security checkpoints and from "visitors' management systems" in access-controlled communities ... The vehicle checkpoints transmit information to IJOP, and "receive, in real time, predictive warnings pushed by the IJOP" so they can "identify targets ... for checks and control."[2]

The IJOP also draws on existing information, such as one's vehicle ownership, health, family planning, banking, and legal records, according to official reports. Police and local officials are also required to submit to IJOP information on any activity they deem "unusual" and anything "related to stability" they have spotted during home visits and policing. One interviewee told Human Rights Watch that possession of many books, for example, would be reported to IJOP, if there was no ready explanation for owning them, such as being a teacher.

Using artificial intelligence, the IJOP began "pushing" suspected criminals, or future criminals, to the police and the government for further investigation. The police were supposed to take action as soon as they received the warning. Sometimes that meant an in-person visit the very same day, a house arrest, or an order that the suspect limit their movement within a perimeter. Sometimes it meant full-on detention or arrest.

One system surveilled fertilizer purchases that could be used to make explosives.

"If a person only buys five kilos of chemical fertilizers, but suddenly [the amount] increases to 15 kilos, then we would send the frontline officers to visit [the person] and check its use," a police researcher told the Chinese media.[3]

That was what had happened to Maysem when she was ordered to take a civics class in the summer of 2016. The system had predicted she might have become "radicalized" in Turkey.

"But the problem was that I could know nothing for sure," she said. "How could I be sure that the police really knew that much about me? What if the systems weren't as good as they claimed?

"The government made me uncertain because the way they acted was so opaque. Making someone uncertain is as good as making someone scared. Better to behave and assume they're watching you."

And that was the role of the panopticon.

[ ]

As I spoke with Maysem and interviewed dozens of other Uyghurs, I could see that the scope and mission of the IJOP was to become a massive dragnet rather than a supply of actionable counterterrorism enforcement. Later, through Abduweli, who had his own contacts elsewhere, I got a document dump of dozens of confidential Communist Party papers in Chinese. They offered a glimpse inside the workings of the government unlike anything we'd seen before. The documents, released in two batches that journalists called the Xinjiang Papers and the China

Cables, were being circulated among the press and diplomatic community.

"One day, I got the documents [the China Cables] from someone on WhatsApp," Asiye Abdulaheb, the Uyghur woman who helped leak the documents, told me from her home in the Netherlands, where she's been a citizen since leaving Xinjiang in 2009. "I was active on social media campaigning for Uyghur causes, and someone sent [them] to me because my profile was big, and I could spread the word." Abdulaheb, formerly a government worker in Xinjiang, said she wasn't concerned about having her name printed, because having a public media profile protected her from reprisals.

"I realized how important these documents were, so I posted them on Twitter. But to my surprise, no one listened."

Not for a while at least.

She began contacting researchers and journalists and sharing the documents. And now, the same online tools the Chinese government was employing to oppress a population were used to expose its atrocities.[4]

The Xinjiang leaks were a bombshell. They were a peek behind the veil of government power, unmasking the thinking and decision-making processes of China's leaders in Xinjiang. They also suggested that the system had dissenters even within government ranks. Why else would a government official have leaked the documents to Abdulaheb, and by extension to the foreign media, risking imprisonment and even execution in China?

Immediately, China's intelligence operatives started to plot against Abdulaheb and her family.

"My ex-husband got a call from an old friend in Xinjiang. He convinced him to travel to Dubai to meet up."

At first, Abdulaheb and her ex-husband had agreed traveling anywhere was a bad idea. But the friend persisted, offering to pay for her husband's ticket and hotel.

Finally, he agreed.

"When he traveled to Dubai, Chinese security officials met him at the hotel. They were waiting for him."

"We know who you are. We have a lot of people in the Netherlands and we can get you," said one intelligence operative, according to Abdulaheb. "Out here in the desert, dead people can get buried and never found."

After threatening him, they tried to convince him to hack his ex-wife's computer.

"They gave him a USB drive and said, 'This USB stick has movies and photos of your old family in China. Put it in the computer and you can see your mother.'"

He assumed the USB stick contained malware of some kind that would grant them access to his ex-wife's computer.

"He came back to the Netherlands and told us what happened. We called the police and gave the USB to the security bureau." The government cleared the USB of malware and returned it to them later.

Meanwhile, their family received death threats online.

[.]

The Xinjiang leaks covered the years from 2013 to 2017, and were exactly the bombshell I needed to get inside the terrifying IJOP system. The documents were typically monotonous, listing the numbers of suspicious people reported through the joint operations platform, and pinpointing their locations. One document in China cables leaked to me, for instance, told of "24,412 suspicious persons, including 16,354 in Kashgar, 3,282 in Hotan, 2,596 in Kezhou and 2,380 in Aksu." But these lists were in fact a trove of information.

"Anytime you come across a student with ideological problems or abnormal emotions, estimate the situation and deal with accordingly," read one document leaked to me.

"Students" was the double-speak term for camp inmates. "Build and develop a secret force, act on information, and prevent students from cooperating together to make trouble."

The "secret force" appeared to mean that the camp guards should convince detainees to spy on each other.

"Dorm areas and classroom areas must be fully covered by surveillance technology. Absolutely no blind spots."

And then there were instructions on how to "cleanse the ideology" of the students.

"Effectively resolve ideological contradictions and work on bad
emotions," one document stated. "Help students understand the
illegality of their former behavior, criminality, and other dangerous activities. Psychological counseling plays an important role in
correction."

Outside the camps, in cities like Kashgar, Maysem's hometown,
there was also documentation on how to control and surveil the
population.

"When rolling out the 'Integration' platform," the advice read,
referring to the IJOP system, "use technological means to pay
close attention to families and other unknown figures in households. Use these technological means to inquire, investigate and
thoroughly sort out issues."

For people who had fallen to the rank of "untrustworthy" under Xinjiang's social credit system, the documents urged the police to gather extra data on them, and then insert the data into the
system, which would determine if they should be detained for a
pre-crime and taken to a camp.[5]

Pre-crime, or "predictive policing" as it was officially called,
was the result of the AI using an algorithm to guess who might
commit a crime in the future. The state system, the IJOP, notified
police officers when it had found a pre-crime suspect and urged
them to investigate further or detain the target. Having relatives
overseas, praying, fasting, and engaging in religious activity were
all indicators that someone would commit a pre-crime. Uyghur
refugees compared it to the film *Minority Report*, based on the 1956
novella by Philip K. Dick about a police commissioner from the
pre-crime division investigating a man who's supposed to murder
someone in the coming week.

And how deep did that surveillance go? Yet another piece of
the puzzle was coming to light. I learned exactly what kind of
data was being gathered when the Dutch computer hacker Victor

Gevers found the datasets on who was monitored and tracked, strangely available to the public, with no privacy restriction for the people being watched.

The unsecured database was created by SenseNets, a facial recognition developer that was 49 percent owned by SenseTime, one of China's big two facial recognition firms. (SenseTime exited its ownership around the time the data breach came to light.) The database consisted of information on 2.5 million people, mostly in Xinjiang. It contained their name, sex, ethnicity, ID number, birth date, and employer. As alarming was the revelation that the database exposed the locations of 6.7 million trackers that residents had passed in the previous twenty-four hours, revealing where the residents had been. "Trackers" meant cameras, handheld devices equipped with cameras and used by the police, and ID scanners. They were located in mosques, hotels, internet cafes, and police stations.[6]

The trackers, Gevers said, "make up part of this artificial intelligence–based security network which uses face recognition, crowd analysis, and personal verification."[7]

SenseNets claimed to have a partnership with Microsoft.

"Microsoft is not involved in a partnership with SenseNets," a Microsoft spokesperson told CNBC after Gevers published his findings. "We have been made aware SenseNets is using our logo on its website without our permission, and we have asked for it to be removed."[8]

Later, Gevers found another unsecured online database, this time consisting of millions of social media profiles across China, and their WeChat usernames. The database included speculation on whether women were "breed-ready."[9]

Maysem was aghast at the scope of surveillance. But she wasn't surprised, after having lived through it.

The data provided a preponderance of evidence that the Chinese government was targeting people on mobile apps, in the campaigns Irfan and other Uyghur technology workers had told me about.

Since July 2016, the Chinese government had been targeting users of the mobile app Zapya, developed by a start-up in Beijing, that encouraged users to download the Koran and share religious teachings with friends and family.[10]

One government document urged the surrender of "those in possession of a small amount of [content related to] state separatism, violence and terror, religious extremism, 'hegira' audio/video, or other illegal propaganda materials, but who have transmitted [such materials] between family members to watch or read, without any other serious circumstances."[11]

"Whenever the police stopped us, they would check our phones," Maysem told me. "Zapya was one of the apps they were looking for. If they saw Zapya, we'd be marked down as suspicious. And maybe we'd be sent to a reeducation course."

The Chinese government wrote in the leaked documents that more than 1.8 million Uyghurs were using Zapya, including four thousand "unauthorized imams."[12]

In another alarming development, after checking their phones for banned content, police had begun asking or forcing people to download a new smartphone app called Jingwang Weishi, or "Web Cleansing." A research team at the nonprofit Open Technology Fund (OTF) analyzed the app and found it extracted the basic information on a phone, including its IMEI (international mobile equipment identity) and manufacturer, making the phone easy to track and monitor.

"The app scans the device's external storage for files looking for those it deems as 'dangerous,'" OTF wrote. "If a file is identified as 'dangerous' it prompts the user to delete the file."[13]

BuzzFeed News also reported in April 2018, based on Chinese state media sources, that police had begun installing the app Citizen Security on the phones of regular people. The app allowed smartphone users to instantly send tips to the police, should they spot something suspicious: a man with a beard, or an unusually large prayer service.

"Authorities at the Urumqi Police Department encouraged everyone to download and install Citizen Security," said one official Chinese-language report. "This could help turn all citizens into whistleblowers, and form a strong support system for the anti-terrorism campaign." The Chinese government claimed the app yielded more than thirty thousand tips in its first three months of use in 2017.[14]

As she recited her weekly propaganda in class, Maysem became more and more paranoid. Not because people were observing her, but because the machines, calculating and devoid of feeling, were. How omniscient and intelligent was this computer system that never stopped watching her? Did it see her social media accounts, her smartphone usage, and her text messages?

"When you're cut off from information, from the truth, you're in a constant state of guessing and you begin to see danger everywhere," Maysem told me. "You really don't know who's watching, who's listening, who to trust. Your friends, your family—even they might be the ones out to get you."

CHAPTER **13**

Called to a Concentration Camp

*The Kashgar region is the front line in anti-terrorism
and maintaining social stability.*

—XI JINPING

By August 2016, the whispers lit up like fireflies across Kashgar. One day, it was the police force, out in a larger presence. The next, an armored vehicle—or two or three—parked on the occasional street corner with soldiers standing outside it, watching the passers-by. More and more "convenience police stations" were also popping up on street corners in Kashgar; and soon there were more than 950 stations in Urumqi, where Maysem occasionally stopped on a layover for a flight to Ankara.[1]

"Changes are coming," people told each other. Rumors were spreading that the Communist Party wanted harder, stronger leadership.

Maysem wandered Kashgar, where she saw old neighborhoods where friends lived suddenly fenced in. Ghettoized, they had to show their ID cards to enter and exit. "Construction workers showed up suddenly, without telling anyone, and put fences around neighborhoods overnight. They woke up wondering what happened," Maysem said.[2]

Purchasing simple household items like kitchenware and groceries became a hassle. Eventually, knife salesmen were required to pay thousands of dollars for a machine that turned a customer's ID card photo, ethnicity, and address into a QR code, a type of barcode that could be scanned with a smartphone for information, which was then lasered into the blade of any knife they sold.[3] That way, the data and identity of knife purchasers were etched into the knives they bought, a precaution should a terrorist go on a knife-attack spree.

"But it can't get that much worse," people told Maysem. Their reasoning was that the government had tapped out all its surveillance tools. What else could it possibly do to limit their people's freedom?

Maysem was in her monotonous indoctrination class when the instructor began talking about a new arrival in Xinjiang.

"Chen Quanguo will be leading our region," her teacher said. "A respected commander, he will guide us in the fight against the three evils of terrorism, separatism, and religious extremism."

Maysem's mother had also heard of the new arrival. "There's a new leader coming," she said that night.

"He was a comrade who worked in Tibet," her father replied. "He ran the security operations there."

Tibet, the predominantly Buddhist region just south of predominantly Muslim Xinjiang—the "roof of the world" as it was known for its colossal Himalayas—had been the center of alarming crackdowns for the previous five years. Life there had not been easy for its 3 million people, who had lived under Chinese communist rule since 1951. At that time, China had invaded and annexed the region, then sent Tibet's charismatic spiritual leader, the Dalai Lama, into exile.

Chen Quanguo, who pioneered the use of convenience police stations in Tibet, was now in his early sixties.

Chen served as an artilleryman in the army, then worked at a car factory. He entered politics at a young age and rose fast in the 1990s, getting promoted every year, a feat in China's unforgiving political arena.[4] One Uyghur who met him at a security conference told me he had an exact and calculating demeanor. He didn't tolerate mistakes.

He had a habit of swimming laps every afternoon, but little was known about him. He was a secretive man, with little public profile, even by the standards of China's opaque politics.

"At public events, Chen fits the bill for a party cadre with a sweep of jet-black hair, somewhat drawn features, and a tendency to deliver long speeches interspersed with tongue-twisting party jargon. . . . Despite a 40-year career, a search through his official speeches failed to throw up any ambitious slogan, joke or personal anecdote attributable to him," the *South China Morning Post* in Hong Kong reported.

But in Xinjiang, where he was now stationed in the regional capital of Urumqi as of August 29, 2016, his reputation was already well known.

One tactic he practiced was to personally walk around the capital, inspecting the city. He would call the police claiming there was an emergency. Then he would wait, counting down the seconds on his watch, curious to see how long they would take to arrive. He wanted faster, more responsive, more vigorous policing.[5]

[ ]

"**One day, the street administration** called me on my phone," Maysem recalled. It was September 2016, about a week after Chen Quanguo took over in Xinjiang.

"Please come. We have important things to talk about today," said an official.

"Usually, I went to the street administration with my mother," Maysem told me. "But that day I went alone, since Mom was sick."

When she arrived at the local government building, pretty much every Uyghur student she knew who'd studied or lived abroad was waiting in the check-in line. In turn, Maysem approached the man at the counter.

"Everyone who's back from a foreign country has to report to a reeducation center," the officer told her. "There's an important meeting. You should attend. You're going to have to study at this place for one month." The officer didn't explain what the "place" was.

"One month?!" Maysem shouted. "I have to go back to school!" She expected to return to Turkey to complete the final year of her master's degree just two weeks later. "You're telling me I have to leave my real graduate school to study your stupid propaganda?"

The officer apologized for not knowing anything more, and said he couldn't help her return to Turkey in time for her graduate schooling.

Ms. Ger, the neighborhood watcher, was also present at the government building, observing everyone who filtered in and out.

She pulled Maysem aside. Maysem was unsure if she was trying to be helpful or menacing. Ms. Ger was always polite, but untrustworthy.

"Good, you're still in China. We were wondering if you had left. Big changes are coming. You need to remember that this isn't my doing—it's the doing of Chen Quanguo. The gossip is that he is making big plans. I don't know what comes next, but I want you to know this before your reeducation."

Maysem was ordered to get in the back of a car for a ride to the reeducation center. She had no opportunity to go home and get clothes for the month.

As they drove, Maysem passed her old high school. Then her neighborhood. She saw her grandmother's former house and her local park. She saw the traditional adobe homes and the wall surrounding Kashgar's old city. She began to realize she'd made the grave error of surrendering control and following orders too quickly. She had no idea where she was being taken.

After an hour's drive, she saw her destination coming into view. Her heart jumped into her throat.

"There were camouflaged soldiers with guns. I also saw policemen wearing black special forces uniforms. People had assault rifles and giant sticks." She later identified these as spiked electric-shock batons.

"I exited the car. The building was a high school, but clearly it was refurbished and changed into something new. I was escorted by police officers. They checked me with their metal scanners and then ushered me to two black iron doors."

Maysem read the sign above the doors:

"The defense of our nation is the duty of every citizen."[6]

After she had passed through, the doors behind Maysem suddenly slammed shut.

"I am a citizen. I love my country. I will make my nation great," read a slogan on the wall.

"I would learn that the purpose of this place was to bring all 'backwards' people into the modern lifestyle—to stop people like me from becoming terrorists."

At the end of the hallway was another door. Suddenly it opened, and out popped a police officer.

"Come, come," he ordered.

Maysem entered an eerie lobby manned by a receptionist, with cameras in each corner of the room.

"Why did the neighborhood administration send me here?" she asked. "What do I have to do?"

"Don't ask questions. You sit here and wait," the receptionist snapped back.

Ten minutes later, a few dozen elderly, well-dressed men and women flooded in, escorted by guards.

"What is the meaning of this?!" shouted an older woman wearing ostentatious jewelry. "Do you know who I am?! My husband works for the vice governor!"

Around ten officers in black SWAT uniforms stood at the front of the room, where one announced the start of the "political re-education course," a mandatory indoctrination session in the re-education center that would run for six hours a day. The crowd was livid.

An officer in the room shouted at everyone to be quiet.

"We have a problem," he explained to the crowd. "This place is getting dirty. We have to clean up. Who wants to volunteer?"

Some younger women volunteered to clean the desks and scrub the floor, thinking it would earn them the goodwill of the police.

"You!" an officer said, pulling Maysem out from the crowd of about fifty people. "You look like the youngest person here! You can wash the windows."

"That was the start of another problem," Maysem said. "I was the youngest, so I kept getting singled out for extra work. I told them that the officers at the previous building said we'd be studying politics, not cleaning windows."

The guards were unimpressed. "You'll meet with our supervisor," one told her.

When Maysem sat down with the reeducation center's supervisor in a nearby office, he asked her bluntly, "Do you have any important relatives?"

"I come from a good family," Maysem said.

"You're cleaning the windows," the officer responded, unimpressed. "We're only trying to help you."

Maysem refused. The supervisor pulled out a stack of forms from his desk and called someone.

"We've got a young girl here. She doesn't want to clean the windows. So how about you educate her for a while?"

The officer escorted Maysem back through the hallway and outside. As she left, the other inmates appealed to the authorities.

"Give her a break," said one woman. "She's just a young girl."

Outside, a police car arrived.

"Take her to the detention center," the supervisor ordered the driver. Maysem had heard the police use the term "detention center" before, and she assumed it referred to some sort of propaganda course, similar to the class she had been attending that summer. Little did she know "detention" now meant much more. "She'll be comfortable there."

"It was about 11 A.M.," Maysem remembered, "and by now, I was really angry. Then I went between frustration and sadness. I sat in the back of the car and looked outside at my hometown. Then, out of nowhere, I started crying. I couldn't control it."

After a short ride, Maysem arrived at a second camp, the one the guards called the "detention center," a larger compound with large steel doors and more SWAT officers roaming the perimeter.[7] She passed through an eerie hallway with paintings of sad women in veils on one wall and happy women wearing dresses and high heels on the other wall. She entered the lobby, was processed through the computer system, then was pushed to the floor by guards who forced her into the tiger chair in the courtyard, and left.

When the guards returned, they removed the straps and ordered Maysem to stand. "You're going to raise your arms and stand still for another few hours," said one.

Maysem did as she was instructed, standing still in the court-yard. A police officer stood behind her with a baton.

"You know what happens if you move," he told her.

[ ]

A few hours after Maysem was taken to the second camp, her mother answered the door to a group of policemen. They informed her that her daughter was being held in a "reeducation center" to "cleanse her mind of ideological viruses," and handed her government papers confirming the nature of her internment.

She immediately tried to think whom among her friends and contacts she should approach, to either get Maysem released or to get better treatment for her. She called old friends in the government, asking for favors and promising to somehow pay them back in the future.

Maysem's mother had contacts in the assistant mayor's office. She stormed through the doors of the building where his office was located, and showed his receptionist the police papers describing Maysem's internment. "She hasn't even been charged with a crime!" she exploded.

The middle-aged receptionist looked at her as if this was nothing special, and finally agreed to let her meet an aide to the assistant mayor. He too was unimpressed and unhelpful.

"We have to take care of five thousand women in the centers. The orders come from the top, not from our office," the aide said. "And why is your daughter special? We know that a lot of people are being shipped off for detention. We've met a lot of concerned parents. But this isn't something that we can control."

But Maysem's mother would not give up.

[ ]

After two hours, the guards told Maysem to release her still posture and escorted her to a cell about the size of a living room, around thirty-three square yards. It held about twenty other women, watched over by two cameras.[8]

The women seemed vacant to Maysem; they stood or sat staring blankly into space. "I didn't talk to them, and they didn't talk to me. No one trusted anyone."

Maysem's instinct was right.

"The police usually appointed a cell boss, whose job was to manage the cell, watch the prisoners, and tell the guards if they broke any rules, like fighting with the other cellmates or not studying the propaganda hard enough. I didn't know how the cell worked yet, so I kept to myself."[9]

That night, Maysem couldn't sleep. Next to her bunk bed was a bucket in which the female prisoners urinated and defecated throughout the night. The stench was awful.

I really hope I'm not here long, she thought. *I really hope Mom can do something.*

[ ]

Maysem was still awake when the alarm bell rang at 6 A.M. Bright fluorescent lights went on in her cell. The women tumbled out of bed.

After a quick shower, the first order of the day for the women was to line up in formation outside in the courtyard. There they performed calisthenics and stretches while a female voice read an eclectic mixture of instructions and propaganda over the loudspeakers.

"Now stretch to the right! Stretch to the left! Hold!

"Repeat after me! Love our Chairman Xi Jinping! Love the Communist Party! Let us free ourselves of the viruses in our minds!"

The prisoners repeated the phrase and the announcer went on:

"Let us purify the mind, cleanse ourselves of ideological viruses! We must all be good patriots who love our country!"

Then began another morning routine. The prisoners were ordered to stand behind a line and bend their knees, ready to sprint. A female guard stood beside them.

"Go!" she shouted.

For one minute, the prisoners sprinted around the courtyard until they arrived at their prize: slices of moldy bread laid out on plates on the ground. Maysem was hardly athletic but pushed herself, not knowing whether she'd be punished for failing to run fast enough.

"Stop!"

The women stopped and took a breather.

"And now we'll announce the winners!" The guards picked out a dozen or so women whom they thought ran the fastest and hustled the hardest. Maysem was among the winners.

"And now your reward."

The guards took all the women to the canteen and gave them breakfast: the slices of moldy bread they had sprinted toward and boiled water. Those who ran too slowly were required to skip breakfast as punishment.

"I refused to eat it," Maysem told me. "I was worried about getting sick from the bread. And the water was discolored. It had white fog. I worried the guards had tainted it."

Next was the first of two indoctrination courses that day. Maysem entered the classroom and immediately noticed the cameras in every corner, pointed at the students, able to read their facial gestures or what they wrote in their notebooks.

At 9 A.M., the teacher entered the room. She stood at the front, behind a partition of metal bars, surrounded by two guards positioned near each wall. All the students opened their notebooks in unison, as if on cue. The teacher turned to a group of men.

"When you were growing up," she asked, "did you ever see a cell phone?"

The students gestured, seemingly in unison, that they had not. One man stood up.

"We had no food. We had no electricity, no water. We didn't have technology. We didn't even know what a TV was," he said in a matter-of-fact, robot-like voice.

"We are thankful to our party and government."

He sat down.

"Look at the successes of the Chinese people!" the teacher exclaimed. "Look at the difference. Our great nation has built your towns, schools, roads, and hospitals. Look at all our technology! Before you had nothing, and you did nothing to better yourselves when you had the chance. Our great Chinese people brought you into the modern world!

"Now, we'll begin our law class."

Maysem gazed around the room at the blank faces of the students, who seemed conditioned not to say anything independent.

"Here in China, our legal system guarantees the equality of all minorities," the teacher said.

"The Soviet Union," she went on, "was full of minorities. But it didn't have a good policy to protect those minorities. So the Soviet Union collapsed. But China lives strong. China will protect you, and China will care for you.

"Both my parents had seven or eight siblings. We were poor. But the government led us the right way with the one-child policy," she said of China's longtime policy of limiting the number of births per family.

"Today I am prosperous, and I can give my two children whatever they want. We must thank our government.

"You all have sharp minds. You're smarter than all those other people still out on the streets. You've all been overseas. That's why our great nation brought you here. I am so proud to meet all of you every day because I can see your intelligence.

"Now, let's try an exercise."

The teacher placed two water bottles on the desk. One was empty and one was full.

"I say the full water bottle is full of water. I also think the empty bottle is full of water. What do you think?"

One student raised his hand and stood up.

"Both water bottles are full!"

"Good!"

Maysem was trying to process these bizarre mind games.

It's like she's trying to brainwash us into thinking this hellhole prison is great, she thought. *Everything is good because she says it's good—she wants us to doubt our own realities.*[10]

She peered around the room at the other students, who remained mute and expressionless.

I have to find ways to keep my mind sharp. I have to find a weakness in the system.

Maysem's quest to find a weakness in the system seemed impossible at first. The rules, regulations, and "tests" were haphazard and arbitrary, making little sense. It was as if they were designed to frighten the detainees, throw them off guard, and pressure them into signing a confession or snitch on their cellmates before their cellmates snitched on them.

One at a time, the detainees sat down in front of two tables holding miniature models. The table on the left had models of a house and a yard, arranged in no pattern at all. The table on the right held miniature models of an AK-47 assault rifle and a grenade, again laid out sloppily with no order in mind.

"You were supposed to rearrange the models of the house, trees, and bushes into a yard, like in real life," I was told by another Uyghur detainee interred in Maysem's concentration camp. "Then, the testers asked you to rearrange the models of the AK-47 and grenade so they looked right, somehow. But how can an assault rifle and grenade look 'correct' on a table?

"I later learned that if you touched the fake gun and fake grenade and started moving them around at all, you failed the test and were declared a terrorist because you seemed comfortable touching weapons. Luckily, I didn't touch them because I didn't know what to do."

The punishment for failure was a day or more in isolation, followed by a repeat of the test.[11]

After two morning hours of activities like this, the teacher told them to begin their daily writing ritual.

"Now that class is finished, you need to do the usual drill: write seven pages of reflection on our course today," the teacher announced. It was 11 A.M. They had one hour.

All the students calmly began writing, pouring out words whose only purpose was to flatter their teacher and political leaders. Maysem learned this by peering at other students' notebooks.

"I love my government … I love my country … I love my brilliant teacher … I am a bad person who has made mistakes … I am happy to learn the right thought from my brilliant teacher."

Every student seemed to be writing pretty much the same thing at the same time. The teacher was looking around when she spotted Maysem without a notebook.

"Where's your notebook?" she asked.

"I never got one."

That was the weakness, Maysem realized. In their quest to monitor, document, and control everything, the country's leaders had erected a ludicrously bureaucratic police state. The camps, hastily repurposed from high schools and other buildings, were overcrowded and disorganized. The police-state bureaucracy couldn't keep up with the sudden swell of inmates, and needed more time to organize a functioning system of concentration camps.[12] This meant that occasionally people fell through the cracks of the reeducation system, unable to get a simple item like a notebook.

"The policeman had sent me to this detention center on a whim, because I complained to him about having to clean the windows," she explained.

But he hadn't put Maysem through the right steps in the bureaucracy to register her as an inmate at the higher-level concentration camp. Maysem was only registered for the lower-level reeducation center where she was supposed to study Communist Party governance for six hours a day. And because Maysem wasn't properly written into the system, the authorities hadn't prepared a notebook, uniform, or the usual kit for her. They didn't know what to do with her.

"It gave me a little hope. Maybe I could somehow game the system, and get out."

The teacher, realizing something was amiss, asked the guards to escort her to the camp's "political officer." Maysem entered the office of a tall man with a worn face.

"I was scowling. I was so angry at the pointlessness of the class, and it showed on my face."

Rather than give Maysem a notebook and pencil, he immediately launched into a lecture.

"I can see from your file that you're highly educated. Master's student, university studies in Beijing, high test scores, many years overseas. You speak multiple languages. Your neighbors say you're always reading books."

Maysem didn't respond.

"I know you think your teacher is just some kind of elementary school teacher, that this is all beneath you. But she is your boss, and I am your boss. You will remember that that's why you're here."

Maysem rolled her eyes.

The political officer slammed his hand on a pile of papers. "I don't want to see that look on your face ever again."

"My feelings are none of your business," Maysem snapped back.

"Look around at everyone," the political officer said. "Nobody has feelings here. They don't show hatred. They don't show passion. When the guards beat them, they don't cry. Look at all the students writing in their notebooks. There's no difference between them. You can see their minds are one—they've been cleansed of their viruses.

"Now, I apologize that we were unable to put you through our orientation course. It's because you haven't been registered here. We called your neighborhood administration office and we're working on fixing that. But you are new here. You will learn with time. And while you're here, I don't want to see any of that emotion on your face. Now you may go."

Escorted by guards, Maysem returned to the classroom, where she spent the remainder of the hour gazing at propaganda slogans on the walls, since she didn't have a notebook. The bell rang and the students closed their notebooks and headed off for lunch. They sat in prearranged groups of four at each table. Before being allowed to eat, they stood and sang China's national anthem, "March of the Volunteers." Lunch was a small bowl of boiled vegetables and white rice. When the hour was finished, guards escorted the students, who walked in groups of four in near-perfect unison, back to their cells. They were permitted a thirty-minute nap under strict conditions.

"We were allowed to sleep only if we kept our beds tidy. But our beds had to be tidy even *while* we were sleeping," she said. "If we didn't sleep, or moved around too much, or whispered and talked, the guards would punish us, either with a beating or by denying us lunch the next day. The only way to keep our beds neat was to sleep sitting up."

Maysem was exhausted. And sitting upright, she couldn't sleep.

After thirty minutes, the guards returned.

"Why isn't that girl sleeping?" one of them said to the other cellmates, pointing to Maysem. "You will teach her our rules. Now, we will punish all of you."

The guards forced the cellmates, except Maysem, to stand perfectly still for thirty minutes. If one of them moved, they'd all have to start over.

"Look at what you did to them," a guard shouted at Maysem. "This is your fault!"

After the ritual ended and the guards left, Maysem apologized to the other prisoners.

"Please don't worry," one of them said. "They always punish us for a different reason. Today they blamed you. Tomorrow they'll find a strand of hair on the floor."

From 2 P.M. to 4 P.M., the women joined the male inmates for a series of classes that included "Islam," the "constitution," "national unity," and the "life and thought of Xi Jinping," Maysem said.

This time, a man claiming to be a religious leader entered the classroom.[13] Maysem braced herself for another bizarre propagandistic ramble.

"None of you realize what religion really means, what Islam means," he told them. "Praying, fasting—none of this is suitable for modern life in our great nation.

"We are the surgeons who operate on your brains, your ideology. Your minds are poisoned. Now, we will give you medicine. You must be grateful to our great nation for this medicine."

Maysem was about to roll her eyes again, but remembered the cameras and the warning of the political officer that morning: *Don't show emotion.*

Better to stay flat-faced, she thought. *Wouldn't want my cellmates to get punished again, because of me.*

"Look at the typical Muslim village," the "religious leader" continued. "The husband is a poor laborer. The woman doesn't work. The children don't go to school because they're held back by religion and poverty.

"It's your fault that you're here. Think about your families. Their lives were disrupted because you held the poison of your ideology in your minds. You needed to come here to cleanse yourself. And now your families might be suffering because you are gone. Maybe they can't find a job. Maybe your kids had to stop school. It is your fault. It is your fault.

"You don't know what religion really is. You don't know. You don't know. You really don't."

At the end of the droning lecture, the students opened their notebooks and calmly began writing their seven-page summaries. The "religious leader" called on one student to present his writings.

"I regret the wrong life I have lived," the student announced. "Thank you to the Party. You gave me everything. You are like my parents; you are my father and mother in one. You are the sun, you are the moon, you are the mountains. I don't believe in heaven or hell. You are my only heaven. I will only follow you. Please lead me forever, so I may find the way."

[ ]

That night, Maysem struggled to sleep. In an all-male cell nearby, she overheard an argument break out between a prisoner and a guard.

"What's this rolled inside your cigarette?! Thief!"

Accused of smuggling something that Maysem couldn't quite overhear, guards stormed into the cell and beat the man.

When morning came, a guard entered her cell and called out Maysem's name.

"Come with us." Maysem worried that a similar punishment awaited her.

The guards escorted her to a lobby-like space near the front door. As she entered, she was overwhelmed with joy. Her mother was there.

CHAPTER 14

Mass Internment

Thoroughly reforming them towards a healthy heart attitude.
—CHINESE OFFICIAL IN XINJIANG, AUGUST 2017

Maysem's mother had managed to locate the camp and convince the resident political officer to give her just one meeting with Maysem.

"She had golden rings, sharp clothing, and makeup." Maysem recalled. "She wanted to convince the camp officials that she was someone important, worthy of taking seriously."

Her mother had brought her a change of clothes. Maysem, unregistered, still didn't have a proper uniform.

"Wear this," her mother said.

"How did you find me?" Maysem asked.

"We don't have much time together," her mother said. "But I'll tell you what's happening as fast as I can."[1]

Maysem's mother had spent an entire night outside her neighborhood's government office. Then she'd spent hours pleading with an administrator to let her meet the mayor himself, not an aide to the assistant mayor as before, and plead her case.

"I just want to see her once," she begged, according to Maysem, recalling her mom's story. "I just want to know where she is."

"That's a state secret," the administrator replied sternly. "We have to care for matters of national security."

"She's no threat to national security!"

"We have so many girls to deal with in the reeducation centers. We can't help you."

Maysem's mother had hoped that by waiting outside all night, in the breezy autumn air, she could catch the first people coming to work the next morning.

After the office had closed that evening, an administrator had approached her at an outdoor bench, where she was planning to sleep.

"Please go home," she said. "There's nothing we can do this late."

But Maysem's mother had stayed. And when the sun rose the next morning, a man who worked in the building approached her. He explained that the government workers inside had been talking about her that morning.

"You've been here all night?"

"I have to see my daughter."

"I don't know what kind of person your daughter is," he said. "Maybe she's dangerous because she studied in Turkey. Turkey is a Middle Eastern country, you know. Maybe her mind is infected. If she has this kind of infection, she has to stay in a center for one or two years so she can be cured. Trust me, she will come out a better person. This is merely the Situation. We hope you will understand."[2]

At this point "the Situation" was a kind of neutral double-speak Uyghurs were beginning to use to describe the emerging police state, to avoid getting in trouble. They could not say "mass detentions," "atrocities," or a "repressive government." As I sat with Maysem, I remembered all the times, while traveling in Xinjiang and Turkey, that locals and Uyghur refugees had called their plight "the Situation." "The Situation is not good," explained a businessman back in 2017. "But I am in favor of the government's efforts to improve the Situation."[3]

Maysem's mother wasn't sure whether or not the government worker actually believed what he was saying. Was he really indoctrinated?

Having failed to win over the local government bureaucrats, Maysem's mother raced home—her husband had just returned from a vacation in the mountains, after receiving the news of Maysem's detention.

"He wouldn't stop crying," her mother told Maysem. "Maybe you don't feel his love for you, but he truly does love you."

Maysem's father, the Communist Party bureaucrat, paced around the house, then called an old friend.

"You must understand the Situation. I can't interfere in the business of these training centers," was the message he got from his friend. "Public security will find a way to freeze my salary or send *me* to a center."

After much deliberation, Maysem's parents decided their only hope was to go back to the government office the next day and plead their case, this time with paper evidence.

"Mom and Dad approached the front desk of [the local government office] with all their old ID cards, passports, marriage certificates, diplomas, and a family tree. They had documents on everyone from our family," Maysem told me. "They wanted to show that I came from a good upbringing and that I wasn't a security threat. They learned how hard it was to prove a negative—to prove you're innocent when you're assumed guilty."

"Every daughter is like your daughter," a minor party boss retorted, a different official from the day before.

Her mother decided to appeal to the bureaucrat's feelings, to try to make her daughter stand out.

"I know your daughters are at a boarding school," she said. "They're far away, aren't they? You want them to be educated, hard working. They're vulnerable, being so far away. You don't have much control over what they do and what happens to them. How would you feel if they finished class one day and then they were taken away and accused of terrorism? And you're all the way here, thousands of [miles] away?"

That party boss, it turned out, came from a scholarly background and was as respected in the community as Maysem's mother. As a scholar trying to educate his kids, he saw something of himself in Maysem's mother, because she had instilled the values of education and the love of literature in her own daughter, Maysem believed.

"Mom told me that he took one look at her, and then picked up the phone and called some contacts. Mom wasn't sure who exactly he called. But, somehow, he was able to get her access to the camp to meet me."

Sitting in the camp with her daughter, her mother consoled Maysem.

"Don't be afraid," she told her daughter. "Don't let anyone convince you that you did anything wrong. Sometimes, life throws hard things at you. But you will only come out stronger."

When her time was up, she gathered her belongings and, before heading out, left Maysem with a simple statement: "This experience is a gift. I am so proud of you."

[ ]

Adrian Zenz was an anthropologist and leading researcher on Xinjiang. He gained his information from public tender documents posted in Chinese by the Chinese government, police, and contractors. He found that, from 2016 to 2017, security spending in Xinjiang had increased by 92.8 percent, as schools, police stations, and sports centers were refurbished and turned into detention centers.[4] By the end of 2017, Zenz wrote, "reports emerged that some ethnic-minority townships had detained up to 10% of the entire population, and that in Uyghur-dominated Kashgar Prefecture alone, the number of interned persons had reached 120,000."[5]

"I estimated that the centers held anywhere from a hundred thousand people," he told me, "to just more than a million," nearly one-tenth of Xinjiang's 11 million Uyghur population.

That was an early estimate, from when Zenz began his research based on public tender documents published online between 2016 and 2018. He later raised the higher end of his estimate to 1.8 million people detained in the centers since the spring of 2017.[6]

Other former detainees and camp employees, lucky to escape, came forward with stories about the conditions in the camps once they were out of China.

"From the beginning of 2018, I worked in what is called in China a political camp. In fact, it is a prison located in the mountains." These words were spoken by Sayragul Sauytbay at her sensational trial in Kazakhstan.[7] She was an ethnic Kazakh woman from China hired as a teacher at a camp in northern Xinjiang in November 2017. She then escaped across the border to Kazakhstan. In July 2018, Sauytbay sought asylum in Kazakhstan, where she urged its government not to send her back to China, arguing that she was under threat of torture.

Sayragul said: "I thought I would be killed. I thought I would get the death penalty in China for exposing the camps.

"About twenty-five hundred [people] were imprisoned in my camp in the mountains. It had very high-tech AI surveillance rooms and devices. In one room where these people were imprisoned, there were four cameras at four corners. There is one more camera in the middle. So five cameras in total. In addition, the hallways were full of cameras.

"In each cell, one person had about one square yard to themselves. One room was about sixteen or seventeen square yards. Each cell had about sixteen, seventeen, or twenty people.

"Everyone was monitored twenty-four hours a day."[8]

"The cameras could hear everything, and the guards said there were floor sensors that could sense our movements. If we made a sound," explained Omir Bekali, a Kazakh national detained in another camp, "the guards would beat us with [rubber] spiked batons." He showed me the scars on his back, which he said came from torture and beatings.

Omir, a Kazakh citizen born in China, had visited China on a business trip in March 2017. "I went to see my family in China. Then the authorities showed up at my house and took me away. They said I endangered state security.

"I spent eight months in the police detention center. I didn't even get a trial. Then the police asked me to sign a confession in November [2017] and said I would be freed. I signed the confession, but instead they sent me to a concentration camp for a month. They put me in the tiger chair and they also chained me to the floor . . . A few dozen men were crammed into a single room, with cameras watching them, and they had to sit uncomfortably. They were chained down to the floor in a single position for hours or days.

"Everything we did was watched and heard. The Communist Party knew everything about us."

Omir told his captors that he was not a Chinese citizen and didn't belong in the camp. He had been a citizen of Kazakhstan since 2008. It made no difference. His jailers responded that he was a suspected terrorist who needed to purify the mental viruses in his head, and the fact that he was born in China was enough evidence to detain him. The Chinese government released him on November 24, 2017, only after the Kazakhstan government complained.[9]

[ ]

Maysem was actually at risk of being sentenced to forced labor if she remained unpurified, as part of a government project to ostensibly teach discipline and loyalty to detainees who, as the guards told Maysem, had "infected minds."

Wealthy coastal provinces in China were home to factories that made Nike sneakers and iPhones. But as China's economy grew and its population aged, more people had left their factory-floor assembly jobs and graduated to the white-collar class.[10] China was facing a labor shortage.[11] So where would it turn?

Uyghur detainees were China's solution for reinvigorating its workforce, helping the economy, and imparting discipline among the inmates, as guards put it to Maysem. When in 2017 the government expanded a program called Xinjiang Aid, and began shipping Uyghur detainees to factories across China, it claimed it was working toward "inter-ethnic fusion" and "poverty alleviation."

In total, the Australian Strategic Policy Institute (ASPI) identified eighty-three companies that benefited from Uyghur workers transferred through labor programs. They included Amazon, Adidas, Calvin Klein, Gap, and Tommy Hilfiger. Over the next two years, until 2019, more than eighty thousand Uyghurs would be transferred out of Xinjiang to work, "and some of them were sent directly from detention camps," ASPI reported. It described the numbers involved as a conservative estimate.

Amazon later said it stopped sourcing from an "entity," without naming the entity, after the US government added it to a sanctions list in July 2020.[12] Adidas said it advised suppliers to suspend yarn purchases from yarn maker Huafu, pending an investigation. The parent company of Calvin Klein and Tommy Hilfiger said it intended to increase scrutiny of groups that supplied raw materials. Gap said it worked with two suppliers who used yarn from mills in Xinjiang and was sorting out and reviewing its relationships there.[13]

Apple was another American company that benefited. It had connections to at least three factories in its supply chain that employed Uyghur laborers forcibly transferred from the camps.

ASPI found that, between April 28 and May 1, 2017, seven hundred Uyghurs were transferred to the city of Nanchang to work at a factory run by O-Film. O-Film made cameras for the iPhone 8 and iPhone X. In December 2017, Apple CEO Tim Cook visited another O-Film factory. According to an Apple press release, Cook praised O-Film for its "humane approach towards employees" during his visit. He also said that workers seemed "able to gain growth at the company, and live happily."

Apple's manufacturing partners expanded their use of Uyghur labor in September 2019, according to a local government document stating that 560 Uyghur workers had been transferred to the Foxconn factory that made half the world's iPhones. Foxconn, a major Apple partner, had taken part in the Xinjiang Aid scheme.[14]

Apple said it launched an investigation into O-Film. "Apple is dedicated to ensuring everyone in our supply chain is treated with dignity and respect," an Apple spokesman said in a statement. "We have found no evidence of any forced labor on Apple production lines and we plan to continue monitoring." In late 2020 or early 2021, Apple reportedly dropped O-Film as a components supplier over accusations of its involvement in forced labor.[15]

Another company that claimed to make components for an Apple supplier, Highbroad Advanced Material Company, signed an agreement with a local government to employ one thousand Uyghur workers each year for three years.[16] Highbroad makes components for flat-panel displays, and counts among its other customers HP, Mercedes-Benz, Dell, LG, and Volkswagen.[17]

HP didn't respond to media requests for comment after the report was released. Dell and LG said they saw no evidence of forced labor in their supply chains, but that they would investigate.[18] Volkswagen, which runs a plant in Urumqi, said it had "direct authority" in all areas of its business and "respects minorities, employee representation and social and labor standards."[19]

ASPI also believed that another benefactor of Uyghur labor programs was Nike. ASPI found that in January 2020 six hundred mostly female Uyghur detainees were transferred to the Taekwang Shoe Factory in a town called Laixi, where they were put to work making Nike sneakers. The detainees were barred from going home for holidays, and had their ideology monitored by a "psychological dredging office." "Blessed are those who work here in Laixi!" read a sign posted in the factory.[20]

"We have been conducting ongoing diligence with our suppliers in China to identify and assess potential forced labor risks related to employment of Uyghurs, or other ethnic minorities from XUAR [Xinjiang Uyghur Autonomous Region], in other parts of China," Nike said in a statement. "Based on evolving information, we strengthened our audit protocols to identify emerging risks related to potential labor transfer programs. Our ongoing diligence has not found evidence of employment of Uyghurs, or other ethnic minorities from XUAR, elsewhere in our supply chain."[21]

Xinjiang supplies 20 percent of the world's cotton used in products such as garments and footwear. In 2018, three regions within Xinjiang forcefully transferred at least 570,000 people to do grueling cotton picking by hand for the bingtuan, Xinjiang's paramilitary force.[22] After the findings became public in December 2020, the United States banned cotton imports from the bingtuan, accusing it of "slave labor."[23]

"The reported situation is of a scale, scope, and complexity that is unprecedented during the modern era of global supply chains," the Retail Industry Leaders Association, a trade lobbying group consisting of leading clothing brands, announced in a statement with other industry groups, after the details of the labor transfers were made public. "Accepting the status quo is not an option."[24]

[ ]

In December 2017, the Communist Party began Becoming Family Week, a project that placed one million party cadres in Uyghur family households. Government propaganda called these placements "family reunions." But they were really an effort to put government workers in the quarters of Uyghur men and women, where trusted bureaucrats could spy on Uyghurs and share their beds and meals.

Becoming Family Week was an experiment that expanded into a full-on homestay program. Government workers lived with their host families every two months for five days at a time. If local family households refused to take part, they were deemed terrorists and swept away to a concentration camp.[25]

As reports of human rights atrocities emerged around the world, China attempted to whitewash its reputation and deflect attention from the situation in Xinjiang.

"Xinjiang fully respects and effectively guarantees the civil rights of its citizens in accordance with the law, by respecting and protecting life and property, safeguarding the right to a fair trial, and promoting free expression," read a government white paper released on June 1, 2017, titled "Human Rights in Xinjiang— Development and Progress."

"Life and property are respected and protected. Since the 1990s, violent terrorists, nationalist separatists, and religious extremists have plotted and committed a series of violent terrorist crimes, causing loss of life to and damaging the property of people of all ethnic groups."[26]

"Many people say from the bottom of their heart: 'The happiest Muslims in the world live in Xinjiang,'" wrote an official in a state newspaper, the *Xinjiang Daily*, in August 2017.[27]

Eventually, the Chinese government began inviting foreign journalists, United Nations officials, and other foreign-government officials to visit the camps. The United States objected to a visit by the UN's counterterrorism chief to Xinjiang, fearing it would help legitimize the human rights travesty.

"Beijing continues to paint its repressive campaign against Uyghurs and other Muslims as legitimate counterterrorism efforts when it is not," a top US diplomat said in response to the UN visit in 2019.[28]

"The problem in China is that all the foreign news about Xinjiang is censored all over the country. So most Chinese citizens don't know the real story and think we're terrorists," Maysem confirmed. "But China can try to influence the storytelling around the world by sending out its propaganda at the UN, where it's not censored. When I was in the camp, I had no idea if anyone outside knew what was going on, and that was saddening.

"We were like a blank space on the map."

[ ]

As we spoke in Ankara in November 2019, three years after her internment, Maysem picked up a copy of 1984.

"This man was so smart. How could an Englishman write a book seventy years ago that predicted my experience? 'War is peace, freedom is slavery, ignorance is strength,'" she recited, repeating the mantra of the fictional nation of Oceania.

"These words were so intelligent. George Orwell saw the future. He saw our world, the world of the Uyghur people. He writes about the strategy of newspeak."

"Newspeak has been used by all kinds of authoritarian governments," I said. "What makes the Uyghurs different?"

"Technology. We've had many authoritarian governments since 1984 was published [in June 1949]," Maysem explained. "The Soviet Union, Mao's China, North Korea, the Iron Curtain. But what sets this apart is that our technology is finally good enough to mimic science fiction books, down to the exact technologies that the old authors thought would happen.

"When you combine the technology with the old authoritarian tactics, everything that Orwell talked about—the newspeak, the big screens that showed party propaganda, the harsh punishments and concentration camps, and the constant monitoring of a population—are suddenly amplified.

"Back then, those leaders used force and violence to repress their people. Today, with technology, they don't need violence like they used to. They can control a population, brainwash its people, and strip them of their humanity to become subservient."

"Like a panopticon?" I asked, recalling the term other Uyghurs and experts in authoritarianism had used to describe their regime.

"Exactly," she said. "But in the old days, you needed a human guard for the panopticon. Humans can doze off, make mistakes, maybe show a little compassion. It's an imperfect system.

"In our new world of artificial intelligence, the stakes are so much higher. We don't always understand how a machine comes to conclusions about people. You can be late to class one day. And a machine will watch you through the camera and somehow, with all the data it's gathered from the entire country, it'll conclude you're about to rob someone. Then the police will sweep in and detain you under predictive policing.

"But the police, I learned, aren't always thinking about what they're doing. Their job is to take orders. And once we humans resign from critical thinking, we're in trouble."

[ ]

From her own incarceration, Maysem was able to learn a good deal about the surveillance systems at concentration camps. Occasionally, a proud party administrator liked to brag to the prisoners about their capabilities, either to scare them or, Maysem thought, in some twisted way to impress them.

"We can see everything and hear everything," a guard told Maysem. "The floors have sensors. We know where people are walking. We know when they're urinating. The cameras are everywhere and they know exactly what everyone is doing. We can see every detail. Including what you write."

Then there was the AI system, just one element of the broader Sky Net surveillance system across China. Guards occasionally explained what that was capable of too.

"It can figure out when you're distracted in the classroom," said one guard. "It can see when you're concentrating. That's how the AI system can help us figure out what to do with each prisoner."

Cameras were installed in the female bathrooms and showers. Male guards, Maysem said, watched these camera feeds from a control room, able to hear every sound. She knew because she once managed to peek inside the open doorway of a control room that contained monitors displaying the camp's camera feeds.

Maysem was wary of the other prisoners and spoke to them minimally; she didn't trust anyone. In the cell and the courtyard, the canteen and the classroom, it was as if a gray cloud of computing had blanketed everything. Humans were machines, and machines were human, able to perceive the world around them through facial recognition technology—at least that's how it felt to Maysem.

"The humans had no personality, no being, no soul," Maysem told me. "I started to realize the machines were more human than the humans. The government essentially told us that they held the secrets to our safety. They understood the big brain, the way things worked. They controlled the technology, and therefore we had to fall in line."

[ ]

China's AI firms made huge financial progress from the surveillance state. In December 2016, Megvii, the facial recognition start-up founded five years earlier with the help of Microsoft Research Asia alumni, raised $100 million from investors.[29] Tencent, the developer of WeChat, started out the year worth $180 billion and went on an investment spree. It poured more than $21 billion into a variety of start-ups—anything from online gaming to ride sharing to gene sequencing.[30]

Finally, China's disparate start-ups, growing in wealth and influence, had the potential to build a nationwide ecosystem that could bring together big data, facial recognition, and AI.

Go, the board game beloved in China, kick-started China's AI engine.

For years, AI engineers had believed Go was so hopelessly complex—it has 361 pieces—that it would be impossible to write a software program that could win over a human. The number of possible positions on the board exceeded the number of atoms in the known universe, requiring incredible computing power and pattern recognition.[31]

Google, which had been investing in AI since its founding in 1998,[32] bought the start-up DeepMind in early 2014. And Deep-Mind, founded by three brilliant technologists including a child chess prodigy, made an AI software program called AlphaGo.[33]

Its programmers wanted to see if AlphaGo could learn to play this incredibly complex game on its own, without a human hand. So they developed a new AlphaGo program that didn't need any data inputs whatsoever. It would learn the game all by itself, and then go head-to-head with world champions.

What happened was startling. After only seventy hours of playing matches with itself, the new AlphaGo program reached a level capable of beating top human players. Then, after a reboot, it took AlphaGo only forty days to learn the sum of humans' knowledge of Go. After that it beat the previous, most advanced, version of AlphaGo 90 percent of the time.

The developers were puzzled. Even they had little idea how the new AlphaGo got so smart in such a short time.

These discoveries potentially had enormous implications. If similar levels of AI were applied to other areas, they could upend the way we worked, lived, drove, went shopping, ate, and even conducted diplomacy and fought wars. AlphaGo's AI system, after all, closely mimicked the thinking behind warfare and could have battlefield applications. In China, few were paying attention until AlphaGo was put to the test against Go grandmasters, most of whom were based in East Asia.

"Humans, as it turned out, would have held the system back. The achievement was architecting a system that had the ability to think in an entirely new way and to make its own choices," the technology forecaster Amy Webb wrote. "It was a sudden, unexpected leap, one that portended a future in which AI systems could look at cancer screenings, evaluate climate data, and analyze poverty in nonhuman ways—potentially leading to breakthroughs that human researchers never would have thought of on their own."[34]

By the time I watched AlphaGo beat the eighteen-time world champion, South Korean Lee Sedol, it was advancing toward a capability called "general AI," meaning AI not constrained to a single purpose. It could be put to use for so much more than games.

Observing the match at the Four Seasons Hotel in Seoul, in March 2016, I slowly came to realize how important this moment was. "AI has the power to do so much," a Go player told me at the match, commenting on each move. "Clearly, the AI has become smarter than the humans."

Lee Sedol resigned the first three of five games. Then AlphaGo resigned one, prompting an audible sigh of relief in the audience. During game five, Lee Sedol sat there befuddled, head in hand, with no clear way to victory. When he signaled his resignation, the audience gasped.[35]

"This changes everything," an AI developer in the audience said to me. "Everything."

The Chinese government, I soon learned, was both impressed and aghast that a machine, owned by an American firm no less, could win at a game so tethered to its national culture. Chinese-Taiwanese AI investor Kai-fu Lee called it "China's Sputnik moment," a reference to the Soviet Union's October 1957 launch of Sputnik, earth's first man-made satellite. Fearing that its international rival was far ahead, the United States had then kicked off the space race that culminated in the Apollo missions to the moon.

In its turn, China now saw itself needing to catch up to a technologically advanced world power. The team of government policy makers, handpicked by Chairman Xi to execute the grand strategy that would allow China to catch up to the United States in technology, was given a new target. They had to beat America and turn China into a global leader.[36]

CHAPTER 15

The Big Brain

The internet age will promote the development of human life,
production and productivity.

—XI JINPING, SPEECH MADE DURING VISIT
TO TENCENT, DECEMBER 7, 2014

"**As I thought about my time** in the camp, I could see the irony about how people live under this system," Maysem said. "Everyone must become a robot to survive, with no feelings." However, she soon learned that not everyone was brainwashed. Some were faking it.

Maysem observed a prisoner in her classroom, Mr. Behram. Mr. Behram looked like he was in his sixties. Occasionally after singing patriotic propaganda songs, he would stand up and sing a silly children's song, breaking up the reverent atmosphere. The guards would burst in and beat him with batons. But he didn't flinch. He kept singing until he was dragged out. One time when he reappeared in the classroom the next day, with bruises and an arm cast, he sang a children's song again, only to again be beaten and dragged off.

Maysem was in her cell getting ready for her next class when the sound of men crying in a nearby cell startled her.

"Shut up, be a man, don't cry!" shouted a guard as he beat them.

Then the doors to Maysem's cell opened and guards escorted in an old lady, who appeared to be in her seventies. She had just been detained and was about to begin her "vocational training" in the camp.

"This place is so barbaric!" the frail woman shouted at the guards. "It's like the days of Chairman Mao! No law, just idiot police!"

Exasperated, she sat down on her bed as the cell doors shut automatically. After she calmed down, she told her story quietly.

"Those crying men in the other cell are my sons," she explained. "The police showed up to our house today. I was with my three sons, and their kids were also at the house. But there was a problem. The police knocked on the door for a regular security check. They peeked inside and saw so many kids. They knew that my sons broke the child policy.

"The police barged in and asked for their records and scanned them in their smartphones."

The police clearly intended to seize the children and put them in state orphanages, where they'd undergo political indoctrination.

"I'm retired! I'm just an old lady! Why are you harassing the kids?" the woman protested.

"It's a matter of population control, miss," an officer responded with sinister calm.

When she told him to "Get out of my house!" the police put the old lady in cuffs, along with her three sons.

"By the authority of the public security bureau, you are being detained under 'predictive policing,'" an officer explained, invoking the term for pre-crime. Maysem continued her recollection of the old woman's story. "You will be sent to a detention center where your thoughts will be harmonized."

"I've been sick. I'm not in good health," she told Maysem and the other cellmates. Maysem could see she had a hard time walking, and that she couldn't quite hear what people were saying around her. Most of the other twenty cellmates were present.

The group could hear guards in the nearby cell talking with each other about the three sons, and then beating them again.

"Who do you think you are to cry around here?" an officer shouted.

"Someone tell them to stop," the old lady said. She began panting. Then she grabbed her chest and collapsed on the bed.

"She's having a heart attack!" Maysem shouted. The doors opened and guards walked in, unconcerned.

"She's faking it," a female guard suggested. "We see a lot of cases like this. Don't help her."

The officer brandished a spiked rubber baton in front of the cellmates so they would not be tempted to intervene.

"Help her and I'll break your skull."

Maysem approached the collapsed old woman, only to be rebuffed again by the guard. Her breathing was labored as she lay on the bed, her eyes seemingly empty as if she were unconscious.

"I'd never seen anyone have a heart attack before," Maysem told me. "I felt helpless."

The guards ordered the cellmates to leave for their indoctrination class.

"What were we supposed to do at that moment? It's an impossible situation," Maysem said.

After sitting through two hours of propaganda, they returned to their cell. The old woman was gone. Her three sons, meanwhile, were being forced to stand motionless in the courtyard for an hour.

A guard stood behind the three men. He also carried a spiked rubber baton.

"We never heard what happened to the old woman. I hope they treated her and sent her home. I could only be optimistic, because that's the only way to get through that place," Maysem said. "That's when I realized that I might not get out of there alive. Now I knew that I had to survive."

The next evening, after indoctrination classes, Maysem was winding down for the day when guards pulled her aside and escorted her into a sparse room. Inmates had been taken to that room before. They always came out bloodied, bruised, and traumatized.

"There was a man sitting at the interrogation table," she recalled. "He looked like he was expecting me."

Four cameras pointed at Maysem as she sat down in front of him.

The man was the scholarly minor party boss her mother had spoken to a few days earlier. He apparently knew something was wrong with Maysem's case, and had come out to see what was really going on.

"It's just you and me," he said to Maysem. He insisted that the cameras had been turned off. Maysem of course assumed it wasn't true.

"I only want to see what kind of a person you are."

"I'm a student," Maysem responded. "This is all a mistake."

He pulled out a notebook and began reading.

"Do you know any separatists in the Middle East? Terrorists and extremists?"

"Of course not."

"What do you think of our country's strategy there?"

Maysem wasn't sure how to answer at first, because each question could be a trick. She channeled her mother's thinking, since she always said the right thing at the right time.

"I think it's fine for a nation to protect its interests," Maysem said, giving a vague reply that drew on her studies. "What country doesn't want to protect itself?"

"Tell me about the history of the East Turkestan Independence Movement," said the academic, referring to the group China claimed was instigating terrorist attacks on its soil.

Maysem had no connection to it. *If I pretend like I don't know anything about it, they won't believe me, since I'm already at a camp,* Maysem thought, weighing the consequences. *If I say I know about them, I'll be accused of terrorist connections, because I study in the Middle East.*

"I know we need to fight them. They're a terrorist group."

The party boss pulled out a Koran, the Islamic holy book.

"Do you believe in God?"

"Yes."

He opened the Koran, originally written in Arabic, translated into Chinese. "Kill them wherever you encounter them, and drive them out from where they drove you out, for persecution is more serious than killing."[1]

The party boss put down the book and looked up at Maysem.

"As you can see, this is a verse about fighting. What do you think about jihad?" he asked.

"Jihad is something I do every day," Maysem snapped back. "It's a spiritual struggle. When I wake up in the morning and I'm tired, I am fighting a jihad within myself to get to class and study. When I take an exam, that is my jihad. It is about being just and fair and true to yourself in the face of adversity. People think it's just about violence. But that's wrong. Everyone fights jihad within themselves, even kids."[2]

"And how do you know all that?"

"My mom taught me about all religions, not just Islam."

The party boss took down notes.

"And what do you think about bilingual education?" He was referring to the government's policy of teaching Mandarin Chinese to Uyghur schoolchildren.

"I think everyone should be able to speak two languages."

"What differences do you see between Turkey and China? Between the people and cultures?"

"Of course China is my home. We are hard working and we're respected. Back in Turkey, people are lazy and the place is dirty." Maysem felt she had no choice but to insult Turkey, no matter that she longed to return to her temporary home.

"And what do you think about our detention center?"

"I want to leave. Why would you even ask?"

"You think you'd be allowed to leave with no reason? You haven't proven your innocence."

"It's hard to prove a negative," Maysem replied.

"The government always does something with a purpose. Do you think we would put you here with no reason?"

The party boss stood up, put on his coat, and prepared to leave. He had one last word of advice.

"Think about the reason you're here." He exited, and Maysem was escorted back to her cell.

[ ]

Near the end of 2016, executives at Megvii, the maker of facial recognition technology, huddled in their one-floor office space in Beijing. They pored over their accounting books. They'd been expanding, investing, being aggressive, looking for ways to build the crime-fighting system of the future. But they were far from posting a profit large enough to achieve their dream of becoming the brains behind the digital operations for every industry that needed it, or justify an initial public offering that would make them rich.

"We were falling into a downtime," one executive told me. "We weren't posting strong revenues. Everyone was expanding so fast and so they had debts to pay off. We were changing our direction several times a year, and replacing a lot of employees. It was a hard time. But we managed to survive for one reason: AlphaGo."[3]

Just over a year after beating South Korean Lee Sedol, AlphaGo was ready to take on the world champion, the Chinese player Ke Jie, who agreed to compete against AlphaGo over five matches.

After three grueling days and on his third and final game, Ke Jie capitulated. He had lost them all.[4]

"No human on earth could do this better than Ke Jie," wrote AI expert and investor Kai-fu Lee, "but today he was pitted against a Go player on a level no one had seen before."[5]

The match was a turning point.

One month later, on June 27, 2017, China passed a curious new law, rubber-stamped by its legislature. The national intelligence law, as it was called, alarmed many Uyghurs in contact with me. It opened the possibility that all citizens could become spies at the state's behest.

"All organizations and citizens shall support, assist, and cooperate with national intelligence efforts in accordance with law, and shall protect national intelligence work secrets they are aware of," read Article 7.

"National intelligence work institutions shall use scientific and technical techniques, increasing the level of distinction, screening, synthesis and analytic assessment of intelligence information," stated Article 22.[6]

Four months later, on October 18, 2017, Chairman Xi Jinping took the podium at the much watched Nineteenth National Congress. This was a gathering of elite Communist Party delegates who came together to plan national strategy for the next five years, and choose new leaders. With AlphaGo's latest victory, China's leaders knew they had to speed up their development of AI technology.

"We will work faster to build China into a manufacturer of quality, develop advanced manufacturing, promote further integration of the internet, big data, and artificial intelligence with the real economy," Xi announced, "and foster new growth areas and drivers of growth in medium-high-end consumption, innovation-driven development, the green and low-carbon economy, the sharing economy, modern supply chains, and human capital services."[7]

Then the government got to work, creating a "national AI team" to realize the dream. The ministry of science and technology selected four companies: AI giants Baidu, Alibaba, and Tencent, the trio called the BAT, along with voice recognition specialist iFlyTek. Later, they would add intelligent vision firm SenseTime.[8]

The Chinese government had supported many AI companies for a decade or more, with finances and political backing. Government support for AI was expanding to unseen levels; there was a gold rush. Numerous Chinese technology executives told me it was better to jump on the bandwagon right away and worry about the implications later. If they didn't move fast, the competition would beat them to it.

At Megvii, many executives agreed that now was the time to seize on government backing, expanding at any cost to defeat its competition, SenseTime.

"You must understand that start-ups are pushed along by history. We are the hostages of history, not the creators of it," I was told by a Megvii research and development executive.

"Our breakthrough came through when we got government funding after AlphaGo," he said. "Megvii got an injection of $430 million. Now we're five or six times bigger, and we expanded from our little one-floor office."

"First we need to survive as a business, and then we can build our moral values. We can't use one perspective imported from another country [the US] as a living standard for all human beings," he told me. "If one standard fits all, then a business wouldn't be able to survive. I'm not saying who is right or wrong."

At SenseTime, executives concurred. They wanted to beat Megvii.

"The key is getting as much market share as possible, so we have a strong position," a SenseTime employee told me. "If we don't seize the opportunities earlier than others, we'll be in a tough position if we have to chase them afterwards. So our strategy is to get more projects out at any cost."

They weren't fussy about the use their technology might be put to.

"If you are close to the government, you get more government projects to help increase your market share. Being close to the government is a must-do."

When journalists asked AI developers whether China would deploy AI to curtail human rights, they got a somewhat similar response: that's not our business.

"As a venture capitalist, we don't invest in this area, and we're not studying deeply this particular problem," Sinovation Ventures chief Kai-fu Lee later told *60 Minutes*.[9]

By 2017, China was on a path toward runaway AI development, abetted by the state. No longer were commercial businesses like SenseTime and Megvii at the forefront of strategy on how to develop these technologies—for messaging apps, surveillance, and online shopping—then selling their services to the government as they were needed. Now, the government was consolidating AI strategy under the dictates of national interest. Companies had to get on board or be left behind.

CHAPTER 16

The Bureaucracy Is Expanding to Meet the Needs of the Expanding Bureaucracy

The object of persecution is persecution. The object of torture is torture. The object of power is power.

—GEORGE ORWELL, *1984*

After a week at the camp, Maysem was lying awake in bed, pondering the mission entrusted to her by the party boss: to figure out why she was there. She wasn't sure what to say about why she was imprisoned. The party boss, the guards told her, would return the next morning.

She drifted in and out of sleep, her mind racing, thinking about what her mother would say. As she drifted off again, she saw herself standing outside the camp. Then her mother showed up on a bicycle.

"Time to go!" she said.

When the alarm bell jolted her awake, Maysem realized she had been dreaming. The doors opened and after her morning exercise routine and breakfast, Maysem was again escorted to meet the party boss at 9 A.M.

He cut to the chase.

"Why are you here?"

"I'm too proud," Maysem said. "I'm the favorite in my extended family. I always get the attention. I don't know how to treat people. I always thought I was nobler, more important.

"I looked down on your officials. I thought they were stupid and uneducated. But I realized that I'm the uneducated one, because I looked down on the Party."

"What do you think about your classmates?"

"I thought they were uneducated too. They didn't think anything about our laws and customs. They never grew up reading or doing hard mental work. Now they study five hours a day. They're becoming useful citizens for our nation."

"As much as you are progressing here," the official announced, "we cannot let you leave yet. You still have more studying to do."

Maysem was crushed. The seeming impossibility of escaping began to dawn on her.

The system wants me to admit I'm crazy and wrong, she thought. *But once I admit I'm crazy and wrong, I have to stay longer because I've just admitted I'm crazy and wrong.*

"I was worried that everything I was admitting was going into the computer systems," she said. "Were the machines concluding that I was a terrorist because I was willing to talk about my flaws? Did I just shoot myself in the foot?"

Anxious and uncertain, Maysem was escorted to her morning propaganda class, where she was mocked by the guards.

"Here's your notebook and pen," the teacher announced, finally giving her the materials she needed for studying.

Maysem's spirits sank.

"A notebook and pen meant I was officially an inmate. I was no longer outside the system. That was it. I could stay here for years, even die here."

She looked around the classroom. Everyone was staring at her, an outcast whose hopes and dreams had finally been crushed.

She peered down with dread at her notebook. The lined paper before her pulled her into the depths of the labyrinth—an inescapable hell of rote where Maysem would be forced to unlearn her own mind, submitting to the orders of the machine trying to remake her.

"Love the Party, love the Country!"

Maysem put pencil to paper, prepared to inscribe the mindless chants of her classroom teacher, with the futile hope of being released months or years down the road.

I submit to the Party. The Party is my mother and father, she imagined herself writing. *I have been arrogant. I have been wrong. The Party, my parent, will protect me. I submit, I give myself up to you, my protector and savior. You are the sun, you are the moon, you are the mountains and the ocean.*

Maysem broke out of her morbid daydream. She looked at the blank page before her. The students around her were writing their usual seven pages of self-criticism and recitation. She longed for the openness of the pastures and oasis she had grown up with. But now was the time to suppress that instinct to be an individual.

Pencil in hand, Maysem submitted and began writing. Moments later, the doors to the classroom were flung open. She looked up from her notebook. A small scrum of guards was staring at her. As usual, they held their spiked rubber batons. Maysem knew what that meant. She'd been caught. She'd disobeyed the Party, somehow. She prepared for her punishment.

"You're coming with us," said a guard.

"There's a car waiting for you."

The camp chief didn't have a friendly look on his face. Maysem remained seated, wondering what he was talking about.

"I said there's a car waiting for you."

Maysem felt her mind go numb. Nothing seemed to add up anymore. If a car was waiting for her outside, surely the driver had orders to take her somewhere even worse.

"We got a call from the local administrative office. There was an error. You're being reassigned."

The camp chief looked like he'd been scolded, Maysem recalled.

"I struggled to piece together exactly what he was saying," she told me. "I sat there not sure what to think. Was it a trick?"

Like every other order the camp leaders had carried out, this one seemed to make no sense. It was as if they were trying to make her doubt her own reality even more.

Why give me a notebook and pencil and then order me to leave?

Two guards helped Maysem from her seat. They nudged her forward, trying to get her to walk.

She resisted at first, worried about what was coming. The cameras seemed to follow her as she walked. And then she exited through the eerie cement hallway. Along one wall, the paintings of oppressed women wearing veils seemed to cry out to her. On the other side, the women in high heels and modern clothing were out and about shopping and eating, seemingly aloof to Maysem's presence. Then guards outside the camp opened the final doorway and the sunlight overwhelmed her. *What now?* she wondered. *Will they take me away and torture me?* The guards ushered Maysem into the car. She looked back at the camp as they drove off, wondering if or when her fellow inmates would ever get out, and if they'd given up hope for good.

They drove past traditional adobe homes on which Kashgar was built. Maysem realized she was back in the city. She glimpsed her high school. Then her friends' homes.

"But I wasn't finished. There was still one more step," Maysem told me. "I had to finish the indoctrination class at the reeducation center. The one that I was originally at before they sent me to the second concentration camp . . . that other camp was the detention center."

She was ushered into the reeducation center. The students were delighted by her return; they dropped their pencils and clapped when she joined them. After the brief euphoria, the teacher asked for quiet in the classroom. Maysem sat down and got to work as a student. She only had a few more weeks left before graduation.

She hoped that one day she could get back to Turkey, back to her university, her boyfriend, her normal life.

"But something was off. I couldn't think, and I couldn't feel," Maysem told me. "I was muted inside."

Every time a critical thought or a flourish of imagination floated into her head, she shut it down.

Dangerous, she thought. *Shut up. Don't think. Just do.*

The next couple of weeks of classes were a dull routine. It was as if every day was the same, as if time had stopped. The students sauntered along, submissive to each day's rote obligation. After six hours of class every day, they went home to prepare dinner for their families. They would go through the same process the next day.

At some point every day, the teacher would show propaganda videos of patriotic students marching in formation, and random people on the street praising China or standing before the Chinese flag. They were generally utterly featureless, but one day the teacher showed a documentary that included a face Maysem recognized: "It was my professor Ilham Tohti."

"Ilham Tohti, who has been sentenced to life in prison, is a terrorist and extremist," Maysem recalled the documentary saying. The video showed Tohti in handcuffs, standing before a judge and receiving his sentence. "Ilham Tohti used his position as a professor to infiltrate our nation and infect the minds of our students and people. The Party stands against enemies such as Ilham Tohti, who are a cancer for the nation."

Then the film showed a series of interviews with Professor Tohti's former students. Maysem was taken aback. She knew them from the time she audited his class.

"I studied under Ilham Tohti," said one student, a man in a polo shirt. "I quickly realized that Professor Tohti was a terrorist who had infiltrated our minds. Now that I'm at a reeducation center, the Party is teaching me to cleanse my mind of Ilham Tohti's virus."

"The three viruses of terrorism, extremism, and separatism once existed within me," proclaimed another student. "The virus was spreading, thanks to Professor Ilham Tohti. But the Party cured me. The Party set me on the right course."

"Love the Party! Love the Country! Down with the scoundrel Ilham Tohti!"[1]

One by one, the students in the documentary denounced their professor.

Once it was over, the teacher told the class to begin the old routine: open their notebooks and write seven pages of reflections on Ilham Tohti.

"I have reflected on the teachings of the Party," Maysem wrote. "I was wrong. The Party is great. The nation is great. Reactionary intellectuals have infiltrated our nation to infect my mind and soul. The Party is my father and mother, and the Party has corrected me."

She was tired. She just wanted to go home.

"I was ready to leave. The class was almost finished. We only had three days left. And now that I was graduating, I had to plot my way out of China—to freedom." Maysem finished her final day of class and left the other students behind, who were forced to stay longer for whatever transgressions they stood accused of.

"The Situation was deteriorating quickly. Every day I heard stories about this or that brother, father, mother, friend disappearing into a camp," Maysem said. "The police showed up in the middle of the night and took them.

"I was lucky. I got out of my reeducation course early, right before things took their absolute worst turn."

Maysem and her mother organized a meeting at the main Kashgar government office with a local official who could grant Maysem permission to leave the country. She had, after all, successfully graduated her indoctrination course and purged her mind of nefarious thoughts.

The official presented Maysem with a bewildering list of documents that needed to be submitted to every office imaginable: the office of the neighborhood administrator, the office of a local police officer, the office of a party political officer, the office of … on and on.[2]

"You need all their signatures and stamps," he explained.

"Mom and I spent hours and hours gathering the forms: my birth certificate, housing registration, documents proving my attendance at my elementary school through university, even the death certificates of my grandmother and grandfather."

Finally, Maysem was ready for the endless visits to bureaucrats to plead for their signatures. For each one she had to endure the monotony of standing in a long line, then explaining her case in great detail before the signature was granted.

"Why do you need to leave China?" this or that officer would ask her. "What business do you have in the Middle East?"

"I completed my political training in China, and I showed I was a loyal citizen," she would respond, pointing to her coursework at the reeducation center and the fact that she graduated as evidence of her patriotic dedication. "I have to finish my graduate school overseas, in Turkey. I'm already enrolled."

Each time, a bureaucrat looked carefully through the paper, and double-checked for any missing documents or signatures. Occasionally, they made a phone call or two to confirm the procedure and legality of what they were doing—allowing a young woman to leave when the city was increasingly on lockdown. And there was the occasional "payment," or bribe, passed under the table.

Maysem knew time was running out to escape China.

"I saw that Chen Quanguo was starting to step up the police measures," she said. Each week there were more patrols, more convenience police stations, more cameras, and more disappearances. "The software, the AI . . . I could feel it getting more sophisticated."

"You've been lucky," Maysem's mother explained. "But we need to get you out of here. We need to get you to safety."

Maysem's mother determined that her daughter must leave before the entire country shut down on October 1 for China's independence day holiday, which celebrated the Communist Party's seizure of power after the civil war.[3]

As soon as the paperwork was complete, Maysem's mother bought a plane ticket for Maysem's flight from Urumqi to Ankara. But since Maysem lived in Kashgar, she needed to get to the regional capital first—not an easy task.

"Let's take the bus," her mother said. "It's a full-day ride, twenty-four hours."

On the packed bus where people could overhear them, they were careful what they said. The subject of Maysem's overseas study was off-limits.

"Remember that when you go back to the world," her mother said, using deliberately vague language, "you have so much to show. You can be a voice. We'll be all right back here in China."

"And what about Dad?" Maysem asked.

Her relationship with her father was still difficult, much of it unresolved. They hadn't healed some of their past pain.

"Remember that he loves you too."

He was the one who had burned Maysem's small library of books. Could she forgive him? Had he actually saved her from a worse sentence, should the authorities have found those books? Maysem wasn't sure.

It was midnight when she and her mother disembarked in Urumqi. Maysem had a small bag full of documents; her mother had brought only her purse. They didn't want to signal at the police checkpoints that Maysem planned to leave the country. Even though she had her documents in order, the police might act arbitrarily to detain her again.

The two women approached the airline check-in counter. As she examined Maysem's passport and documents, the employee at the desk had a perplexed look.

"There's a problem with your ticket," she said, picking up the phone and dialing.

"You bought this ticket in June 2016," the employee explained. "You changed it three times. But you didn't get the right permission each time."

Maysem's mother, hoping for the day her daughter would be free, was the one who had changed the ticket's departure date three times, when Maysem was required to attend her propaganda course and then was detained in the two camps. Maysem, it turned out, was supposed to be getting all those government permissions while she was in a concentration camp.

"Seriously?" Maysem asked.

It was another Catch-22 designed to keep people like her under control. You can't get properly registered for an airline ticket because you're in a camp, and you can't leave the country because you can't get a plane ticket.

Standing in the middle of the empty airport, Maysem felt exhausted. She was ready to give up.

"I'd gone all that way, been through all that suffering. And I couldn't escape because of some dumb bureaucratic problem with my ticket," she said.

"Plus, it was now October 1. The employee told us there were no airline workers at the office who could help settle this. We'd have to wait. And waiting any longer could mean more imprisonment."

To Maysem, the system had succeeded in what it was built for: bureaucratic oppression.

Her mother had a flight back to Kashgar the next day, but she forgot about her own ticket and decided to stay with Maysem in Urumqi.

"Let's think. We can figure this out in a day. We can get you out another way."

They finally discovered a bus due to depart Urumqi with connections to other busses that would eventually reach northern India—a four-day ride that meant going west around the harsh Taklamakan Desert, past Kashgar where she had just come from, and through smaller towns and villages near Tibet that eventually led into India. Luckily, not only did India have relaxed visa rules for Chinese citizens, but also Maysem would be able to pay for an Indian e-visa on her smartphone.[4]

From India, Maysem could then book a flight to Turkey. It was risky. The Chinese border guards could easily stop her before she entered India, if she was deemed suspicious.

"This will be the last time we'll see each other for a long time," her mother told her just before Maysem boarded the bus. "But remember the gift you've been given. The experiences you had were a gift, because now you will be safe, you will grow, and the world will see what is happening."

They hugged. Maysem turned around and watched her mother pass into the distance, becoming a dot against a backdrop of skyscrapers and ramshackle buildings. And soon she looked out into the vast dark stretch of desert, empty and forlorn, the place where ancient treasures were rumored to be buried, where adventurers and spirits had long roamed.

The magic of Kashgar and the expanse of the Taklamakan Desert that suffused Maysem's childhood were gone. The festive crowds no longer gathered at the desert's edge every year, converging on shrines and the tombs of martyrs and warriors. Kashgar, the farmland, the oasis—all were barren, devoid of life, a shell. The state had removed minarets from some mosques and razed other mosques completely. Parking lots, gardens, and even a public restroom stood in place of the mosques and cemeteries where the graves of Maysem's centuries-old ancestors once lay.[5] People on streets and dirt roads wandered like corpses, seemingly unsure of who they were and where they came from, or were going.

Maysem knew she could never go back.

She closed her eyes and saw the ancient epics, with their heroes and villains waging battles using magic and sorcery. She remembered poetry readings and concerts. She recalled her family's weekend outings, when they fed on delicious meats and the days were filled with joyous chatter. And then she said goodbye.

CHAPTER 17

The Prison of the Mind

Once their mental state is healthy,
they will be able to live happily in society.

—MENTAL HEALTH COUNSELOR IN XINJIANG

In the fall of 2016, Maysem's boyfriend, Arman, was on his way to teach a class when he got a phone call from an unknown number. He didn't pick up the first time. Then the number called again.

"Hello?" he asked.

"I'm here. I'm okay."

It was Maysem, phoning from India. It was the first time in four months she and Arman had been able to speak, the first time in months they could be reasonably sure the Chinese government was not harvesting the contents of their call.

"I have so much more to tell you. I'll be there soon."

A few days later, Arman waited at the airport arrivals gate. Maysem approached him slowly, then embraced him. But she said nothing.

[ ]

Something had changed in Maysem after she left the camp. She later recounted to Arman that when she was on the bus out of China, people asked her where she was from. Suspicious of spies and informants everywhere, she didn't trust them, nor did she want to speak. Talking made her tired because it required thinking, and thinking was risky.

"Kashgar," was her only terse reply.

"That place is on lockdown," said one man. "How did you get out here?"

"You're a very lucky young girl," said an older woman.

After Maysem had flown out of India and arrived in Turkey, she had to approach an immigration officer to get her passport stamped. She didn't want to say anything to this man either.

"Where are you from?" he asked.

Maysem stared blankly. She hesitated, reluctant to speak before a figure of authority, the person who, back in China, would have had total power over the future of her family and her career.

"What brings you to Turkey?"

No answer.

The immigration officer looked at Maysem's Chinese passport. She had a student visa, and she was enrolled in a well-known graduate program at the university. Everything looked fine.

"I'm a student," Maysem finally said. "I'm just coming back from the summer break." The immigration officer stamped her passport and let her through. She took a taxi to her apartment.

Back home, "I stumbled around my apartment with baggy, dirty sweatpants and didn't shower."

She didn't want to get out of bed in the morning. She failed to show up to class.

Arman started to understand how lucky Maysem was to have left China, even though she never told him exactly what had happened. Starting on October 19, 2016, just weeks after her escape from Xinjiang, millions of Uyghur residents were told to report to local police stations, where they were required to surrender their passports. Police departments posted the announcements online, saying no new passports would be issued. The Uyghurs were stuck in China, perhaps for life.

But Maysem didn't feel lucky. She felt like a runner struggling to sprint through slushy, muddy snow.

"That year, from late 2016 to 2017, I pretty much slept the entire year," she told me. "Everywhere I looked, I saw authority. When someone asked me a question, I thought they were interrogating me, that I had to hide something. When I picked up my smartphone or opened my laptop, I felt like a machine was watching me, judging me, thinking about me.

"Why hold a deep conversation? Why read something and then talk about it with other people? Complexity and humanity were risky bets."

Maysem had become so skilled at faking her disdain for emotion and critical thought—her tactics for survival—that now, in a very real sense, she couldn't think or feel at all.

"I felt like a computer. I was programmed to take in the environment around me and then spit out a calculation for my own preservation" was how she put it.

Moping around her unkempt, increasingly dusty apartment, Maysem occasionally picked up a book, out of boredom. She opened *The Time Traveler's Wife*, an old favorite, but immediately put it down. She checked her home for cameras and surveillance devices.

Whenever she peered out her window and saw a police car with lights flashing, or the local police officer on patrol, she got frightened and went back to bed.

She also refused any occasional invitations from friends, professors, or well-wishers who wanted to help her out of her slump, telling them: "I have to sleep. I don't have time for that. Find someone else."

Maysem's friends reacted at first with anger and sadness. They assumed Maysem was no longer interested in their friendship.

"That was hurtful," one friend told her.[1]

Finally, Arman persuaded her to attend a small gathering of friends for dinner and tea.

"I went in a dress that I'd been wearing for days," she said. "It was knotty and dirty. I looked like I'd been begging on the street."

She walked in and felt the friends turn to her in discomfort, unsure what had happened.

Over time, she began opening up to Arman and other fellow students.

"But something strange happened. I would tell them about the concentration camp. But I would tell my story from the third person. I would tell it as if I was talking about someone I knew."

Confused, her friends only had more questions. They didn't seem to understand what she was saying to them.

"Are you sad because your friend had all this happen back in China?"

One night, Maysem woke up sweaty and gasping. She felt her hand move to her chest. *Am I dying?* she thought. She whispered an Islamic prayer recited by those who believe they are dying: "Verily we belong to Allah, and verily to Him do we return."[2]

The pain in her heart was unbearable.

[ ]

"There's nothing wrong with you," the doctor told Maysem after doing a series of tests. "How are you feeling lately? Everything okay at home?"

Maysem didn't respond. The doctor, sensing something psychological was going on, told her to seek counseling.

But Maysem still didn't want to talk to anyone. Luckily, her mother was writing her text messages, offering a small dose of comfort as she struggled to get her life back together.

"Today, we had a nice big lamb dinner and way too much wine," her mother joked, sending a photo of tipsy houseguests eking out whatever joy they could feel as their situation got worse. Her mother's messages arrived only about once a month. That was it. And they lacked detail. It was the only way to hide from the authorities, who were detaining citizens messaging family members living outside China.

"I miss you," Maysem wrote back almost every time.

Once, she received no response. A month later, Maysem's phone vibrated.

"Don't message us. It's not safe," her mother said. "It's too dangerous to call. Never call us again."

Maysem didn't respond. Then she got one more message.

"Maybe we won't talk again for a long time. But one day, if you can come back and be with us, call this phone number." Her mother sent her a family member's number that she believed would be relatively safe.[3]

That was the last Maysem heard from her.

It was impossible to find out the truth of what had happened.

"And that's when it hit me that I was totally alone."

Her mother had sacrificed herself so she could get Maysem to safety and freedom. She put herself in danger. She stayed behind with the family when she could have also escaped.

Finally, Maysem realized that she didn't really have a choice. She remembered her mother's words when she'd come to the concentration camp with a care package of new clothes:

"This experience is a gift. I am so proud of you."

"How could I get this far, only to give up?" Maysem said to me. "The police state was winning. They destroyed me, even as I sat thousands of miles away, totally free."

Pointing to her temple, she said, "Up here, I was still a prisoner."

It was time to get her life back in order. Through the darkness, Maysem began remembering the people who were sources of light, able to resist tyranny with the slightest gestures of passion, joyousness, and comedy. She remembered Mr. Behram, the old man who kept singing a kid's song even as he was beaten by the guards. And she remembered what he once announced in defiance to the classroom.

"You can make fun of anything except death," he said, paraphrasing a Uyghur proverb. "Because when you're dead, well, you can't make fun of anything. Satire is a part of being alive."

Maysem realized she had a purpose. She had to make use of the "gifts" the police state, ironically, had handed her: strength, the ability to survive hardship, an opportunity to tell the world what was happening.

She sought counseling and told her story to a psychologist. As she released her emotions in retelling what had happened, Maysem felt she was taking control of her feelings of oppression and loss for the first time. She was no longer the passive victim she had been turned into, receiving inputs and delivering outputs.

"Finally, I was beginning to feel alive again. And now I understood why we carry our stories with us. Stories, the ability to tell a story and to understand one, is what connects us."

[ ]

As Maysem began reconstructing her experience and coming to terms with it, she started realizing the importance of family and of a community of friends—the people who helped her, the people who looked out for her in hard times, even while she might be angry and bitter against them—and of country.

"I put my family in a place of danger and unhappiness," she said. "They did everything in their power to help me escape. And I left them. We are in a state of constant guilt. It's a torture of the mind, worse than a torture of the body, that traps you. And that's what the police state is designed to do."

Then she envisioned a much better world.

"Imagine if we lived in a nation that was content and happy, a place for democracy and participation, where everyone was empowered to think freely and make their own decisions. People's love for their community would push them to sacrifice themselves for their country and for future generations. They'd stand up to any difficulty and defend their country and community against threats. They would create art, literature, scientific discovery . . . all this comes from a society where people feel safe, free, and empowered. They have freedom of thought and freedom of speech.

"And that is the importance of a strong republic, a strong nation that can protect its people from tyrants."

But she could not see such a world being offered to the Uyghurs.

"I've always hoped that this would end with something great. But now I think Big Brother will control everything. People will forget about love, about God. Everyone's lives will be arranged in advance by the government."

After putting her studies on hold for the academic year, Maysem began embracing the truths of her new life. She got out of bed and showered every morning, bought new clothes, and threw away the old dresses and sweatpants she had worn for days at a time.

In the fall of 2017, a year after escaping from China, she returned to her studies. The professors immediately recognized that bright well-spoken woman who'd been in their classes before.

Her next step was to marry her boyfriend, Arman. After a day outdoors and a candlelit dinner at home, he had proposed. They got married in a small ceremony held in Turkey.

Maysem's life was back on track. Then one day, hoping for news of her mother back in Xinjiang, she opened her smartphone and checked her mom's social media profile on WeChat.

There was a status update next to her profile picture.

"Having a good day and we're doing well," it read.

Maysem was taken aback. She knew that no one could send a direct WeChat message to her from China. The authorities would intercept it and promptly take away anyone who had contact with someone in a foreign country, especially a person like Maysem, an enemy of the state who had spent time in a prison camp.

Nonetheless, Maysem's instinct was to respond on WeChat. Maybe she could communicate with her mother that way.

"Just married!" she wrote as her status update.

Hours later, her mother posted a status update.

"Proud of my daughter!"

Maysem posted a new profile picture that showed her with Arman.

"Growing up!"

"I love the Communist Party and my family!" her mother wrote.

"Communist Party is great," Maysem joked, knowing that Chinese authorities were bad at catching irony.

"Dad's well. Great things ahead" her mother replied. Because Maysem knew her mom's figures of speech and inflections, she was sure it was actually her mom and not the Chinese government hacking her mom's WeChat account.

The exchanges continued for about eight weeks. Maysem woke up in the morning to new status updates and new profile pictures from her mother. Her mom's profile pictures showed Maysem's old neighborhood behind her, her high school, the grocery store, and everything that was familiar from home.

Then, as suddenly as they had begun, the updates stopped. Maysem posted fresh updates to see if she would receive a reply.

"History class is so interesting," she posted for all to see. But after days and then weeks and then months, there was no further response from her mother.[4]

Alone again, Maysem thought.

One day, after lunch, Maysem's phone vibrated. She picked it up. A woman who called herself Alfiya, whom Maysem didn't know, claimed in a WeChat message that her family was being "cared for" and that Maysem should "come home."

"Your neighborhood is looking great these days," she wrote, sending a photograph of Maysem's old street corner. "People really like you. Your friends and family all want you to come back."

Maysem's heart dropped. "Alfiya," she knew, was a government agent. And the perfect police state had managed to get in touch with her, probably using the WeChat profile updates. Maysem wondered how long they had been monitoring the covert "status updates" she had been posting.

"And then I knew for sure," Maysem said, "that my family had been taken away to the camps."

[ ]

Alfiya kept up her stream of gentle nudges, always polite and reserved in her WeChat messages.

"Here is my apartment," Alfiya wrote, attaching pictures of her kitchen and living room. She seemed to want to get Maysem to open up to her.

She sent a picture of her balcony.

"Don't you see? Things are well here."

"Thank you. Why are you sending me these photos?" Maysem responded.

"People are looking out for you. We're all a community."

Maysem realized she could not afford to ignore the strange dialog, let alone become shrill or accusatory or abusive. Her family's well-being might depend on her reasonableness and her apparent willingness to be positive about China. It required constant

self-control, especially when, as she increasingly did, Alfiya became unnaturally curious about Maysem's personal life.

"Where do you live now? Ankara, Turkey?" she asked. Clearly,
someone in Maysem's family had revealed her place of residence,
or it had been found through the data on her mother's phone or
social media profiles.

Maysem replied, but vaguely. "I'm studying," she wrote.

Alfiya kept prodding. "Here's the local market. Had a nice time
today!"

She asked Maysem to send photos of the fellow Uyghurs who
lived in Ankara as refugees or residents.

Maysem sidestepped that request entirely.[5]

CHAPTER 18

A New Cold War?

No country is permanently strong. Nor is any country
permanently weak. If conformers to law are strong,
the country is strong; if conformers to law are weak,
the country is weak.

—XI JINPING, QUOTING CHINESE PHILOSOPHER HAN FEI TZU

On October 29, 2019, Maysem, Arman, and I, along with a girl-
friend of hers, hopped in a car for a day trip to visit Anitkabir
("memorial tomb"). Situated atop a hill, the mausoleum houses
the remains of Mustafa Kemal, the independence leader who
founded the Republic of Turkey. To people of Turkic background,
he is also known as Ataturk, or "father of the Turks."

We passed through the Lion's Road, a long walkway bordered
by sculptures of lions. We watched ceremonial soldiers goose-step-
ping in formation. Then we entered the mausoleum and stood before the Ataturk's sarcophagus, as soldiers laid a wreath on it.[1]

At first I thought the trip was just a kind of touristic visit to see
Turkey's heritage and monuments. Then I realized the symbolism
this place carried for my Uyghur friends.

"Is this what it means to have your own country? Ataturk
wanted a Turkey that could stand strong," Maysem said as we
walked around looking at historical exhibits. "It was supposed to
be a modern republic. No more superstition, no religion in government. The government should build schools and roads and
hospitals, and keep its people educated and healthy.

"And the military? In the past, the Ottoman Empire had become weak." Maysem spoke about the empire that dominated the

Middle East from the fifteenth to nineteenth centuries. "And the British invaded in World War I. They wanted to make this place a satellite, control the oil supplies. But Ataturk wouldn't stand for it. He believed in his people and he taught them that they could stand up for themselves."

"Turkey," I pointed out, "was not a democracy. It became authoritarian under Ataturk."

"That's not the point," Maysem's friend chimed in. "Yes, we want a democracy. But the point of Ataturk is that he shows what it means to have your own country. Your country is what protects you. It gives you rights and responsibilities as a citizen."

Maysem gazed in admiration at a statue of Ataturk, then said:

"A people should be united. They should share a common goal, a vision for who they are and where they came from and what they hope for in the world. But we, the Uyghurs, we have nothing.

"We're broken. We have a government that's divided us, turned us against each other, and even outside China, we don't trust each other. We don't want to work together to fight back.

"And how about America? How about George Washington and Abraham Lincoln? Or Martin Luther King? How do you think they achieved what they achieved? They united so many Americans under a vision of what it means to be free and equal. And Charles de Gaulle? Nelson Mandela? Gandhi?"

Now I could see how Maysem viewed her Uyghur world. It had no grand story, nothing to strive for—it was a fallen world.

"We're broken because we have no leader, no hero. They're all in prison."

"And who is the leader that you want?" I asked.

Both women, Maysem and her friend, snapped back almost in unison:

"Ilham Tohti."

"He's not only a scholar," Maysem said of her professor, now serving a lifetime prison sentence. "He's a leader. He can stand up at a podium and go on and on with charisma. He can't be corrupted. I believe he would die for what he believes in.

"But we live in a time where people all over the world are turning on their leaders, their democracies, their countries. Our leaders lead through fear and anger. They create rage in the people. They don't respect laws and speech. So I don't know if we'll ever have a leader like our teacher."

From the hill, we looked over the city, which had first been the center of an independence movement and was now Turkey's capital. The evening was setting in. The orange-purple sunset reflected brilliantly off the mausoleum. For a moment, I was blinded.

"We should get going," Maysem's friend said. "This place is closing."

[ ]

Uyghurs living all over the world told me in interviews that they carefully tracked developments in China, praying for a breakthrough in the Situation.

Maysem was among them. For more than a year, since July 2018, Huawei, Magvii, SenseTime, Hikvision—companies that helped build the surveillance state that imprisoned her—had become targets of the US government, as well as of dozens of other governments.

Nevertheless, China's tech companies stood behind their capabilities and promised a better future, at least to the public.

"What we've accomplished [once] happened only in movies," SenseTime head of product development Yang Fan told *Forbes* in 2018. He boasted of the company's early accomplishments. Sense-Time was building a database of 10 billion images and videos to help identify faces, many collected from online. In the gritty city of Chongqing, it had identified sixty-nine suspects and caught sixteen fugitives in forty days.[2]

Rumors were spreading that Huawei, which not only sold cloud computing services that helped in surveillance operations in Xinjiang,[3] but also developed facial recognition software that alerted police when it recognized a Uyghur person,[4] was about to have its first smartphone released in a carrier deal with AT&T. If this venture succeeded, Huawei, now the world's third-largest phone vendor behind Apple and Samsung, had a shot at joining the club of influential and prestigious brand names in America.

Instead, Huawei's attempt to land on American shores had the opposite effect. It all began on January 9, 2018, as Huawei CEO Richard Yu was preparing his speech at the Consumer Electronics (CES) show in Las Vegas. He would be unveiling Huawei's new Mate 10 Pro phone in the much anticipated partnership with AT&T.[5]

"When we got to CES, AT&T officially backed out, and they were very clear with us that they were being pressured by the US government," Teri Daley, former Huawei vice president of public relations, who helped with preparations for the event, told me.

"[CEO] Richard [Yu] went on stage as planned and announced the product. When he got to the slide that showed the channels and AT&T was missing, there was an audible gasp from the US tech media."

"AT&T's cancelling its deal to use our phones. It's a big loss for us, and also for carriers, but the more big [sic] loss is for consumers, because consumers don't have the best choice," Yu said in an impromptu outburst after his scripted speech finished scrolling on the teleprompter. "We win the trust of the Chinese carriers, we win the trust of the emerging markets . . . and also we win the trust of the global carriers, all the European and Japanese carriers."[6]

Huawei's dream of becoming another Apple or Samsung was crushed. "Huawei was going to be the poster child of the US-China trade war," Daley said. "The US government had been working on it since 2012, if not before, so they were highly organized."

Criminal court proceedings against Huawei, unsealed a year after the fact, were released to the public. They showed that the US government had accused a Huawei employee of, with the direction and backing of Huawei corporate headquarters, entering a Washington-based T-Mobile laboratory in May 2013. He was on what seemed like a comically bizarre secret agent mission. He removed the arm of a testing robot called "Tappy." Tappy's job was to rapidly tap at new phones and analyze their quality before the phones were released on the market.

Tappy was the envy of the mobile phone industry because of its fast, accurate, and efficient testing capabilities. T-Mobile kept

Tappy on lockdown. Only certain employees from its partners were allowed access.

After taking the robotic arm to his hotel, the Huawei employee measured and photographed it that night. At first, he denied being in possession of the arm when T-Mobile employees unsurprisingly noticed it had gone missing. The next day, he told T-Mobile he "found" the arm in his bag.[7] Huawei said it fired two employees for the debacle. A lawsuit and criminal proceedings ensued.[8] In 2017, a civil court verdict awarded T-Mobile $4.8 million in damages from Huawei.[9]

"This indictment shines a bright light on Huawei's flagrant abuse of the law," Assistant US Attorney Annette L. Hayes in Seattle claimed of the criminal case she helped bring forward in January 2019, two years after the civil verdict.[10] Prosecutors claimed, based on an internal email obtained from Huawei, that Huawei's offices in China had launched a formal policy of giving bonuses to employees who stole confidential information from other companies.[11]

With the alleged plot to steal Tappy's arm unmasked, the resentment and frustration with Huawei's alleged corporate espionage exploded into a full-on trade war between China and the United States. The US stance was representative of Western nations' growing resistance to the arrival of Chinese technology giants deeply enmeshed in the web of surveillance and control they had helped create back home.

On May 2, 2018, four months after the Huawei product unveiling, the Pentagon banned the sale of devices from Huawei and another Chinese firm, ZTE, on US military bases around the world.[12] Three months later, Australia announced a ban on the planned rollout of Huawei's 5G network that would help power coming advances in artificial intelligence and big data, fearful of Chinese surveillance and spying through the new network.[13]

Huawei, however, was still growing. It announced it had shipped 100 million phones worldwide during the first half of that year.[14] On August 1, Huawei replaced Apple as the world's second-largest phone seller.[15]

[ ]

As Chinese technology spread around the world, back in China momentum was building to unify "social credit"—the system that ranked the "trustworthiness" of citizens for loans, jobs, apartment purchases, and even vacation discounts—under a single umbrella, drawing on data from China's private firms, along with government court documents and arrest records.

In early 2018, the Bank of China, the country's national central bank, began reining in control of social credit from the eight private firms that had been developing the social credit system for the previous four years.[16]

Now that the state had elevated its control of the system, the results were fast and efficient. That year, travelers were blocked 17.5 million times from buying airline tickets and 5.5 million times from buying train tickets, because their social credit scores were too low.[17] People were blocked 290,000 times from acting as corporate lawyers or being hired to work in senior management.[18]

And the rollout, at least at the beginning, had a good reception from the Chinese public. In an online survey of twenty-two hundred people in China, carried out in Beijing and Shanghai from March to August 2018, researchers at the Free University of Berlin found that older people and "more socially advantaged citizens"—wealthier, educated city dwellers—were most in favor of social credit. In fact, the higher the income, the higher the approval. These people felt social credit helped promote honest business dealings, since everyone was being watched and graded.[19]

[ ]

As a trade war between Trump's America and Xi's China raged, the two dined together in Buenos Aires, Argentina, on December 1, 2018, agreeing to a ninety-day truce. According to Trump, China agreed to address the practice of requiring foreign companies to hand over trade secrets and intellectual property. Trump also claimed China agreed to buy $1.2 trillion worth of American products. China has never confirmed the terms of the informal dinner agreement.[20]

More than seven thousand miles away, at Vancouver International Airport near Canada's Pacific coast, Huawei CFO Cathy Meng, the daughter of Huawei founder Ren Zhengfei, disembarked from her Hong Kong flight. She was preparing to transfer to a flight to Mexico, when Canada's Royal Mounted Police detained her. They questioned her about her trip and also Skycom, Huawei's business in Iran.[21] The US government believed Skycom was Huawei's "unofficial subsidiary," which Meng used to obtain prohibited US technologies for Huawei's business in Iran, and also to move money out of that country.[22]

"You're saying I committed fraud in the United States?" she responded, according to a court filing.

After searching her bags and questioning her for three hours, Meng was arrested based on an extradition request from the United States.[23] The US Department of Justice accused her of violating sanctions on Iran and defrauding the British bank HSBC, when she allegedly misled the bank in a meeting about Skycom's activities in Iran.[24]

After concluding his dinner with President Trump, Xi Jinping learned about the arrest. The news was delivered to the Chinese government after Meng called Huawei's chief legal officer.[25] Furious, the Chinese government summoned the Canadian and American ambassadors for an explanation.

The arrest caused a sensation in China, where it was widely seen as a coordinated attack against a company that had become a symbol of national technological might. China's vice minister of foreign affairs, Le Yucheng, said that Meng's arrest "severely violated the Chinese citizen's legal and legitimate rights and interests, it is lawless, reasonless and ruthless, and it is extremely vicious." He warned of "serious consequences" if Meng was not released.[26]

Three days after the rebuke, the former Canadian diplomat Michael Kovrig was in Beijing when he was detained for "endangering national security."[27] He was later charged under the 2015 national security law,[28] the same law that gave the government sweeping powers and was deployed in China's building of the Xinjiang surveillance state.

Hours after Kovrig was arrested, I opened my Twitter feed to news that a longtime acquaintance of mine, Canadian-born Michael Spavor, whom I knew from my time visiting North Korea as a journalist, had been arrested at his base in a town in China's northeast, on the same charge of endangering China's national security.

A lively and gregarious expatriate in China, Spavor opened a company that ran cultural and athletic exchanges with, of all places, North Korea, a country whose people he loved and wanted to help by setting up sports matches between North Korean and Western athletes.[29]

One of few Westerners to meet North Korea's dictator Kim Jong Un, Spavor arranged two of Dennis Rodman's infamous trips to that country, where "the Worm" got smashed with the dictator and sang him happy birthday. "Marshal, your father and grandfather did some fucked up shit," Rodman announced to Kim Jong Un, toasting him with a drink, "but you, you're trying to make a change, and I love you for that."[30]

(Change never happened.)

Another time, Spavor organized a professional wrestling match, bringing the legendary retired WWE wrestler Antonio Inoki, then a politician in his home country of Japan, to North Korea. A colorful man of intrigue who once negotiated the release of Japanese hostages in Iraq, Inoki was famous for a ritual in which he slapped his fans hard across the face, believing this channeled his warrior's spirit to the receiver.[31]

Now Spavor, cheerful and light-hearted, was missing.

"We see the arrests as an attack on us," a Canadian diplomat involved in the efforts to release Spavor and Kovrig told me in all seriousness. "Kovrig was a diplomat until recently. China is sending a message."

China didn't attempt to cover up the fact that it was taking hostages in retaliation for Meng's arrest.

"Those who accuse China of detaining some person in retaliation for the arrest of Ms. Meng should first reflect on the actions of the Canadian side," the Chinese ambassador to Canada, Lu Shaye, wrote in an opinion essay in the *Globe and Mail*.[32]

"They needed a Canadian who could be plausibly accused of violating some kind of international sanctions—that is, a Canadian dealing with North Korea or another heavily sanctioned country," the respected North Korea expert Andrei Lankov, a professor at Kookmin University in South Korea who also was acquainted with Spavor, told me. "Sanctions were important because this is what Americans accuse Wang Mengzhou of. 'You take our hostage, so we will take two of your [citizens] hostages!'"

The two were held in prison, under constant surveillance. They were interrogated for six to eight hours every day, and slept under bright lights kept on constantly, a form of psychological harassment.[33] When Canadian consular officials were granted visits to Spavor and Kovrig, the two were disoriented and confused, the Canadian diplomat familiar with the visits told me.[34]

I watched in shock as the news unfolded, getting updates from people in my circle of friends that included Spavor. At the same time, diplomats, investors, and businesspeople confided in me that they no longer felt their previous confidence operating in China. Many were wondering if they too would be taken hostage one day.

"The Chinese government is taking a really strange and conflicting stance," a hedge fund investor told me. "They say that these Chinese companies [such as Huawei] are private and are subject to the same laws as everywhere else. Then the government says, 'You will bow to these private companies or we will retaliate against you.'" China seemed to admit in its foreign policy that Huawei was an arm of China's national interest and had state protection.

The hedge fund investor reminded me of a story I knew well from my time as a foreign correspondent in South Korea and North Korea. In 2017, South Korea's retail giant Lotte offered a plot of land in South Korea for a US-built missile defense system.

China had long protested the deployment of that new THAAD missile system and sought to prevent it.

Once Lotte made the offer, China shut down Lotte stores in China citing fire code violations, opened lengthy tax balance sheet investigations, seized at least one property, and delayed licensing approvals.[35] Lotte stores in China were vandalized and boycotted. China was a valuable retail market in which Lotte was hoping to expand, having invested $9.6 billion.[36] But that year Lotte Mart, its department store business, lost $1.78 billion.[37]

The fearful, jittery sentiment was reported by dozens of other businesspeople with operations in China. Another hedge fund investor told me: "We've done an exhaustive internal assessment, and we believe that in the past three or four years, Chinese technology firms have seen an incredible transformation. They're not only technology developers anymore. They're arms of the state."

China was flexing its muscles at a moment of unprecedented global interconnectedness. Never before had so many nations and peoples been tied together through emerging technologies in AI, data networks, and mass data-gathering, and yet so divided between two powers. The Trump administration, proving the point, then retaliated.

Just over a month after Meng's arrest in Canada, the Trump administration was considering drafting an executive order that would ban US companies from using telecommunications equipment made by Chinese firms Huawei and ZTE.[38] Senators Mark Warner and Marco Rubio proposed a bill that would create a new government body called the Office of Critical Technologies and Security. It would coordinate efforts to fend off the threats posed by foreign technologies from China, Russia, and elsewhere.[39]

Finally, after much speculation, on May 15, 2019, President Trump released his Executive Order on Securing the Information and Communications Technology and Services Supply Chain, which declared that "foreign adversaries are increasingly creating and exploiting vulnerabilities in information and communications technology and services, which store and communicate vast amounts of sensitive information, facilitate the digital economy, and support critical infrastructure and vital emergency services, in order to commit malicious cyber-enabled actions, including economic and industrial espionage against the United States and its people."[40]

The executive order banned American companies from doing business with foreign firms believed to be working for foreign governments seeking to undermine American national security and technology.

The implementation of the executive order saw Huawei, Sense-Time, Megvii, and others all hit with US government sanctions over time, on allegations of national security concerns as well as involvement in human rights abuses. American businesses like Microsoft and Google could still sell software to Chinese firms that used American-made operating systems, like Windows and Android, on their hardware devices. But they needed to apply for a government license before they could sell to Huawei.[41] And the sanctions quickly damaged Huawei's businesses. Google pulled its Android operating system from Huawei phones, requiring Huawei to develop its own buggy and flawed operating system called HarmonyOS.[42]

"The biggest blow for Huawei was . . . when the U.S. government put Huawei on the [sanctions] list," Huawei's former public relations vice president Teri Daley told me.

The fear was that Chinese companies could be turned into spying operations, by installing "backdoors" or flaws that would allow for spying and hacking through Huawei equipment.[43]

Meanwhile, the US Department of Justice released its own data containing disproportionally large numbers of industrial espionage and patent infringement cases it had opened, numbers that had been growing over the past decade.

"More than 90 percent of the Department's cases alleging economic espionage over the past seven years involve China," said Deputy Attorney General Rod J. Rosenstein, announcing charges against three Chinese hackers. "More than two-thirds of the Department's cases involving thefts of trade secrets are connected to China."[44]

The sensational scandals, trials, and criminal charges kept piling up. Poland arrested a Huawei employee accused of spying.[45]

And in January 2019, the United States brought forward twenty-three indictments against Huawei, accusing it of fraud and trade secret theft.[46]

[ ]

I was trying to keep up with the tit-for-tat trade war, shocked at the response from China, which began issuing bold threats against governments that refused to work with Huawei, all while claiming the company was a private enterprise and that its affairs were its own business.

"If the Canadian government does ban Huawei from participating in the 5G network, then as for what kind of repercussion there will be, I'm not sure, but I believe there will be repercussions," Chinese ambassador Lu Shaye said at a press conference. The Canadian government should "make a wise decision on this issue."[47]

CHAPTER 19

The Great Rupture

China will always remain the builder of world peace,
a contributor to global development, and upholder
of international order.

—XI JINPING

The "technology cold war" between the United States and China was nothing like the cold war between the United States and the Soviet Union. The emerging trade war was more intricate and complicated. No Iron Curtain and no Berlin Wall separated the communist from the capitalist world. Markets were open and trade was flowing, and elite communist cadres sent their children to Ivy League schools. Silicon Valley and China didn't exist in separate bubbles. They relied on each other for components, hardware, software—even talent, since incredible numbers of Chinese software developers were trained at Stanford and MIT.

The United States and China were bound at the hip, and yet appeared to be preparing for a prolonged campaign of technological and economic struggle.

[ ]

At a congressional hearing in May 2019, Democratic congressman Adam Schiff said that the "coupling of innovation and authoritarianism is deeply troubling and has spread beyond China itself . . . Export of this technology gives countries the technological tools they need to emulate Beijing's model of social and political control."

Republican congressman Devin Nunes warned at the same hearing of "Chinese adoption and exportation of invasive surveillance measures designed to optimize political control."[1]

The Trump White House, however, cared little about the plight of the Uyghurs.

One month after the congressional hearing, in June 2019, President Trump and Xi Jinping attended the opening dinner of the G20 summit of governments and central bankers. There Chairman Xi explained to Trump "why he was basically building concentration camps in Xinjiang," recalled his national security advisor John Bolton in his book, *The Room Where It Happened.*

"According to our interpreter, Trump said that Xi should go ahead with building the camps, which he thought was exactly the right thing to do."

Only the interpreters were present, so the news didn't get out until Bolton wrote about it later.

Bolton and his colleagues, including Vice President Mike Pence and Secretary of State Mike Pompeo, were concerned Trump was eliminating the repression of the Uyghurs as a reason to sanction China. Considerations like the need to promote democracy and human rights seemed to matter little to the Trump White House.[2]

The trade war was shaping up to be a fractious realpolitik battle between two sides that each wanted a bigger piece of the world's economic and technological pie.

[ ]

Until the fall of 2020, evidence for the perfect police state in China consisted of Uyghur refugee testimony, satellite photography, and other open-source documentation that pieced together the story.

But the trade wars changed all that. Suddenly, as the US government and private research centers released the details of their own investigations, a flood of documentation suggested the deep connivance of many Chinese technology firms in creating the monstrosity in Xinjiang. Despite repeated denials, their involvement, with the full knowledge of what they were getting into, was beyond any possibility of doubt.

Huawei had always claimed it was not involved in the repression in Xinjiang. "Our contracts are with the third parties. It is not something we do directly," a Huawei executive responded to a British lawmaker in a June 2019 parliamentary hearing, when asked if Huawei operated in Xinjiang.[3]

But Huawei and other Chinese tech firms were inextricably involved.

"Together with the Public Security Bureau, Huawei will unlock a new era of smart policing and help build a safer, smarter society," a Huawei executive stated on a government website, according to Chinese media. The website was announcing a new agreement with Huawei in Xinjiang. In 2018, the government signed another deal with Huawei to build an "intelligence security industry" lab in Urumqi.[4] It provided police in Xinjiang with technical support and promoted "success cases" like a data center in Aksu, a historic town in Xinjiang.[5]

All this happened even as the United States and other countries were ratcheting up sanctions against Chinese tech firms.

"Huawei's work in Xinjiang is extensive and the company works directly with the Chinese Government's public security bureaus, and police forces, in the region," ASPI researchers concluded.[6] The US government concurred when it sanctioned Huawei:

"Specifically, these entities have been implicated in human rights violations and abuses in the implementation of China's campaign of repression, mass arbitrary detention, and high-technology surveillance against Uyghurs, Kazakhs, and other members of Muslim minority groups in the XUAR [Xinjiang Uyghur Autonomous Region]," the US Department of Commerce wrote in a filing, adding twenty-eight companies to the sanctions list in October 2019.[7]

SenseTime and Megvii, two of the world's most valuable facial recognition start-ups, were also sanctioned.[8] SenseTime, the firm backed by Qualcomm and Fidelity Investments, set up a smart policing joint venture in Xinjiang in 2017, called Leon

Technology, then sold its ownership stake in 2019. Leon claimed it was responsible for 50 percent of Safe City projects in Urumqi and "construction and maintenance of surveillance infrastructure for 3000/5600km of Xinjiang's borders with neighboring countries."[9] The *New York Times* reported in April 2019 that SenseTime and Megvii built algorithms the government used to track Uyghurs.

SenseTime said its "relevant teams" were not aware the technology was being used for profiling. Kai-fu Lee's Sinovation Ventures, Megvii's backer, told the *New York Times* it had relinquished its seat on the board and sold part of its stake in Megvii.[10]

A 2016 Chinese article by the Chinese Security and Protection Industry Association, a group with the backing of the ministry of public security, reported that Megvii's SkyEye facial recognition software for locating criminal suspects was being deployed across China, including in Xinjiang.[11]

Although similar clues had been published in obscure Chinese-language news websites for a couple of years, the English-speaking world began to take notice as the sanctions conversation became public. Like SenseTime, Megvii denied those reports and voiced strong opposition to its inclusion on US sanctions. "To the company's knowledge, around 1% of its total revenue was derived from projects in Xinjiang in 2018 [and] no revenue was generated in Xinjiang during the six months ending on June 30, 2019," it said in a statement.[12]

Yet the US government and private nonprofit research institutes continued to uncover what appeared to be smoking-gun evidence against Chinese tech firms that had operated in Xinjiang.

Hikvision is the world's largest maker of surveillance cameras. The video surveillance industry website IPVM reported that Hikvision won a $53 million contract to build a facial recognition system in one Xinjiang county, including for its detention camps.[13] At local mosques, Hikvision broadcast state-approved sermons through its video conferencing system and monitored mosques with its cameras.[14] Agence France-Presse obtained a tender document from 2017 showing that thirty-five thousand Hikvision cameras monitored schools, offices, streets, and mosques, ensuring imams maintained a preapproved government line in their preaching. Hikvision won several other bids like this throughout 2017.[15]

The US sanctions list read like a who's who of the companies that had built China's burgeoning technology ecosystem over the previous decade. Every company named protested its inclusion on the list. It was the obligatory theater in the technology wars.

[ ]

By 2018, the rift was quite evident: both sides were in the awkward position of breaking off their technology ecosystems into two separate spheres of influence.

One sphere consisted of countries that wanted access to China's technology and infrastructure—authoritarian countries like Russia and Venezuela, and poorer nations, like Ethiopia, that sought the preferential access and cheaper prices China was offering for its Safe City and One Belt, One Road projects.

The other sphere consisted of the wealthier nations of the West—the "Five Eyes" (Australia, New Zealand, Canada, UK, US), plus the European Union and Japan. These countries were home to Nokia, Ericsson, Amazon, and Google.

As the year wore on, dozens of countries found themselves in the difficult position of having to choose one side or the other. Many opted for China. For most countries, the centerpiece of this decision was determined by which company they wanted to build their nation's next-generation data network. A government could hire Huawei to build a 5G network, or hire a Western company like Finland's tech company Nokia or Sweden's tech giant Ericsson. The 5G network promised a high-speed network with blazing-fast data speeds that could sustain AI, smart manufacturing, smart cities, and other emerging technologies. It was the twenty-first century equivalent to building the railroads and airlines of the past—a boon for the economy, the engine and symbol of national economic progress.

"Widespread 5G connectivity will eliminate information islands, boost the prosperity of a digitalized sharing economy, promote changes to existing production methods and lifestyles, and finally improve people's quality of life," Huawei wrote in a white paper.[16]

By the middle of 2018, the United States and its allies expressed their reservations over granting a 5G contract to Huawei. The US pressured its European Union allies and Australia to not sign 5G deals with Huawei,[17] and later began working with Ericsson and Nokia to see if they could build more secure and trustworthy alternatives.[18]

"Developing our own secure 5G networks will outweigh any perceived gains from partnering with heavily subsidized Chinese providers that answer to party leadership," said US Secretary of Defense Mark Esper.[19]

Australia went forward with a ban in August 2018, crippling Huawei's business there. Huawei Australia reported a 78 percent decline in profits, down to $4.2 million, for 2019,[20] and squarely blamed the Australian government. The ban angered the Chinese government; its ambassador called it a "sore point or thorny issue."[21]

The UK, meanwhile, came under Chinese political pressure not to ban Huawei products. "It will send a very bad message not only to Huawei but also to Chinese businesses," China's ambassador to the UK, Liu Xiaoming, told the BBC. That decision could lead to "bad effects not only on trade but also on investment."[22]

The UK tried to find a path down an increasingly narrow middle road, restricting Huawei to building the noncore parts of the 5G network and limiting its access to nonsensitive parts, thereby reducing the security risks. But that decision irritated the United States, Britain's biggest ally.[23] The US government opened a review into what the presence of Huawei networks meant for the security of US military bases and equipment in the UK, and considered pulling out reconnaissance aircraft and not basing certain stealth jets there.[24]

Poorer nations saw the benefits of working outright with China, and rejecting American assistance.

5G, Safe Cities, and AI, after all, could be put to incredible use fighting crime and improving the quality of life, not just oppressing and surveilling people and building a dystopia as in Xinjiang, they reasoned. The governments of many poorer nations concluded that the potential for more intelligent traffic control, law enforcement, and public education outweighed the security concerns.

The Center for Strategic and International Studies, a major think tank in Washington, DC, concluded in a report that the countries embracing Huawei's Safe Cities technologies shared three characteristics: they were somewhat democratic or not democratic; they tended to be Asian and African; and they were "middle-income countries," meaning not rich but not poor. Pakistan, Bangladesh, Kenya, and Malaysia all embraced Huawei Safe Cities programs.[25] China expert Sheena Chestnut Greitens, a nonresident senior fellow at the Brookings Institution in Washington, DC, built a dataset on China's surveillance and public security platforms being adopted around the world. She concluded: "Countries that are strategically important to the PRC [People's Republic of China] are comparatively more likely to adopt it, but so are countries with high crime rates."

The United States, Greitens believed, might have underestimated the speed and scope of the spread of China's Safe City programs. "We don't know exactly how many of these Safe City programs Huawei has rolled out and in what number of countries," she wrote. Huawei claimed in its own report that seven hundred cities had adopted Safe City programs in one hundred countries and regions.

"The number likely falls between one Western think-tank estimate of 52 countries in 2019 and Huawei's self-proclaimed 100 countries, possibly a marketing exaggeration," Greitens concluded.[26]

But whatever the number, authoritarian leaders were soon deploying Huawei systems to crack down on their opponents.

The government of Uzbekistan announced at a security meeting in May 2019 that it had signed with Huawei to develop a Safe Cities system with 883 cameras in the Uzbek capital—and here the Uzbek government went into full-bore Orwellian language— to "digitally manage political affairs."[27] In Uganda, the *Wall Street Journal* reported in August 2019, Huawei technicians helped the government access the Facebook pages and phones of opposition bloggers who criticized the president.[28]

Huawei denied the allegations, as it routinely did. But the company acknowledged it took a hands-off approach from the ethical and civil rights implications of selling their technologies to authoritarian governments.

"Huawei develops technology, not public policy. That is the role of policy makers and legislators," said the director of Huawei's Southern Africa division.[29] It was the evasive moral equivalent of "I just make guns and sell them. I don't shoot them."

And many of the poor and middle-income countries that joined China's One Belt, One Road project, hopeful it would be an alternative to American meddling, realized they were facing another problem: a debt trap from Chinese loans.

China's economic expansion had dramatically slowed since 2010. It lacked the largesse to manage big domestic infrastructure projects as well as hand out cheap incentives abroad to nations wanting its technology or engineering. China's "debt-trap diplomacy," as people began calling it, seemed to be a new feature of One Belt, One Road.

"Through its $1 trillion 'one belt, one road' initiative, China is supporting infrastructure projects in strategically located developing countries, often by extending huge loans to their governments. As a result, countries are becoming ensnared in a debt trap that leaves them vulnerable to China's influence," wrote Brahma Chellaney, the prominent Indian geopolitical strategist who coined the term "debt-trap diplomacy." He believed that One Belt, One Road wasn't designed to support local economies, but to secure China's access to natural resources or open the market for China's "low-cost and shoddy export goods."

"In many cases, China even sends its own construction workers, minimizing the number of local jobs that are created."[30]

Ecuador took out $19 billion in Chinese loans for bridges, highways, irrigations, schools, and, most prominently, a major dam called Coca Codo Sinclair, touted as a solution to its energy shortages that would lift the country out of poverty. Ecuador agreed to repay many of the contracts in oil, not cash, handing over 80 percent of its oil exports to China. China received that oil at a discount and could resell it at a profit.

A national scandal ensued. Two years after opening, "thousands of cracks are splintering the dam's machinery. Its reservoir is clogged with silt, sand and trees. And the only time engineers tried to throttle up the facility completely, it shook violently and shorted out the national electricity grid," the *New York Times* reported in December 2018. Meanwhile, Ecuador had to scramble to pump enough oil to repay its debt to China. It drilled deep into the Amazon rainforest, already suffering from deforestation, cut social welfare spending, and closed down government agencies.

"The strategy of China is clear," Ecuador's energy minister told the *New York Times*. "They take economic control of countries."[31]

Elsewhere, China was exerting sinister pressure on One Belt, One Road beneficiaries that refused to bow down to its political desires.

Kazakhstan, an oil-rich and strategic country of 18 million people on the northwestern border of China's Xinjiang, was home to popular resentment over China's influence.

In November 2015, Kazakhstan passed a so-called land reform law that would allow foreign citizens to rent land for twenty-five years, an increase from the previous limit of ten years. In many countries, such changes to the law wouldn't sound like a big deal, and could actually liberate the market. But Kazakhstan shared a border with China, and anxious Kazakh farmers feared many Chinese investors would arrive and, in effect, buy up their land with a twenty-five-year lease that the government could then extend by decree, turning them into indentured servants to China.

The BBC reported that in April 2016 about one thousand to two thousand people took to the streets in protest in each major Kazakhstan city, a significant number for a nation that pursued a total lockdown on dissent.[32]

Kazakhstan's dilemma was that Chinese government–owned companies had amassed controlling stakes in Kazakh oil and gas firms.[33] In addition, Kazakhstan was a founding member of the Shanghai Five, the group of Eurasian countries that in 1996 had committed to improving security and fighting terrorism.[34] It couldn't afford a head-on diplomatic collision.

But China didn't just exert pressure on governments. It went after critics personally. Starting in 2016, Serikzhan Bilash, based in Almaty, the Kazakhstan capital, headed a nonprofit activist group called Atajurt ("Fatherland"). The group helped promote the messages of the former Kazakh camp worker in China, Sayragul Sauytbay (mentioned in an earlier chapter). In July 2018, two years after the anti-China protests, Sayragul was on trial and faced possible deportation back to China. She stood accused of illegally crossing the Chinese border into Kazakhstan, where she then leaked Chinese state secrets on the detention camps and their technologies. Her trial became a much watched sensation in Kazakhstan.

"I was terrified," she told me. "I thought I could get the death penalty back in China."

In August 2018, the judge gave Sayragul a six-month suspended sentence. She was granted asylum in Sweden.

After the trial, Sayragul and her allies were intimidated and made to feel they were under physical threat. One night, someone snuck into the garden of her lawyer's home and killed the lawyer's dog. On March 9, 2018, four mysterious men showed up at Serikzhan Bilash's Atajurt office. They refused to identify who sent them, ordered his staff not to record them, and then abruptly left. The staff filmed their getaway.

That night, Bilash, wary for his safety, checked into a hotel hoping for a reprieve. When he didn't answer his phone the next morning or show up at the office, his staff went to the hotel, only to find him missing. The hotel staff were unwilling to say what had happened. His colleagues feared he'd been abducted.

Soon Bilash's wife got a call from an unknown number. It was Bilash, who said that the previous night he'd been forcefully taken from his hotel and flown to Astana, a city six hundred miles away, by government authorities who never identified themselves.

"My wife was so worried," Bilash told me. "She called me over and over, and she was shocked that I would disappear so suddenly."

The police then indicted Bilash with "inciting ethnic discord," pointing to a video in which he said the word "jihad" in a vague, innocuous way, calling for an "information jihad" against China's policies. He faced seven years in prison.

He told me that in August 2019, "I accepted a plea bargain. I agreed to end my activism as part of the deal. I signed it under pressure."[35]

Bilash moved to Turkey and carries out his activism there.

[ ]

Not every nation, however, feared Chinese influence. Some welcomed it.

Pakistan had been a steady American ally during the Cold War. But in the war on terror, the United States complained it was unreliable, helping the Taliban militias in Afghanistan even as Pakistan publicly sided with American military operations.

Pakistan was struggling to emerge from decades of instability that the United States made worse with its military interventions in Afghanistan. And Pakistan had its own complaints about the Americans, who launched drone attacks on suspected terrorists, on an almost nightly basis, in its territory.

"We have learnt over time that the Americans are terrible when it comes to honoring their promises," a former Pakistani government minister told the *Financial Times*.[36]

China seemed like a strong alternative, a counterweight.

"Our friendship is higher than the Himalayas and deeper than the deepest sea in the world, sweeter than honey," read a banner in the Pearl Continental Hotel in Lahore, Pakistan's second-largest city, when it hosted a conference to promote a new project called the Pakistan-China Economic Corridor. Chairman Xi described the corridor as his pet project, and "the project of the century," a plan to invest $55 billion for infrastructure that included twenty-one power plants to fix chronic power shortages.[37]

Pakistan stopped buying some advanced American weapons and began buying Chinese attack submarines, and codeveloping a new fighter jet with China.[38]

China, in launching a scramble for power in Central Asia, stood to benefit from the raw materials that would help build its technology.

In 2016, China accounted for more than 80 percent of the production of rare earths like dysprosium, terbium, and yttrium, used to make batteries and laptops. But China's Central Asian neighbors offered even more opportunity for miners seeking the rare earths that would power the technologies of the future, along with the oil that could keep industry booming.

"While futurologists and networking pioneers talk about how the exciting world of artificial intelligence, Big Earth Data and machine learning promise to change the way we live, work and think," wrote the Silk Road historian and Oxford University professor Peter Frankopan, "few ever ask where the materials on which the digital new world come from—or what happens if supply either dries up or is used as a commercial or a political weapon by those who have a near-monopoly on global supply."[39]

CHAPTER **20**

You're Not Safe Anywhere

The sense of gain, happiness, and security among the people
of all ethnic groups has continued to increase.

—XI JINPING

In April 2019, I was in Istanbul when chatter began going around that Uyghurs in Turkey might no longer be safe. Turkey, for its part, had been the only major Muslim nation to condemn China's treatment of the Uyghurs.

"It is no longer a secret that more than one million Uyghur Turks incurring arbitrary arrests are subjected to torture and political brainwashing in internment camps and prisons," said a spokesman from Turkey's foreign affairs ministry in February 2019. "We call on the international community and the Secretary General of the United Nations to take effective measures in order to bring to an end this human tragedy in Xinjiang."[1]

"That is a good announcement," Abduweli Ayup confirmed to me. "But we don't know how long Turkey will hold that position. Remember, Turkey is an authoritarian nation, and it benefits from Chinese money. It could sell out."

Once a staunch US ally during the Cold War, when it protected the southeastern flank of NATO from Soviet influence, Turkey's economy began slowing and in 2018 hit a crisis that devastated its currency. The situation was made worse by a trade stand-off with the United States. The Trump administration sanctioned Turkey in August 2018 and doubled steel tariffs to 50 percent. Relations between the two countries were sour, in part because of Turkish military campaigns in Syria against the Kurds, a US ally, and the arrest of an American pastor who ran a mission church on the west coast. (He was later released.)[2]

Turkey did what many nations did in a similar position, faced with US condemnations and suffering from economic malaise. It turned to China. Turkey got a $3.6 billion loan from China in 2018 to help fire up its energy and transportation industries,[3] and then got a $1 billion transfer from China's central bank in June 2019.[4] But what did Turkey promise in return?

"I don't trust the government here," Abduweli told me. "I'm worried they're going to sell out to Chinese money and deport all the Uyghurs." It had happened in Egypt almost two years earlier, after all. He confided that he was planning to leave for Norway on a writing grant, where he would ask for asylum.

"I'd feel safer in a strong, secular democracy that wouldn't bow to Chinese pressure and money, and that will allow me to practice my faith freely. Democracy is the only way. Citizens must treasure what they have and protect it."

Abduweli was right to be concerned for his safety. He had a high profile in his community, and Uyghurs with high profiles often met with sad endings. Almost all of them had been either outright accused of espionage in the local news, smeared in government propaganda campaigns back in China, or deported back to China, sometimes under mysterious circumstances.

One morning, I woke to frantic WhatsApp messages from Abduweli. The hammer had come down: a nationalist Turkish newspaper had splashed him on its front page, accusing him of having connections to the CIA.[5] Then he'd started getting threats from a terrorist group.

"We're in danger," Abduweli said. "The hand of China has arrived."

He had to leave at once. Abduweli followed his exit strategy. He traveled to Paris in April 2019, and then Bergen, Norway, in July 2019. There he requested asylum. He was homeless, but free.

[ ]

Four months later, Abduweli's fears about Turkey were confirmed. In August 2019, Turkish authorities deported a Uyghur family to Tajikistan, where they had citizenship. Upon their arrival at the Tajikistan airport, they were handed over to Chinese authorities. Activists claimed to the *Financial Times* that forty Uyghurs in Turkey had lost their residency, out of a community of thirty thousand.[6] Many of them, Abduweli told me, had no valid passport. After their old passports expired, the Chinese embassy refused to issue them new passports in Turkey, which he believed was a way of pressuring them to return home.

Ironically, Middle Eastern Muslim countries, many of them outright dictatorships that ruled under Shariah law, were reluctant to criticize China's treatment of the Muslim-majority Uyghurs. They chose instead to benefit from China's largesse: the One Belt, One Road and Safe Cities programs, and Chinese surveillance technology. They were in effect joining China's technological and geopolitical sphere of influence, after more than a century of European and American dominance in the region. Uyghurs everywhere told me of their fear and alarm over these developments.

"Too many countries are making a big mistake," one former Uyghur detainee told me. "They are replacing one colonial power with another."

The divisions between the pro-West and pro-China coalitions became apparent when members of the UN Human Rights Council released two letters on Xinjiang in July 2019, one opposing China's treatment of the Uyghurs and the other supporting it.

The first letter read:

We call on China to uphold its national laws and international obligations and to respect human rights and fundamental freedoms, including freedom of religion or belief, in Xinjiang and across China. We call also on China to refrain from the arbitrary detention of and restrictions on freedom of movement of Uyghurs, and other Muslim and minority communities in Xinjiang.[7]

It was signed by representatives of Canada, Norway, Japan, the UK, and pretty much every European democracy. The United States didn't sign the letter because it had withdrawn from the Human Rights Council just over a year earlier. Stable and prosperous democracies stood by their values when it came to criticizing China's surveillance apparatus in Xinjiang.

The other letter, a rebuttal signed by representatives of Muslim Arab nations including Qatar, the United Arab Emirates, Kuwait, Egypt, Saudi Arabia, and Syria, along with various dictatorships in South America, Africa, and Asia, told a very different story:

> Faced with the grave challenge of terrorism and extremism, China has taken a series of counter-terrorism and deradicalization measures in Xinjiang, including setting up vocational education and training centers. Now safety and security has [sic] returned to Xinjiang and the fundamental human rights of all people of all ethnic groups there are safeguarded.[8]

[ ]

By the summer of 2019, Maysem had put her life back together. She said to me that telling her story felt like therapy, a way of coming to terms with the suffering in her past. "But I also worry," she confided in me. "We won't be safe in Turkey forever."

She hoped to join a PhD program in the United States.

"That," she said, "is my dream. I want to live the life of the academic."

Until then Maysem was concerned that the clock was ticking— she too might end up in trouble in Turkey. Almost every month during 2019 and 2020, I opened my news feed with alarm at the numbers of Uyghurs being detained, sometimes deported back to China. Another Uyghur writer I interviewed, Abdurehim Imin Parach, was sitting in a Uyghur restaurant in Istanbul one day in March 2020, when plainclothes police came in and detained him without any explanation.

"They took me to a cold building. It was hundreds of miles away," he told me. "And then they released me for no reason [three months later]. They told me not to criticize China."

What does the future hold? An axiom among China watchers is that we should assume the Communist Party will behave in other places as it behaves at home. The export of Xinjiang-style social controls would be a worst-case, but hardly unimaginable, scenario.

Stop the Panopticon

With the onset of totalitarianism, world wars, and genocides in the twentieth century, several of our most prescient writers concluded the world was headed toward a dystopia if we failed to act. In his 1932 book *Brave New World*, Aldous Huxley imagined a world government that indoctrinated children into a rigid caste system, giving them a euphoric drug that made them forget the despair of their twenty-sixth century dystopia.[1] Seventeen years later, in 1949, George Orwell published *1984*, imagining a more overt and fascistic government that controlled its people through a panopticon.[2]

Other books were even more accurately prophetic of life today. In the lesser known *Stand on Zanzibar* published in 1968, the American science fiction writer John Brunner predicted with uncanny accuracy that the world would be overpopulated with 7 billion people in 2010, that its inhabitants would read their news in short bursts and respond with real-time takes on a social network akin to Twitter, that China would emerge as the United States' main rival, and that an African American president named "President Obomi" would sit in the White House.[3]

Those science fiction authors asked the question, "What if?" Their goal was to conceive of a future gone wrong and thus stimulate their readers to think carefully about the decisions immediately in front of them. Decisions that could either propel society toward a dystopian future or help it chart a better course. Xinjiang is the dystopia they imagined.

It's time to abandon the question of "What if?" We should now ask, "What do we do about it?"

We're far behind in figuring out ways to govern the technologies enveloping our daily lives with such prevalence that we often don't notice them. After a decade of advances in smartphone design, social media communication, and e-commerce, the world is on the precipice of another technology revolution. Artificial intelligence, thanks to the superintelligence it can create within specific fields, is shaping up to surpass human capabilities in some areas.

But eminent futurologists and technologists doubt AI will be able to replicate the human brain soon. Nevertheless, to conclude AI will fail in that endeavor, or that the surveillance tactics unrolled in Xinjiang will not reach large parts of the world, is wildly optimistic. AI is already everywhere, barely regulated and poorly understood, surveilling our purchases and clicks and learning how to nudge our behavior. AI can fly and land airplanes, make billion-dollar investment decisions, diagnose electrocardiograms, and guide manufacturing.

"If all the intelligent software in the world were to suddenly stop functioning, modern civilization would grind to a halt," predicted futurologist Ray Kurzweil way back in 2005, when AI was far less pervasive and sophisticated.[4]

So the question isn't whether AI surveillance will permeate our society in the near future. It's whether governments and businesses, which own valuable intellectual property, will have the wherewithal to govern AI in the interests of protecting democracy. Or will they go along with shareholder demands for a greater profit or state demands for more security from pandemics and crime-fighting?

Over the past decade, hundreds of American police departments began rolling out AI and facial recognition systems similar to the ones in China, just not as authoritarian. Nevertheless, the use of those systems has been opaque and rarely audited.

In numerous studies published in 2018 and 2019, the US government's National Institute of Standards and Technology, and other research institutes, consistently found that AI systems were biased against people of color and women. A government study released in 2019 found that Asian and African American men were a hundred times more likely to be misidentified than white men, and that women were more likely to be misidentified than men. Middle-aged white men were almost always identified correctly.[5]

What was going on? Wasn't AI supposed to be law enforcement's superintelligent savior, a check against human biases, ending discrimination? In the United States, the findings underscored a growing realization among our leaders that AI is a reflection of the people who create it. Humans create algorithms and input data for those algorithms, and the algorithms carry their designers' flaws. To make matters worse, we don't entirely understand how our police forces gather their data, whether it's quality data, and how these opaque algorithms process that data. The system has little in the way of checks and balances.

In Xinjiang too "the Situation" cannot be blamed on technological advances, but on the decision to use the technology oppressively and without due restraint or care. That's how innocent people are wrongly identified, falsely accused, and disappeared under ludicrous accusations that they harbor terrorist thoughts.

[ ]

In any case, the West has begun pushing back against deploying the same technologies used in Xinjiang.

First came the departure of the Los Angeles Police Department's (LAPD) use of PredPol, a pioneering program in the field of predictive policing. In July 2019, it announced it was ending the program, which was originally intended to identify neighborhoods with a greater likelihood of property crimes. Other police departments followed the LAPD in dropping the program.

"It didn't help us solve crimes," a Palo Alto, California, police spokeswoman told the *Los Angeles Times*.

But there was still more work to do. Of the eighteen thousand police departments in the United States, sixty of them still used PredPol.[6]

And all the surveillance in the world didn't help China identify in a timely manner the most devastating pandemic in a century: Covid-19.

On December 31, 2019, China reported to the World Health Organization (WHO) a cluster of pneumonia cases in Wuhan, a city in the central part of the country.[7] That "pneumonia," as China called it, was once believed to have originated in a messy, nonhygienic "wet market" selling indiscriminate cuts of raw pork, beef, and chicken displayed in the open air for long periods of time, under little or no regulated conditions. It turned out to be the novel coronavirus Covid-19,[8] which shut down the world and wiped out economic activity for much of 2020.

When Covid-19 reached America and emptied out city centers and beach resorts, the consequences of China's rise as an opaque authoritarian government directly touched American soil. No longer was China a distant, looming police state whose culture and behavior the West could ignore as something that existed a long way away, without any direct consequences. China had become so tethered to the rest of the world through trade, travel, and tourism that nothing, it seemed, could stop the swift, global arrival of Covid-19. The world had to grapple directly with the poor decisions of Chinese leaders who imprisoned whistleblowers reporting the bad news,[9] deployed an army of paid internet trolls to suppress online reports,[10] and delayed a rapid response to the outbreak.[11]

Rather than address the pandemic as a global problem, China's "wolf warrior" diplomats, as they called themselves, launched angry and pointed rhetoric against countries that called for an investigation into whether there had been a cover-up. Chinese state media declared Australia was "gum stuck to the bottom of China's shoe." The Chinese embassy in France falsely accused French nursing-home workers of "abandoning their posts overnight . . . and leaving their residents to die of hunger and disease."[12]

The US consulate in Guangzhou, a city in southeastern China, issued a warning that the Chinese government was discriminating against blacks in China. The government deliberately attempted to give the impression the virus had come from Africa, thus deflecting attention from the fact it had actually originated in China.

"As part of this campaign, police ordered bars and restaurants not to serve clients who appeared to be of African origin," the warning read. "Moreover, local officials launched a round of mandatory tests for Covid-19, followed by mandatory self-quarantine, for anyone with 'African contacts,' regardless of recent travel history or previous quarantine completion."[13]

Zhao Lijian, a foreign ministry spokesman who tussled with foreign officials and journalists on Twitter, even posted a series of tweets suggesting American soldiers brought Covid-19 to China.

"It might be US [sic] army who brought the epidemic to Wuhan," he wrote. "Be transparent! Make public your data! US owe us an explanation! [sic]" The conspiracy theory that US troops brought Covid-19 to China spread rapidly there.[14]

Covid-19 was dangerous not merely because of the threat of the virus itself, but because the suddenness of its appearance was so overwhelming that governments scurried to embrace excessive powers for social control—powers they had no obligation to relinquish.

Some administrations are already showing signs that they will be unwilling to give up their newfound powers, and that they'll use the data obtained in the fight against Covid-19 to surveil political opponents or aid law enforcement. Many of the emergency legal powers don't come with sunset provisions that end them after a period of time. They're effectively permanent unless the government chooses to repeal them. In March 2020, the British Parliament quickly passed a 340-page law giving government ministers the authority, with little oversight, to isolate and detain people indefinitely, shut down airports and ports, and ban public gatherings and protests. The same month, Israel's prime minister Benjamin Netanyahu authorized the country's security agency to track citizens using secret cell phone data developed for counterterrorism. Hungary's prime minister Viktor Orban was given the power under a new law to suspend existing laws, after he declared a state of emergency.[15]

American companies, meanwhile, remained keen on Chinese technology. In the midst of the epidemic, on April 29, 2020, Reuters reported that Amazon had bought fifteen hundred thermal cameras for almost $10 million from Dahua, a Chinese firm blacklisted by the US government for human rights abuses in Xinjiang. Amazon wanted to measure the temperatures of its workers. Amazon didn't appear to violate US sanctions. But the Bureau of Industry and Security warned that "transactions of any nature with listed entities carry a 'red flag' and recommends that U.S. companies proceed with caution with respect to such transactions."[16]

[ ]

George Floyd's death in May 2020 ignited hundreds of police brutality protests in Minneapolis, Chicago, Portland, Washington, DC, and elsewhere during the summer. In the middle of a public debate about how technology could fight a pandemic, the controversy accelerated over how police might be using it.

American technology giants faced a public backlash and government concerns that these technologies were prone to discriminate against minorities, and were being deployed for nefarious means. One AI start-up, Dataminr, helped the police monitor social media posts regarding the locations and actions of social media protesters. Protesters were disturbed because of the company's unusual access to Twitter's Firehose, a feature that allowed Dataminr to scoop up every public tweet once each user clicked "send."[17]

In June 2020, IBM CEO Arvind Krishna wrote a letter to Congress, declaring IBM would no longer develop facial recognition technologies.

IBM no longer offers general purpose IBM facial recognition or analysis software. IBM firmly opposes and will not condone uses of any technology, including facial recognition technology offered by other vendors, for mass surveillance, racial profiling, violations of basic human rights and freedoms, or any purpose which is not consistent with our values and Principles

of Trust and Transparency. We believe now is the time to begin a national dialogue on whether and how facial recognition
technology should be employed by domestic law enforcement
agencies.

Artificial Intelligence is a powerful tool that can help law
enforcement keep citizens safe. But vendors and users of AI
systems have a shared responsibility to ensure that Al is tested
for bias, particularly when used in law enforcement, and that
such bias testing is audited and reported.[18]

Two days later, Amazon announced it was banning police departments from using its facial recognition technology for a year.[19]
Then Microsoft said it would not sell the technology to the police
until the federal government passed a law "grounded in human
rights" to regulate the technology.[20] The surveillance state in the
United States had reached its limits—for the moment.

[ ]

In Xinjiang, the Situation continued to worsen. In July 2020,
Chinese authorities declared a "wartime" state in Xinjiang. Then
the police went door to door. The *New York Times* reported they
warned all residents to stay inside their apartments, and sealed off
the buildings.

Medical authorities had uncovered eight hundred cases of
Covid-19 in Xinjiang, the largest outbreak in China since first reporting the outbreak in Wuhan seven months earlier. With more
than a million people crammed into detention cells with dozens
or more other detainees, Xinjiang was a perfect storm for the pandemic.[21]

Authorities began forcing concentration camp detainees and
regular residents throughout Xinjiang to drink traditional Chinese medicine, even though there was no evidence it had any effect fighting the virus.

The guards at one camp told detainees to strip naked, then to
cover their faces as they were hosed down with disinfectant.[22] The
unusually harsh lockdown measures, even by China's standards,

seemed to have little purpose except to reinforce the power of the perfect police state.

[ ]

The United States and China were working themselves into an increasingly dangerous tit-for-tat, with no way out. In May 2020, the US government halted semiconductor supplies to Huawei, blocking the company from buying the hardware that was the engine of the AI revolution. Huawei's leafy-green campus in southern China fell into a state of emergency, with executives scrambling to find a solution, since its stockpile of chipsets would last only until 2021.[23]

Then, that summer Chinese students at US universities reported being questioned and screened at US airports, even though they had the proper study visas. The students called it harassment.[24]

By declaring a "zero-sum" conflict, the United States was at risk of shooting itself in the foot, chasing out much needed AI talent coming from China. The US maintained a large technological lead worldwide, but that position rested on its ability to bring in smart people.

In June 2020, a study by MacroPolo, a China-focused think tank at the Paulson Institute in Chicago, found that 60 percent of "top tier" AI researchers worked for American universities and companies, and that more than two-thirds of top researchers working in the United States got their undergraduate degrees in other countries.

Furthermore, 29 percent of top-tier AI researchers worldwide got their undergraduate degrees in China, but 56 percent chose to live and work in the United States.[25]

[ ]

China too was guilty of digging itself into the zero-sum predicament that killed whatever trust people around the world had in it. China persecuted the Uyghurs, built a cult of personality around Xi Jinping, passed laws that allowed for sweeping state powers, threatened other countries that raised legitimate concerns over Huawei technology, created an opaque system of poor governance that instigated the spread of Covid-19, and rode a wave of wolf warrior nationalism practiced by diplomats who scolded and threatened other governments for not obeying China's orders.

As the world listed during the dramatic year of 2020, China, buckling down, completed its project of national revival. Under Xi Jinping, it emerged closer to its historical empire, renewed in feelings of national pride and authoritarian rule. Technology was central to the revival. As China moved back in time to reclaim its lineage, its new technologies flung it forward into modernity and enabled its prosperity.

After Xinjiang, Hong Kong was another place where authorities, in a swift clampdown, deployed facial recognition technology against pro-democracy protesters. In June 2020, China's legislature passed a national security law that effectively made Hong Kong—once an administrative zone within China that enjoyed special democratic privileges because it was handed over from the UK in 1997—a part of China. The law banned vague "subversion" against China, and made almost any dissent punishable with prison time.

Authorities deployed the law in a prolonged crackdown, arresting pro-democracy demonstrators, starting with eight elected legislators and a wealthy newspaper owner. The entire pro-democracy opposition party resigned from parliament. Hong Kong was effectively turned into an authoritarian state under Chinese rule.[26]

Armed with a new arsenal of military technologies, China sped up a project of ongoing territorial expansion backed by its national vision. In June 2020, skirmishes between Chinese and Indian military forces in the Himalayas resulted in sixty deaths. India, fearful of Chinese spying and cyber-infiltration, joined the United States in proposing bans on the Chinese-made apps TikTok and WeChat.

In October 2020, China broadcast a video showing a simulated invasion of Taiwan, and sent fighter jets threateningly close to its airspace. China had long sought to "reclaim" Taiwan, ever since anti-communist forces were given control of the island in

October 1945 and the Chinese Communist Party took power in mainland China in 1949.[27] Throughout 2020, China undermined international law by claiming large swathes of the South China Sea, where it harassed American, Indian, Vietnamese, and other countries' naval vessels.[28]

As China continued to strengthen its vast censorship apparatus, it imprisoned a tycoon and two professors who criticized Xi Jinping's leadership and China's response to Covid-19.[29] In November, retaliating against Australia, China imposed tariffs of up to 212 percent on Australian wine, cutting off the industry's biggest export market. China claimed it found evidence of dumping; Australia believed it was being punished for calling for an investigation into the origins of the pandemic.[30]

Now, despite calls by US and European leaders decades earlier to accommodate China's rise, hopes for a detente were dashed.

[ ]

Maysem looked on at China's rise with apprehension.

Dozens of Uyghurs told me they were worried their friends and family would never be released from the camps, and the perfect police state was here to stay.

Yusuf Amet, the former spy we had interviewed more than two years earlier in 2019, revealed his identity on a TV broadcast. He was then targeted for assassination, he believed by a Chinese intelligence operative, in Turkey. At eleven o'clock on the night of November 2, 2020, Yusuf was leaving a friend's home in Istanbul, when an assailant shot him twice in the shoulder. He was hospitalized in critical condition. Turkish police opened an investigation, and as of March 2021 have not found the perpetrator.[31]

In December 2020, Maysem was alarmed to hear China had signed an extradition treaty with Turkey that could pressure Turkey to return Uyghurs suspected of "terrorism." Turkey hadn't yet ratified the treaty, and hadn't said when it planned to.[32]

Maysem's fears of being deported back to China were escalating. If she were found in Ankara, she could be sent back on invented sedition charges, and once again be put into a concentration camp because she dared to speak out against the government in China.

"I'm worried about Turkey. I'm worried that they'll sign the treaty for Chinese money. Investments are important." As of February 23, 2021, Turkey had not ratified the treaty.

[ ]

As the perfect police state spread its influence worldwide, Maysem reflected on the difficulties of starting a new life at a time when she couldn't escape the dramatic events around her.

"This is the police state of the twenty-first century," she said. "We're in a new era. To be authoritarian is different now."

Uyghur birth rates, she pointed out, had plummeted, a government strategy, she and many researchers believed, for slowly and subtly wiping out a population without having to send them to gas chambers and mass graves: the notorious pursuits of twentieth-century tyrants.

Xinjiang was witnessing the consequences of the long-standing policy of requiring Uyghur and other minority women to use birth control and undergo abortions, sterilizations, and medical procedures to insert IUDs, intrauterine contraceptive devices.

"Study [sic] shows that in the process of eradicating extremism, the minds of Uygur women in Xinjiang were emancipated and gender equality and reproductive health were promoted, making them no longer baby-making machines. They are more confident and independent," announced the Chinese embassy in the United States in January 2021, in a usual style of doublespeak.[33]

On January 19, 2021, the US State Department cited forced sterilizations when it declared the Situation a genocide. "I believe this genocide is ongoing, and that we are witnessing the systematic attempt to destroy Uighurs by the Chinese party-state," Secretary of State Mike Pompeo said in a statement. Chinese officials were "engaged in the forced assimilation and eventual erasure of a vulnerable ethnic and religious minority group."[34] The "genocide" designation could lead to stricter sanctions and deepen China's isolation from the West.

Two weeks later, Maysem and Abduweli were aghast, but not surprised, when reports emerged of systematic rape in the camps.[35] "I heard those stories too," Maysem said, though she didn't witness them personally.

Almost three weeks after the rape reports emerged, on February 22, Canada's parliament voted in favor of a nonbinding resolution to recognize the treatment of the Uyghurs as a genocide.

China fervently denied the accusation. "There's nothing like genocide happening in Xinjiang at all," responded China's ambassador to Canada, Cong Peiwu.[36] Whatever the label, whether "genocide" or "crimes against humanity" or "human rights atrocity," almost everyone I interviewed agreed that the Situation is the greatest humanitarian disaster of our century so far, and a harbinger of what is to come if we don't learn to cope with the rapid advance of technology.

[ ]

For months, Abduweli had been receiving phone calls from his niece Mihriay. Years ago she had been a teacher at his now-defunct Xinjiang kindergarten, which taught the Uyghur language. "She was so smart. She taught little kids to read in two months." Abduweli said he and Mihriay were kindred spirits on a similar path in life.

In December 2014, Mihriay had moved to Japan to undertake a scholarship, studying languages as her uncle Abduweli did, at the University of Tokyo. Almost four years later, after the Situation deteriorated, the Chinese authorities began harassing her with phone calls placed from Xinjiang. They were upset about Abduweli's subversive online writings from Turkey. She relayed the messages to her uncle. "She kept asking me to stop my work," Abduweli said.

The police then threatened to detain her mother, still back in Kashgar, if Mihriay didn't return home soon. In June 2019, Mihriay relented and went back to Kashgar.

On an unknown date, Mihriay was detained and taken to a concentration camp. On February 23, 2021, Abduweli learned in a phone call from a friend in China that his niece, just thirty years old, had been taken to a hospital under mysterious circumstances, and died. Abduweli believes that because of the circumstances, death from natural causes was incredibly unlikely, and that the authorities were probably involved, possibly in retaliation for Abduweli's campaigning overseas.

"I was a bad example for her," Abduweli said, feeling a weight of guilt. "She wanted to follow me. If I were someone else, just making money, enjoying life, she would be alive. And I realized that no matter what we do, we cannot protect our families in the camps."

Devastated and mournful, Abduweli reminisced on where he's been and where he stands now:

"When I was younger, I gave a lecture at a university, back in China. I said that these technologies will change the world. That nobody can stop free expression, nobody can stop people who want to be free. I spoke this to my students, and I spoke it to my followers. I promised them a better world.

"But I failed. Our technology did not make us free. We live in a digital prison, even if we live in a world that is free outside, in the physical world. The world that we hoped for, it never came."

Maysem, meanwhile, was finding closure in telling her story. She was unsure what the future would hold, but wanted to transcend those worries and get on with her life. "I don't want to relive my story anymore," she told me. "I've worked so hard rebuilding myself. Now I understand what happened to me. It's time to move on."

And so she said goodbye, for now. "But whatever happens next, I've been thinking about what it means to tell a story. A story has a life of its own," she said as we parted ways. "As long as our stories live on, we will live on, too."

Acknowledgments

I could only write this book due to the courage and selflessness of dozens of refugees, academics, diplomats, and foreign correspondents whose testimonies I've been lucky to hear, and whose work I have studied and admired. Many of them were the first to build a body of evidence about the surveillance state of Xinjiang, risking their well-being and careers. This at a time when Chinese money and market access makes it fashionable for Hollywood filmmakers, NBA basketball representatives, and university administrators to censor themselves and their employees.

For example, in October 2019, Houston Rockets manager Daryl Morey tweeted his support for pro-democracy protests in Hong Kong by those who opposed mainland Chinese encroachment on their government, as well as police brutality against protesters. LeBron James responded that Morey was "not educated on the situation."[1] It's an odd position, since the NBA and its players agreed in August 2020 to engage in "meaningful police and criminal justice reform" at home, in America.[2]

In 2020, China became the world's biggest movie market, lucrative for Hollywood because China had 1.4 billion potential viewers. The James Bond movie *Skyfall* was only released in China after the subtitles were changed to mask references to torture by Chinese police.[3] In August 2020, the ending credits of Disney's live-action picture *Mulan* thanked eight government bodies in Xinjiang, including a public security bureau in the city of Turpan, tasked with running concentration camps for the ethnic Uyghur and Kazakh minorities, for their cooperation in allowing *Mulan* to be filmed in Xinjiang.[4]

In June 2020, the teleconferencing software company Zoom suspended three accounts at the request of the Chinese government. The government claimed the accounts were hosting "illegal" online commemorations of the pro-democracy Tiananmen Square uprising in June 1989.

The three accounts weren't even based in mainland China. Two belonged to US-based activists and the third belonged to a Hong Kong–based activist. Zoom said it made "mistakes" and announced: "Going forward Zoom will not allow requests from the Chinese government to impact anyone outside of mainland China." Yet Zoom also said it was building technology that would assist with state censorship in China. "Zoom is developing technology over the next several days that will enable us to remove or block at the participant level based on geography."[5]

Then, in December 2020, the US Department of Justice charged a group of Zoom employees in China with providing the names, email addresses, and IP addresses of users outside China to Chinese intelligence. One suspect also stood accused of fabricating evidence that would have falsely suggested some accounts, which were holding online memorials for the Tiananmen Square protests, promoted terrorism and pornography.[6]

[ ]

I am especially indebted to Abduweli Ayup, Uyghur writer and linguist, who took on this book as my translator and assistant while we both lived in Istanbul, Turkey. He had been tortured in a Chinese detention center because of his writing and advocacy as a proponent of linguistic human rights, specifically for the intergenerational transmission of the Uyghur language and culture. Finally released and able to leave in August 2015, we met, as he continued writing on democracy for his website in Turkey. Then Abduweli began getting death threats from a terrorist group with connections in Syria, and was accused of spying by a Turkish newspaper. In April 2019, he fled Turkey and now lives in Norway.

I met my wife and life partner, Gözde, while researching and writing this book in Istanbul. Soon after I submitted my manuscript, we were engaged on a boat traveling in disputed waters between Turkey and Greece in the Aegean Sea, and had a scenic wedding in July 2020 in Tekirdağ, a Turkish heartland west of Istanbul.

I'm also grateful for all the help I received from Tahir Hamut, Uyghur poet and filmmaker, in 2018. Having heard that his best friend was hauled away to a concentration camp, Tahir barely got his family out of Xinjiang in August 2017, before they too would be targeted for "reeducation," China's euphemism for political brainwashing. Tahir spent more than thirty hours allowing me to interview him, and guiding me through his personal experience of the perfect police state.

Mehmetjan Abudugayiti, my Uyghur assistant in Washington, DC, fled China alone in October 2011. He hasn't heard from his family in years.

The relentless journalists at Radio Free Asia's Uyghur-language service, the nonprofit broadcasting organization in Washington, DC, and Megha Rajagopalan, BuzzFeed News' former China bureau chief, blew open the floodgates with their groundbreaking coverage of Xinjiang in the fall of 2017. Rajagopalan was forced out of China, where she had built her life and career. In retaliation for the incredible reporting by RFA's Uyghur reporters, the Chinese government sent their family members in Xinjiang to concentration camps.

Gene Bunin, a former resident of Xinjiang, was also asked to leave the region. He was accused of being a foreign spy by a newspaper in one country, Kyrgyzstan, and denied entry in another, Uzbekistan, probably because of his meetings in those countries with activists, and his selfless work gathering the stories of Uyghurs, Kazakhs, and other Turkic minorities on his website, shahit .biz. *Shahit* is the Uyghur word for "witness."

James Millward, history professor at the Georgetown University in Washington, DC, was full of encouragement, and offered me a primer on the history of Xinjiang and Central Asia when I first set out to write this book.

Sean Roberts, anthropology professor at my alma mater, George Washington University in Washington, DC, took me inside the cultures and societies of Xinjiang and the "Turkic world"—the landscape of oases, steppes, and mountains that span from western China through Central Asia and the area between the Caspian and Black Seas, ending in Turkey.

Maya Wang, China researcher at Human Rights Watch, published invaluable reports. I spoke with Maya when a group of Uyghurs was attempting to escape from Egypt, where they were being hunted down by Egyptian police, aided by Chinese agents. She helped me put together a letter for an asylum court that would vouch for their story so they could find refuge in France.

Omer Kanat, executive director at the Uyghur Human Rights Project, and Nicole Morgret, project manager there, helped me gather evidence and introduced me to key people in the Uyghur community. Serikzhan Bilash and his activist group, Atajurt ("Fatherland"), based in Kazakhstan, also supplied testimony and introduced me to key Kazakh witnesses for interviews.

Adrian Zenz, a German anthropologist based in Minnesota, amassed a wealth of material based on public tenders and state media documents on the construction of concentration camps.

Victoria Rowe Holbrook and Mücahit Kaçar, two lively and renowned scholars in the field of Turkish literature, generously translated fifteenth-century poetry for this book.

For the conception and production of this book, I am indebted to:

Clive Priddle, my editor at PublicAffairs who was responsible for the publishing of this book. Clive saw an allegory in this story and knew it was time for a book. He and his assistant, Anu Roy-Chaudhury, made my manuscript worthy of publication.

Alan Rinzler, my developmental editor for this and previous work, saw similar promise and helped shape and prune my early notes into a structure and storyline. Will Murphy then gave the book one more edit and helped my prose enormously.

David Halpern, my agent at the Robbins Office in New York, took me on, vouched for me, and believed in my abilities as a writer.

Wen-yee Lee, a talented technology journalist from Taiwan, thoroughly fact-checked my book and contributed research that was difficult to find.

Joshua Kurlantzick, Remco Breuker, Devin Stewart (rest in peace), Genevieve Fried, and Jaan Altosaar generously read and made suggestions on my manuscript.

The Fund for Investigative Journalism graciously granted me the money to help cover travel expenses and investigative reporting costs.

Istanbul, Turkey
February 23, 2021

Notes

Unless otherwise noted, all direct quotations from Maysem, Abduweli, Yusuf, and other Uyghur and Kazakh refugees, along with direct quotations from employees at Huawei, Megvii, and SenseTime, come from the author's own interviews.

Prologue. The Situation

1. When the author visited Xinjiang in December 2017, he first heard the phrase "the Situation" used by Uyghur guides to describe the emerging police state. The author's assistant, Abduweli Ayup, a Uyghur refugee from Xinjiang, first heard the phrase in January 2016, used among Uyghurs who had escaped China and arrived as refugees in Turkey.

2. Radio Free Asia, "Chinese Authorities Jail Four Wealthiest Uyghurs in Xinjiang's Kashgar in New Purge," January 5, 2018, https://www.rfa.org/english/news/uyghur/wealthiest-01052018144327.html.

Chapter 1. The New Dominion

1. Paul Mozur, "Looking through the Eyes of China's Surveillance State," *New York Times*, July 16, 2018, https://www.nytimes.com/2018/07/16/technology/china-surveillance-state.html.

2. Joyce Liu and Wang Xiqing, "In Your Face: China's All-Seeing State," BBC News, December 10, 2017, https://www.bbc.com/news/av/world-asia-china-42248056.

3. Stephen Chen, "How Tensions with the West Are Putting the Future of China's Skynet Mass Surveillance System at Stake," *South China Morning Post*, September 23, 2018, https://www.scmp.com/news/china/science/article/2165372/how-tensions-west-are-putting-future-chinas-skynet-mass.

4. Human Rights Watch, "China: Big Data Fuels Crackdown in Minority Region," February 26, 2018, https://www.hrw.org/news/2018/02/26/china-big-data-fuels-crackdown-minority-region.

5. Albert von Le Coq, *Buried Treasures of Chinese Turkestan: An Account of the Activities and Adventures of the Second and Third German Turfan Expeditions* (London: G. Allen & Unwin, 1928), 37, https://archive.org/stream/in.ernet.dli.2015.279757/2015.279757.Buried-Treasures_djvu.txt.

6. Peter Hopkirk, *Foreign Devils on the Silk Road*, paperback 2nd ed. (London: John Murray, 2016), 9–12.

7. Rian Thum, *The Sacred Routes of Uyghur History* (Cambridge, MA: Harvard University Press, 2014), 2–7, 196–97.

8. Marco Polo, *The Travels of Marco Polo* (New York: Penguin, 1958), 80–81.

9. Jane Perlez and Yufan Huang, "Behind China's $1 Trillion Plan to Shake Up the Economic Order," *New York Times*, May 13, 2017, https://www.nytimes.com /2017/05/13/business/china-railway-one-belt-one-road-1-trillion-plan.html.

10. BBC News, "China to Try Eight People over Deadly Tiananmen Attack," May 31, 2014, https://www.bbc.com/news/world-asia-china-27647842. See also Associated Press, "Urumqi Car and Bomb Attack Kills Dozens," May 22, 2014, https://www .theguardian.com/world/2014/may/22/china-urumqi-car-bomb-attack-xinjiang.

11. BBC News, "Four Charged over Kunming Mass Knife Attack," June 30, 2014, https://www.bbc.com/news/world-asia-china-28085994.

12. BBC News, "Imam of China's Largest Mosque Killed in Xinjiang," July 31, 2014, https://www.bbc.com/news/world-asia-china-28586426.

13. Clifford Coonan, "Suspected Hijackers Die Following On-Board Flight," *Irish Times*, July 3, 2012, https://www.irishtimes.com/news/suspected-hijackers -die-following-on-board-fight-1.527852.

14. Sami Moubayed, *Under the Black Flag: At the Frontier of the New Jihad* (London: I.B. Taurus, 2015), 168.

15. Xinhua, "Respected Imam's Murder Is Anti-Humanity, Anti-Islam," August 1, 2014, http://en.people.cn/n/2014/0801/c90882-8764198.html.

16. Carter Vaughn Findley, *The Turks in World History* (Oxford: University of Oxford Press, 2004).

17. James A. Millward, "'Reeducating' Xinjiang's Muslims," *New York Review of Books*, February 7, 2019, https://www.chinafile.com/library/nyrb-china-archive/ reeducating-xinjiangs-muslims.

18. Thum, *The Sacred Routes of Uyghur History*, 2–7, 171–77.

19. George Soros, *In Defense of Open Society* (New York: PublicAffairs, 2019), 16–17.

20. "Facebook Shows Another Foreign Spy Hidden behind CNRP to Topple the Government," *Fresh News*, August 24, 2017, http://freshnewsasia.com/index .php/en/63667-facebook-2.html.

21. Erin Handley and Niem Chheng, "Filmmaker James Ricketson Charged," *Phnom Penh Post*, June 9, 2017, https://www.phnompenhpost.com/national/film maker-james-ricketson-charged.

22. "Latest Updates: CNRP Leader Kem Sokha Arrested for 'Treason,'" *Cambodia Daily*, September 3, 2017, https://www.cambodiadaily.com/news/nrp-leader -kem-sokha-arrested-treason-134249/.

23. From two Khmer-language news broadcasts in August and September 2017, in possession of the author.

Chapter 2. The Panopticon

1. Nanchang Public Security Bureau, "75 Behavioral Indicators of Religious Extremism," September 8, 2015, http://www.ncga.gov.cn/e/action/ShowInfo.php

?classid=1256&id=5881. The link was taken down on an unknown date, but remains partially translated at Human Rights Watch, "'Eradicating Ideological Viruses': China's Campaign of Repression against Xinjiang's Muslims," September 9, 2018, https://www.hrw.org/report/2018/09/09/eradicating-ideological-viruses/chinas-campaign-repression-against-xinjiangs#_ftn53.

2. *Egypt Independent*, "China to Invest $11.2 Billion in Projects for Egypt's New Administrative Capital," September 4, 2017, https://egyptindependent.com/china-invest-11-2-billion-projects-egypts-new-administrative-capital/. Details of other security and infrastructure agreements from September 2016 to September 2017 can be found at "Egypt, China Sign Technical Cooperation Document in Specialized Security Fields," State Information Service of Egypt, https://www.sis.gov.eg/Story/114496?lang=en-us; and "Egypt, China Sign Three MOUs on Security, Launching New Satellite, Electrical Rail Project," *Enterprise*, September 6, 2017, https://enterprise.press/stories/2017/09/06/egypt-china-sign-three-mous-on-security-launching-new-satellite-electrical-rail-project/.

3. Human Rights Watch, "Egypt: Don't Deport Uyghurs to China," July 18, 2017, https://www.hrw.org/news/2017/07/08/egypt-dont-deport-uyghurs-china#.

4. Human Rights Watch, "Egypt: Don't Deport Uyghurs to China."

5. Al Jazeera, "Egypt Arrests Chinese Muslim Students amid Police Sweep," July 7, 2017, https://www.aljazeera.com/news/2017/7/7/egypt-arrests-chinese-muslim-students-amid-police-sweep.

6. While I was in Washington, DC, I was able to help Asman and his family find refuge in France after they flew to Paris and asked for asylum.

7. Megha Rajagopalan, Alison Killing, and Christo Buschek, "China Secretly Built a Vast New Infrastructure to Imprison Muslims," BuzzFeed News, August 27, 2020, https://www.buzzfeednews.com/article/meghara/china-new-internment-camps-xinjiang-uighurs-muslims. The authors write: "In the most extensive investigation of China's internment camp system ever done using publicly available satellite images, coupled with dozens of interviews with former detainees, BuzzFeed News identified more than 260 structures built since 2017 and bearing the hallmarks of fortified detention compounds. There is at least one in nearly every county in the far-west region of Xinjiang."

8. Lao Mu, "Vocational Education and Training Centers in Xinjiang Represent New Path to Address Terrorism," *People's Daily Online*, September 10, 2019, http://en.people.cn/n3/2019/0910/c90000-9613730.html.

9. Steven Jiang and Ben Westcott, "China's Top Uyghur Official Claims Most Detainees Have Left Xinjiang Camps," CNN.com, July 30, 2019, https://edition.cnn.com/2019/07/30/asia/xinjiang-official-beijing-camps-intl-hnk/index.html.

10. Xinhua News Agency, "Full Transcript: Interview with Xinjiang Government Chief on Counterterrorism, Vocational Education and Training in Xinjiang," October 16, 2018, http://www.xinhuanet.com/english/2018-10/16/c_137535821.htm.

11. Radio Free Asia, "Xinjiang Political 'Re-Education Camps' Treated Uyghurs 'Infected by Religious Extremism': CPP Youth League," August 8, 2018, https://www.rfa.org/english/news/uyghur/infected-08082018173807.html. The journalists obtained an audio recording of an official from the Communist Youth League

in Xinjiang, posted on a Chinese social media group and addressed to Uyghur youth. They translated some of its contents.

12. Austin Ramzy and Chris Buckley, "'Absolutely No Mercy': Leaked Files Expose How China Organized Mass Detentions of Muslims," *New York Times*, November 16, 2019, https://www.nytimes.com/interactive/2019/11/16/world/asia/china-xinjiang-documents.html.

13. In addition to the author's interviews, similar accounts are documented in Allison Killing and Megha Rajagopalan, "What They Saw: Ex-Prisoners Detail the Horrors of China's Detention Camps," BuzzFeed News, August 27, 2020, https://www.buzzfeednews.com/article/alison_killing/china-ex-prisoners-horrors-xinjiang-camps-uighurs.

14. Killing and Rajagopalan, "What They Saw," in addition to the author's interviews.

15. Chris Buckley, "China's Prisons Swell after Deluge of Arrests Engulfs Muslims," *New York Times*, August 31, 2019, https://www.nytimes.com/2019/08/31/world/asia/xinjiang-china-uighurs-prisons.html.

16. Leaked China Cables in the possession of the author. Also see Ramzy and Buckley, "'Absolutely No Mercy.'"

17. Rajagopalan, Killing, and Buschek, "China Secretly Built a Vast New Infrastructure to Imprison Muslims."

18. Rustem Shir, "Resisting Chinese Linguistic Imperialism: Abduweli Ayup and the Movement for Uyghur Mother-Tongue-Based Education," Uyghur Human Rights Project, May 2019, https://docs.uhrp.org/pdf/UHRP_Resisting_Chinese_Linguistic_Imperialism_May_2019.pdf. Media articles and human rights reports frequently misstate Abduweli as having been detained for three years. Abduweli said the correct timeline is fifteen months in four detention centers.

19. The author and Maysem agreed not to state her precise field of study within the social sciences, because that would easily identify her.

20. These accounts are well documented in the author's interviews; some interviewees gave the author recordings of the calls from Chinese agents and relatives back in China. Also see Deutsche Welle (Germany), "How China intimidates Uighurs Abroad by Threatening Their Families," July 11, 2019, https://www.dw.com/en/how-china-intimidates-uighurs-abroad-by-threatening-their-families/a-49554977.

Chapter 3. Sky Net Has Found You

1. Maysem was a child in the 1990s when Uyghurs began asserting their national identity after the Cold War, such as at demonstrations in Ghulja, Xinjiang, in 1997. Police opened fire on the protesters, killing perhaps dozens of them, though the official count was nine deaths. Maysem said she was speaking from her childhood perspective, coming of age in a comfortable and insular upbringing, and part of a politically favored family at a time when the repression of Uyghurs was still nowhere near today's intensity. For more information on the Ghulja demonstrations

and ensuing torture and executions, see this 1997 news documentary from the UK's Channel 4 news at https://www.youtube.com/watch?v=4RUCOrg2Pbo.

2. Human Rights Watch, "We Are Afraid to Even Look for Them: Enforced Disappearances in the Wake of Xinjiang's Protests," October 20, 2009, https://www.hrw.org/report/2009/10/20/we-are-afraid-even-look-them/enforced-disappearances-wake-xinjiangs-protests.

3. Author's interviews with Uyghur extremist fighters in Istanbul, Turkey, from February 2018 to July 2018.

4. Nate Rosenblatt, "All Jihad Is Local: What ISIS' Files Tell Us About Its Fighters," New America Foundation, July 2016, https://na-production.s3.amazonaws.com/documents/ISIS-Files.pdf.

5. Kevin Wang, "Chinese City Bans Beards, Islamic-Style Clothing on Busses During Event," CNN.com, August 6, 2014, https://www.cnn.com/2014/08/06/world/asia/china-beard-ban/index.html. Also see Sina News, "Xinjiang Karamay: Those with Large Beards and Four Kinds of Dressing Banned from Taking Buses (新疆克拉玛依：留大胡须等五种人员禁乘公交)," August 5, 2014, http://news.sina.com.cn/c/2014-08-05/210530635703.shtml. The author's assistant translated the title from Mandarin Chinese to English.

6. Human Rights Watch, "'Eradicating Ideological Viruses.'" The regulations are available in Chinese at Regulations of Xinjiang Uygur Autonomous Region on Religious Affairs (新疆维吾尔自治区宗教事务条例), 2014. Also see Xinhua, "Bans on Wearing Veils, Garment Covering Face in Public Places in Urumqi Are Approved (乌鲁木齐公共场所禁止穿戴蒙面罩袍的规定获批)," January 10, 2015, http://www.xinhuanet.com/politics/2015-01/10/c_1113948748.htm. The author's assistant translated the title from Mandarin Chinese to English.

7. Tom Phillips, "China Launches Massive Rural 'Surveillance' to Watch Over Uighurs," Telegraph, https://www.telegraph.co.uk/news/worldnews/asia/china/11150577/China-launches-massive-rural-surveillance-project-to-watch-over-Uighurs.html.

8. Thum, The Sacred Routes of Uyghur History, 23.

9. Thum, The Sacred Routes of Uyghur History, 16. "I request men of learning that, if there should be any mistakes and faults in this tazkir," reads one manuscript named on page 72, "they should amend them with a kind of postscript and bring them into shape." The region's history, the history that Maysem loved, "is a history created by mass participation rather than experts, more akin to Wikipedia than to the Histories of Herodotus or the Epic of Sundiata," writes Rian Thum, historian of the region and professor at Loyola University New Orleans, on page 15.

10. Tian Han and Nie Er, "March of the Volunteers," 1935, http://english1.english.gov.cn/2005-08/16/content_23523.htm. Translated from the Chinese.

11. Frank Dikötter, The Cultural Revolution: A People's History, 1962–1976 (London: Bloomsbury Press, 2017), i–xix. "Even if, in terms of human loss," Dikötter writes on page xviii, "the Cultural Revolution was far less murderous than many earlier campaigns, in particular the catastrophe unleashed during Mao's Great Famine, it left a trail of broken lives and cultural devastation. By all accounts, during the ten years spanning the Cultural Revolution, between 1.5 and 2 million

people were killed, but many more lives were ruined through endless denuncia-tions, false confessions, struggle meetings and persecution campaigns." Also see Anne Thurstone, *Enemies of the People* (New York: Knopf, 1987), 208–9.

12. Raisa Mirovitskaya and Andrei Ledovsky. "The Soviet Union and the Chinese Province of Xinjiang in the Mid-1930s," *Far Eastern Affairs* 35, no. 4 (2007): 92–103. The Woodrow Wilson Center for International Scholars in Washington, DC, also maintains an excellent online archive of declassified Soviet records, ti-tled "China and the Soviet Union in Xinjiang, 1934–1949," at https://digitalarchive .wilsoncenter.org/collection/234/china-and-the-soviet-union-in-xinjiang-1934-1949.

13. James A. Millward, *Eurasian Crossroads: A History of Xinjiang* (London: Hurst Publishers, 2007).

14. Ezra F. Vogel, *Deng Xiaoping and the Transformation of China* (Cambridge, UK: Belknap Press, 2011), ch. 16, "Accelerating Economic Growth and Opening, 1982–1989," 450–75, and ch. 24, "China Transformed," 693–712, Kindle ed.

15. The optimistic thinking about China in the 1990s and 2000s was reflected in the predominant US government policies, newspaper op-eds, and speeches of the time. For instance, see President Bill Clinton, "Full Text of Clinton's Speech on China Trade Bill" (speech, Paul H. Nitze School of Advanced International Studies at the Johns Hopkins University, Washington, DC, March 9, 2000), recorded by the Federal News Service, https://www.iatp.org/sites/default/files/Full_Text_of_ Clintons_Speech_on_China_Trade_Bi.htm. President Clinton stated: "By join-ing the W.T.O., China is not simply agreeing to import more of our products; it is agreeing to import one of democracy's most cherished values: economic freedom. The more China liberalizes its economy, the more fully it will liberate the potential of its people—their initiative, their imagination, their remarkable spirit of enter-prise. And when individuals have the power, not just to dream but to realize their dreams, they will demand a greater say." Skeptics of China's WTO accession in 2001 were often dismissed as protectionists in Washington, DC, circles. These in-cluded trade lawyer Robert E. Lighthizer, "A Deal We'd Be Likely to Regret," *New York Times*, April 18, 1999, https://www.nytimes.com/1999/04/18/opinion/a-deal -wed-be-likely-to-regret.html.

16. Zheng Wang, *Never Forget National Humiliation: Historical Memory in Chinese Politics and Foreign Relations* (New York: Columbia University Press, 2012), ch. 5, "From Vanguard to Patriot: Reconstructing the Chinese Communist Party," 119–41.

17. Bethany Allen-Ebrahimian, "Meet China's Salman Rushdie," *Foreign Policy*, October 1, 2015, https://foreignpolicy.com/2015/10/01/china-xinjiang-islam-salman -rushdie-uighur/. An e-book version of *The Art of Suicide* is available in the Uy-ghur language at https://elkitab.org/oluwelish_senitiperhat_tursun/. The author gathered additional information on Perhat Tursun's life in interviews with his ac-quaintances, the poet Tahir Hamut, the journalist and historian Eset Sulayman, and linguist Abduweli Ayup. The author could not reach Tursun for an interview because he was detained in Xinjiang in January 2018 and is believed to have re-ceived a lengthy sentence since then, according to the shahit.biz victim database at https://shahit.biz/eng/viewentry.php?entryno=2.

18. Bethany Allen-Ebrahimian, "Meet China's Salman Rushdie."

Chapter 4. China Rises

1. David Kirkpatrick, "How Microsoft Conquered China," *Fortune*, July 17, 2007, https://money.cnn.com/magazines/fortune/fortune_archive/2007/07/23/100134488/.

2. Robyn Meredith, "(Microsoft's) Long March," *Forbes*, February 17, 2003, https://www.forbes.com/forbes/2003/0217/078.html?sh=86a319f6802c.

3. Kirkpatrick, "How Microsoft Conquered China."

4. Kirkpatrick, "How Microsoft Conquered China."

5. Mara Hvistendahl, "China's Tech Giants Want to Go Global. Just One Thing Might Stand in Their Way," *MIT Technology Review*, December 19, 2018, https://www.technologyreview.com/2018/12/19/138226/chinas-tech-giants-want-to-go-global-just-one-thing-might-stand-in-their/way/.

6. Sunray Liu, "Microsoft Builds R&D Dream Team in Beijing," *EE Times*, September 9, 1999, https://www.eetimes.com/microsoft-builds-rd-dream-team-in-beijing/.

7. Kai-fu Lee, *AI Superpowers: China, Silicon Valley, and the New World Order* (Boston: Houghton Mifflin Harcourt, 2018), 4–5.

8. Good Morning America, "Casper: Apple's initial Voice First System from 1992," posted by YouTube user Brian Roemmele on January 20, 2017, https://www.youtube.com/watch?v=8De_KxYt1pQ. The video was first broadcasted on *Good Morning America* in 1992.

9. Wang Jingjing, "The 'Whampoa Academy' of China's Internet," *People* (China), https://www.weibo.com/p/1001643998598932131471. The article is in Mandarin Chinese. Jeff Ding, Oxford doctoral candidate and Rhodes scholar at the Oxford Future of Humanity Institute, translated the article and published it on his online ChinAI newsletter. "But in the spring of 1998, KFL [Kai-fu Lee] was experiencing his own 'failure period' while he was a vice president of a company called SGI in Silicon Valley," reads the article. "Because the products they were making were too far advanced and could not find a market, he was forced to sell his own multimedia company." Ding's translation is available at https://chinai.substack.com/p/chinai-37-happy-20th-anniversary.

10. Kai-fu Lee, *AI Superpowers*, 89.

11. Mara Hvistendahl, "China's Tech Giants Want to Go Global. Just One Thing Might Stand in Their Way," *MIT Technology Review*, December 19, 2018, https://www.technologyreview.com/2018/12/19/138226/chinas-tech-giants-want-to-go-global-just-one-thing-might-stand-in-their-way.

12. Kai-fu Lee, *AI Superpowers*, 16.

13. Also see Richard P. Applebaum, et al., *Innovation in China: Challenging the Global Science and Technology System* (Cambridge, UK: Polity, 2018), 8 and ch. 5, "How Effective Is China's State-Led Approach to High-Tech Development?" The authors sum up China's innovation model as an "often contradictory blend of heavy-handed state-driven development and untrammeled free enterprise."

14. Elizabeth C. Economy, *The Third Revolution: Xi Jinping and the New Chinese State* (Oxford: Oxford University Press, 2018), ch. 3, "ChinaNet," 55–90.

15. Joseph Kahn, "Yahoo Helped Chinese to Prosecute Journalist," *New York Times*, September 8, 2005, https://www.nytimes.com/2005/09/08/business/worldbusiness/yahoo-helped-chinese-to-prosecute-journalist.html.

16. G. Elijah Dann and Neil Haddow, "Just Doing Business or Doing Just Business: Google, Microsoft, Yahoo! and the Business of Censoring China's Internet," *Journal of Business Ethics* 79, no. 3 (2008): 219–34, https://www.jstor.org/stable/25075661?seq=1. The full pledge can be read in English at *China Daily*, "Public Pledge of Self-Regulation and Professional Ethics for China [*sic*] Internet Industry" (中国互联网行业自律公约), March 26, 2002, http://govt.chinadaily.com.cn/s/201812/26/WS5c23261f498eb4f01ff253d2/public-pledge-of-self-regulation-and-professional-ethics-for-china-internet-industry.html.

17. Economy, *The Third Revolution*, ch. 3, "ChinaNet," 63–65.

18. Evan S. Medeiros, Roger Cliff, Keith Crane, and James C. Mulvenon, "A New Direction for China's Defense Industry," 205, Santa Monica, CA: Rand Corporation, 2005, https://www.rand.org/pubs/monographs/MG334.html.

19. Chinese Academy of Sciences, "Issues in Building a National Innovation System," *High Technology Development Report* (高技术发展报告), Beijing, 2005, http://www.bdp.cas.cn/zlyjjwqgl/ptcg/201608/t20160830_4572983.html.

20. James Palmer, "Nobody Knows Anything About China," *Foreign Policy*, March 21, 2018, https://foreignpolicy.com/2018/03/21/nobody-knows-anything-about-china/.

21. Citi Research, "Hangzhou Hikvision Digital Technology," August 4, 2015, https://img3.gelonghui.com/pdf201508/pdf20150805155951188.pdf.

22. Irfan's account of Huawei's involvement in Xinjiang is consistent with the investigations by the Australian Strategic Policy Institute (ASPI) into the activities of Chinese technology firms. See ASPI, "Mapping China's Tech Giants: Huawei," https://chinatechmap.aspi.org.au/#/company/huawei. His account is also consistent with an investigation by IPVM, a news source on surveillance technologies. See Charles Rollet, "Dahua and Hikvision Win over $1 Billion in Government-Backed Projects in Xinjiang," IPVM, April 23, 2018, https://ipvm.com/reports/xinjiang-dahua-hikvision.

23. For a more detailed history of video surveillance, see John Honovich, "Video Surveillance History," IPVM, May 6, 2020, https://ipvm.com/reports/history-video-surveillance.

24. Honovich, "Video Surveillance History."

25. Olivia Carville and Jeremy Kahn, "China's Hikvision Has Probably Filmed You," *Bloomberg Quint*, May 23, 2019, https://www.bloombergquint.com/technology/china-s-hikvision-weighed-for-u-s-ban-has-probably-filmed-you.

26. Irfan drew detailed diagrams for the author that showed how the camera surveillance systems were set up and linked to government and corporate surveillance offices. These diagrams are in the possession of the author.

27. Steven Millward, "5 years of WeChat," *Tech in Asia*, January 21, 2016, https://www.techinasia.com/5-years-of-wechat.

28. Steven Millward, "Tencent CEO: Weixin Group Messaging App Hits 100 Million Users," *Tech in Asia*, March 29, 2012, https://www.techinasia.com/tencent-weixin-100-million-users.

29. Steven Millward, "Just Short of 2 Years Old, WeChat App Surpasses 300 Million Users," *Tech in Asia*, January 16, 2013, https://www.techinasia.com/confirmed -wechat-surpasses-300-million-users.

30. Associated Press, "Number of Active Users at Facebook over the Years," October 24, 2012, https://finance.yahoo.com/news/number-active-users-facebook -over-years-214600186--finance.html. Jemima Kiss, "Twitter Reveals It Has 100M Active Users," *Guardian*, September 8, 2011, https://www.theguardian.com/tech nology/pda/2011/sep/08/twitter-active-users.

31. Zheping Huang, "All the Things You Can—and Can't—Do with Your WeChat Account in China," *Quartz*, December 28, 2017, https://qz.com/1167024/all-the -things-you-can-and-cant-do-with-your-wechat-account-in-china/. The author confirmed features not listed in the article through his own use of WeChat from 2012 to 2016. In 2016, the author stopped using WeChat to protect his sources in China.

32. BBC, "Timeline: China's Net Censorship," June 29, 2010, https://www.bbc .com/news/10449139.

33. Irfan drew detailed diagrams showing the technical aspects of how the WeChat surveillance worked, which are in the possession of the author. Irfan's account of WeChat surveillance is consistent with the author's interview of one other former Uyghur technology worker. It is also consistent with numerous other accounts of Uyghurs detained in China after the police said they found suspicious WeChat usage. See for instance the story of one Uyghur woman detained for her WeChat usage in 2013 in Isobel Cockerell, "Inside China's Massive Surveillance Operation," *Wired*, May 9, 2019, https://www.wired.com/story/inside-chinas-massive -surveillance-operation/.

34. See Amnesty International, "How Private Are Your Favourite Messaging Apps?," October 21, 2016, https://www.amnesty.org/en/latest/campaigns/2016/10/ which-messaging-apps-best-protect-your-privacy/. Amnesty International writes: "Tencent owns the two most popular messaging apps in China, WeChat and QQ, and is bottom of our message privacy scorecard, scoring zero out of 100. Not only did it fail to adequately meet any of the criteria, but it was the only company which has not stated publicly that it will not grant government requests to access encrypted messages by building a 'backdoor.'"

Chapter 5. Deep Neural Network

1. Jessica Brum, "Technology Transfer and China's WTO Commitments," *Georgetown Journal of International Law* 50 (2018): 709–43, https://www.law.george town.edu/international-law-journal/wp-content/uploads/sites/21/2019/10/GT -GJIL190043.pdf.

2. Remco Zwetsloot, "China's Approach to Tech Talent Competition: Policies, Results, and the Developing Global Response," in report series *Global China: Assessing China's Growing Role in the World*, Brookings Institution, Washington, DC, April 2020, https://www.brookings.edu/wp-content/uploads/2020/04/FP_20200427_ china_talent_policy_zwetsloot.pdf.

3. Kai-fu Lee, *AI Superpowers*, 6–8.

4. I am grateful to a former Google AI developer for assisting with the phrasing of this explanation of deep neural nets.

5. Michael Chui, James Manyika, Mehdi Miremadi, Nicolaus Henke, Rita Chung, Pieter Nel, and Sankalp Malhotra. "Notes from the AI Frontier: Applications and Value of Deep Learning," McKinsey Global Institute, April 17, 2018, https://www.mckinsey.com/featured-insights/artificial-intelligence/notes-from-the-ai-frontier-applications-and-value-of-deep-learning#.

6. Andrew Ross Sorkin and Steve Lohr, "Microsoft to Buy Skype for $8.5 Billion," New York Times, May 10, 2011, https://dealbook.nytimes.com/2011/05/10/microsoft-to-buy-skype-for-8-5-billion/.

7. The World Bank, "Individuals Using the Internet (% of Population)—China," https://data.worldbank.org/indicator/IT.NET.USER.ZS?locations=CN.

8. China Internet Network Information Center, "The Internet Timeline of China (2011)," February 19, 2013, https://cnnic.com.cn/IDR/hlwfzdsj/201302/t20130219_38709.htm.

9. Dave Gershgorn, "The Inside Story of How AI Got Good Enough to Dominate Silicon Valley," Business Insider, June 28, 2018, https://qz.com/1307091/the-inside-story-of-how-ai-got-good-enough-to-dominate-silicon-valley/.

10. I am grateful to a former Google AI developer for illustrating the techniques and commercial applications of GPU technologies in an interview.

11. Allison Linn, "Microsoft Researchers Win ImageNet Computer Vision Challenge," AI Blog, Microsoft, December 10, 2015, https://blogs.microsoft.com/ai/microsoft-researchers-win-imagenet-computer-vision-challenge/.

12. Crunchbase, "Series A—MEGVII," announcement of Series A funding round, July 18, 2013, https://www.crunchbase.com/funding_round/megvii-technology-series-a--927a6b8b.

13. Shu-Ching Jean Chen, "SenseTime: The Faces behind China's Artificial Intelligence Unicorn," Forbes Asia, March 7, 2018, https://www.forbes.com/sites/shuchingjeanchen/2018/03/07/the-faces-behind-chinas-omniscient-video-surveillance-technology/?sh=5efc95584afc.

14. Chen, "SenseTime."

15. Ryan Mac, Rosalind Adams, and Megha Rajagopalan, "US Universities and Retirees Are Funding the Technology behind China's Surveillance State," BuzzFeed News, May 30, 2019, https://www.buzzfeednews.com/article/ryanmac/us-money-funding-facial-recognition-sensetime-megvii.

16. Nvidia, "AI Powered Facial Recognition for Computers with SenseTime," posted by YouTube user NVIDIA on June 6, 2016, https://www.youtube.com/watch?v=wMUmPumXtpw. The video was recorded at Nvidia's Emerging Companies Summit in 2016.

17. Aaron Tilley, "The New Intel: How Nvidia Went from Powering Video Games to Revolutionizing Artificial Intelligence," Forbes, November 30, 2016, https://www.forbes.com/sites/aarontilley/2016/11/30/nvidia-deep-learning-ai-intel/?sh=ba1b3777ff1e.

18. Paul Mozur and Don Clark, "China's Surveillance State Sucks Up Data," New York Times, November 24, 2020, https://www.nytimes.com/2020/11/22/technology/china-intel-nvidia-xinjiang.html.

19. Nvidia, "AI Powered Facial Recognition."

20. Nvidia, "AI Powered Facial Recognition."

21. Nvidia, "AI Powered Facial Recognition."

22. Kai-fu Lee, *AI Superpowers*, 104–5.

23. Zhang Ye, "Translation Tech Booms in Xinjiang," *Global Times*, April 26, 2017, https://www.globaltimes.cn/content/1044253.shtml.

24. Danielle Cave, Fergus Ryan, and Vicky Xiuzhong Xu, "Mapping More of China's Tech Giants: AI and Surveillance," Issues Paper No. 24, Australian Security Policy Institute, December 2019, https://www.aspi.org.au/report/mapping-more -chinas-tech-giants.

25. Alexandra Harney, "Risky Partner: Top U.S. Universities Took Funds from Chinese Firm Tied to Xinjiang Security," Reuters, June 13, 2019, reuters.com/ article/us-china-xinjiang-mit-tech-insight-idUSKCN1TE04M.

26. Cave, Ryan, and Xiuzhong Xu, "Mapping More of China's Tech Giants." Also see Huawei Cloud, "Xinjiang Holds Hands with Huawei Cloud, Promotes 'Tianshan Cloud' Application (新疆携手华为企业云 推进"天山云"应用)," December 15, 2015, https://web.archive.org/web/20191119031933/https://www.huaweicloud.com/.

27. *Forbes*, "Ren Zhengfei," https://www.forbes.com/profile/ren-zhengfei/?sh =3516b5cd2e6e.

28. Bloomberg, "Huawei CEO Ren Zhengfei Survived a Famine, but Can He Weather President Trump?," December 10, 2018, https://www.straitstimes .com/asia/east-asia/huaweis-ceo-ren-zhengfei-survived-a-famine-can-he-weather -president-trump.

29. Interview with William Plummer, July 8, 2020, and three other Huawei employees in the United States and China.

30. Chen, "How Tensions with the West Are Putting the Future of China's Sky-net Mass Surveillance System at Stake."

31. National Security Agency, "Why We Care," Codeword "Shotgiant," January 1, 2010, released March 22, 2014, https://search.edwardsnowden.com/docs/Shot giant2014-03-22_nsadocs_snowden_doc.

32. David E. Sanger and Nicole Periroth, "N.S.A. Breached Chinese Servers Seen as Security Threat," *New York Times*, March 22, 2014, https://www.nytimes .com/2014/03/23/world/asia/nsa-breached-chinese-servers-seen-as-spy-peril.html.

33. Sanger and Periroth, "N.S.A. Breached Chinese Servers Seen as Security Threat."

34. Michael S. Schmidt, Keith Bradsher, and Christine Hauser, "U.S. Panel Cites Risks in Chinese Equipment," *New York Times*, October 8, 2012, https://www .nytimes.com/2012/10/09/us/us-panel-calls-huawei-and-zte-national-security -threat.html

35. Natasha Khan, Dan Stumpf, and Wenxin Fan, "The Public Face of Huawei's Global Fight," *Wall Street Journal*, January 19, 2019, https://www.wsj.com/articles/ the-public-face-of-huaweis-global-fight-11547874008.

36. Von Jacob Applebaum, Judith Horchert, and Christian Stöcker, "Catalog Advertises NSA Toolbox," *Der Spiegel*, December 29, 2013, https://www.spiegel .de/international/world/catalog-reveals-nsa-has-back-doors-for-numerous-devices -a-940994.html.

37. Glenn Greenwald, "How the NSA Tampers with US-Made Internet Routers," *Guardian*, May 12, 2014, https://www.theguardian.com/books/2014/may/12/glenn-greenwald-nsa-tampers-us-internet-routers-snowden. Cisco responded by shipping boxes to vacant addresses and fake identities to throw off the NSA. See Darren Pauli, "Cisco Posts Kit to Empty Houses to Dodge NSA Chop Shops," *Register*, March 18, 2015, https://www.theregister.com/2015/03/18/want_to_dodge_nsa_supply_chain_taps_ask_cisco_for_a_dead_drop/.

38. National Security Agency, "HALLUXWATER: Ant Product Data," June 24, 2008, 5, https://www.eff.org/files/2014/01/06/20131230-appelbaum-nsa_ant_catalog.pdf.

39. Paul Sandle and Jane Barrett, "Huawei CEO Says Not Surprised by U.S. Spying Reports," *Reuters*, May 2, 2014, https://www.reuters.com/article/uk-huawei-tech-ren/huawei-ceo-says-not-surprised-by-u-s-spying-reports-idINKBN0DI18B20140502.

40. Keith Bradsher, "Amid Tension, China Blocks Vital Exports to Japan," *New York Times*, September 22, 2010, https://www.nytimes.com/2010/09/23/business/global/23rare.html.

41. Bradsher, "Amid Tension, China Blocks Vital Exports to Japan."

42. Martin Fackler and Ian Johnson, "Japan Retreat with Release of Chinese Boat Captain," *New York Times*, September 24, 2010, https://www.nytimes.com/2010/09/25/world/asia/25chinajapan.html.

43. Yoko Kubota, "Japan Releases China Fishing Boat Captain: Report," Reuters, September 24, 2010, https://fr.reuters.com/article/us-japan-china-idUSTRE68I06520100924.

44. Gary Brown and Christopher D. Yung, "Evaluating the US-China Cybersecurity Agreement, Part 1: The US Approach to Cyberspace," *Diplomat*, January 19, 2017, https://thediplomat.com/2017/01/evaluating-the-us-china-cybersecurity-agreement-part-1-the-us-approach-to-cyberspace/.

45. Reuters, "Google Exit Appears to Benefit Top China Rival, Baidu," April 29, 2010, https://www.nytimes.com/2010/04/30/technology/30baidu.html.

Chapter 6. Do You Think I Am an Automaton?

1. There are many other nuances and complexities to the way the Uyghur and Han people see each other, depending on the person being interviewed. For informative research on this topic, see Tom Cliff, *Oil and Water: Being Han in Xinjiang* (Chicago: University of Chicago Press, 2016).

2. Charlotte Brontë, *Jane Eyre: An Autobiography* (London: Service & Paton, 1897), ch. 23, published online in the public domain from Project Gutenberg, at https://www.gutenberg.org/files/1260/1260-h/1260-h.htm.

3. Andrew Jacobs, "At a Factory, the Spark for China's Violence," *New York Times*, July 15, 2009, https://www.nytimes.com/2009/07/16/world/asia/16china.html.

4. Human Rights Watch, "'We Are Afraid to Even Look for Them.'"

5. Agence France-Presse, "Footage of the 2009 Ethnic Violence in Xinjiang," July 4, 2010, https://www.youtube.com/watch?v=bEz4frMoriA.

6. BBC, "Xinjiang Arrests 'Now over 1,500," August 3, 2009, http://news.bbc
.co.uk/2/hi/asia-pacific/8181563.stm.

7. Ben Blanchard, "China Tightens Web Screws after Xinjiang Riot," Reuters, July 6, 2009, https://www.reuters.com/article/us-china-xinjiang-internet-idUSTRE 5651K420090706.

8. Human Rights Watch, "'We Are Afraid to Even Look for Them.'"

9. Ilham Tohti, "My Ideals and the Career Path I Have Chosen," Pen America, April 9, 2014, https://pen.org/my-ideals-and-the-career-path-i-have-chosen/. The original Chinese version is available at https://s3.amazonaws.com/wenyunchao_ share/Ilham_01.html.

10. Tohti, "My Ideals and the Career Path I Have Chosen."

11. Tohti, "My Ideals and the Career Path I Have Chosen."

12. Cliff. *Oil and Water*, ch. 1, "Constructing the Civilized City," 27–49.

13. Information Office of the State Council, People's Republic of China, "Full Text: The History and Development of the Xinjiang Production and Construction Corps," white paper, October 5, 2014, http://english.sina.com/ china/2014/1004/742790.html. The original Chinese text is available at http:// www.scio.gov.cn/zfbps/ndhf/2014/Document/1382598/1382598.htm. This government white paper is a propagandistic history of the bingtuan. Its claims should not be taken at face value. Rather, it is useful for observing how China sees the history of the bingtuan.

14. Millward, *Eurasian Crossroads*, 178–234.

15. Thomas Matthew and James Cliff, "Neo Oasis: The Xinjiang *Bingtuan* in the Twenty-first Century," *Asian Studies Review* 33 (March 2009), 83–106.

16. Author's interviews in 2017 and 2018 with former Uyghur and Han residents of Xinjiang. Also see Cliff, *Oil and Water*, ch. 5, "Lives of *Guanxi*," 144–48.

17. Ilham Tohti, translated by Cindy Carter, "Present-Day Ethnic Problems in Xinjiang Uighur Autonomous Region: Overview and Recommendations," *Daxiong Gonghui*, https://ilhamtohtisite.files.wordpress.com/2016/09/ilham-tohti_present -day-ethnic-problems-in-xinjiang-uighur-autonomous-region-overview-and-recom mendations_complete-translation3.pdf. The exact publication date is unclear, but the article was posted on the Daxiong Gonghui website sometime after Tohti's arrest in January 2014. Tohti wrote and revised the article from 2011 to 2013.

18. Tohti, "My Ideals and the Career Path I Have Chosen."

19. Tohti, "My Ideals and the Career Path I Have Chosen."

20. Tohti, "My Ideals and the Career Path I Have Chosen."

Chapter 7. The Great Rejuvenation

1. Barbara Demick, "'Red Song' Campaign in China Strikes Some False Notes," *Los Angeles Times*, June 3, 2011, https://www.latimes.com/world/la-xpm-2011-jun -03-la-fg-china-red-20110604-story.html.

2. Austin Ramzy, "The 2010 TIME 100: Bo Xilai," *Time*, April 29, 2010, http:// content.time.com/time/specials/packages/article/0,28804,1984685_1984864 _1985416,00.html.

3. Ian Johnson, "China's Falling Star," *New York Review of Books*, March 19, 2012, https://www.nybooks.com/daily/2012/03/19/chinas-falling-star-bo-xilai/.

4. Pin Ho and Wenguang Huang, *A Death in the Lucky Holiday Hotel: Murder, Money, and an Epic Power Struggle in China* (New York: PublicAffairs, 2013), 165–74.

5. Chun Han Wong, "Chinese Court Commutes Sentence for Gu Kailai to Life in Prison," *Wall Street Journal*, December 14, 2015, https://www.wsj.com/articles/chinese-court-commutes-sentence-for-gu-kailai-to-life-in-prison-1450102422.

6. Jeremy Page, "Bo Xilai Found Guilty, Sentenced to Life in Prison," *Wall Street Journal*, September 22, 2013, https://www.wsj.com/articles/SB1000142405270230 3730704579090080547591654.

7. The author prefers to use the title "Chairman" rather than "President" to describe China's leader because it is a far more accurate translation. The Chinese government translates this title as "President" in English-language materials to give it more respectability and to legitimize authoritarian rule. In reality, the correct translation is "Chairman." See Isaac Stone Fish, "Stop Calling Xi Jinping 'President,'" *Slate*, August 8, 2019, https://slate.com/news-and-politics/2019/08/xi-jinping-president-chairman-title.html.

8. Chris Buckley and Didi Kirsten Tatlow, "Cultural Revolution Shaped Xi Jinping, from Schoolboy to Survivor," *New York Times*, September 24, 2015, https://www.nytimes.com/2015/09/25/world/asia/xi-jinping-china-cultural-revolution.html.

9. US Embassy Beijing, "Portrait of Vice President Xi Jinping," cable, November 16, 2009, https://wikileaks.org/plusd/cables/09BEIJING3128_a.html.

10. Evan Osnos, "Born Red," *New Yorker*, April 6, 2015, https://www.newyorker.com/magazine/2015/04/06/born-red.

11. James Palmer, "China's Overrated Technocrats," *Foreign Policy*, July 4, 2019, https://foreignpolicy.com/2019/07/04/chinas-overrated-technocrats-stem-engineering-xi-jinping/.

12. Economy, *The Third Revolution*, 5.

13. Ibid.

14. François Bougon, *Inside the Mind of Xi Jinping* (London: Hurst, 2018), ch. 1, "The Renaissance Man," 16.

15. Bougon, *Inside the Mind of Xi Jinping*, introduction, "The Chinese Dream," 7–8.

16. Bougon, *Inside the Mind of Xi Jinping*, ch. 9, "Shedding the Low Profile," 184–85.

17. Bougon, *Inside the Mind of Xi Jinping*, ch. 1, "The Renaissance Man," 17.

18. Bougon, *Inside the Mind of Xi Jinping*, ch. 9, "Shedding the Low Profile," 188.

19. "Profile: Xi Jinping: Pursuing the Dream for 1.3 billion Chinese," Xinhua, March 17, 2013, http://english.cntv.cn/20130317/100246.shtml. The author used the translation from Economy, *The Third Revolution*, 4.

20. Wang Jisi, "'Marching Westwards': The Rebalancing of China's Geostrategy," in Shao Binhong, *The World in 2020 According to China: Chinese Foreign Policy Elites Discuss Emerging Trends in International Politics* (Leiden, Netherlands: Brill, 2014), ch. 6, 129–36. The Chinese version of this article was first published in *Global Times* on October 17, 2012.

21. Xi Jinping, "Promote Friendship between Our People and Work Together

to Build a Bright Future," speech, Nazabayev University, Astana, Kazakhstan, September 7, 2013, https://www.fmprc.gov.cn/mfa_eng/wjdt_665385/zyjh_665391/t1078088.shtml.

22. Kent E. Calder, *Super Continent: The Logic of Eurasian Integration* (Palo Alto, CA: Stanford University Press, 2019), ch. 1, "Eurasian Reconnection and Renaissance," loc. 206, Kindle ed.

23. Geoff Wade, "The Zheng He Voyages: A Reassessment," *Journal of the Malaysian Branch of the Royal Asiatic Society* 78, no. 1 (2005): 37–58, http://www.jstor.org/stable/41493537.

24. Peter Frankopan, *The Silk Roads: A New History of the World* (New York: Vintage, 2015). The first 236 pages are an informative introduction to the many empires and peoples of the Silk Road, predating the rise of Europe.

25. Frankopan, *The Silk Roads: A New History of the World*, ch. 13, "The Road to Northern Europe," and ch. 14, "The Road to Empire," 243–279.

26. Howard W. French, *Everything Under the Heavens: How the Past Helps Shape China's Push for Global Power* (New York: Knopf, 2017), introduction, 11–13.

27. Bill Hayton, *The Invention of China* (New Haven, CT: Yale University Press, 2020), introduction and ch. 2, "The Invention of Sovereignty," 12, 50–91. Hayton and many other recent scholars argue that the "century of national humiliation" is an invention by the Communist Party to rob the Chinese people of their agency in creating their own history, a useful tool for an authoritarian regime.

28. Peter Frankopan, *The Silk Roads*, chs. 14–20, 264–398. The second half of the book is an informative survey of the decline of Eurasian empires due to the rise of Europe.

29. Calder, *Super Continent*, ch. 1, "Eurasian Reconnection and Renaissance," loc. 237, Kindle ed.

30. Chris Buckley and Paul Mozur, "What Keeps Xi Jinping Awake at Night," *New York Times*, May 11, 2018, https://www.nytimes.com/2018/05/11/world/asia/xi-jinping-china-national-security.html.

31. Calder, *Super Continent*, introduction, locs. 121–96, Kindle ed.

32. Calder, *Super Continent*, ch. 1, "Eurasian Reconnection and Renaissance, loc. 302, Kindle ed.

33. Kevin Yao and Aileen Wang, "China's 2013 Economic Growth Dodges 14-Year Low but Further Slowing Seen," Reuters, January 20, 2014, https://fr.reuters.com/article/us-china-economy-gdp-idUSBREA0I0HH20140120.

34. The leaked Xinjiang Papers are in the possession of the author. Also see Ramzy and Buckley, "'Absolutely No Mercy.'"

35. Bougon, *Inside the Mind of Xi Jinping*, ch. 1, "The Renaissance Man," 20.

36. Andrew Jacobs, "Beijing Crash May Be Tied to Unrest in Xinjiang," *New York Times*, October 28, 2013, https://www.nytimes.com/2013/10/29/world/asia/beijing-restricts-coverage-after-car-explodes-at-forbidden-city.html.

37. BBC, "Tiananmen Crash: China Police 'Detain Suspects,'" October 30, 2013, https://www.bbc.com/news/world-asia-china-24742810.

38. Andrew Jacobs, "China Strips Army Official of Position after Attack," *New York Times*, November 3, 2013, https://www.nytimes.com/2013/11/04/world/asia/china-demotes-a-military-commander-after-attack-in-beijing.html.

39. Gerry Shih, "AP Exclusive: Uyghurs Fighting in Syria Take Aim at China," Associated Press, December 23, 2017, https://apnews.com/article/79d6a427b26f4 eeab226571956dd256e.

40. Keira Lu Huang, "SWAT Team Leader 'Gunned Down Five Kunming Terrorists in 15 Seconds,'" *South China Morning Post*, March 4, 2014, https://www .scmp.com/news/china/article/1439991/swat-team-leader-gunned-down-five-kun ming-terrorists-15-seconds.

41. Hannah Beech, "Deadly Terrorist Attack in Southwestern China Blamed on Separatist Muslim Uighurs," *Time*, March 1, 2014, https://time.com/11687/deadly -terror-attack-in-southwestern-china-blamed-on-separatist-muslim-uighurs/.

42. Xinhua, "Nothing Justifies Civilian Slaughter in 'China's 9-11,'" *Global Times*, March 2, 2014, https://www.globaltimes.cn/content/845570.shtml.

43. World Uyghur Congress, "World Uyghur Congress Urges Calm and Caution after Beijing Incident on October 28, 2013," October 29, 2013, https://www .uyghurcongress.org/en/world-uyghur-congress-urges-calm-and-caution-after -beijing-incident-on-october-28-2013/.

44. Hannah Beech, "Urumqi: Deadly Bomb and Knife Attack Rocks Xinjiang Capital," *Time*, April 30, 2014, https://time.com/83727/in-china-deadly-bomb-and -knife-attack-rocks-xinjiang-capital/. Also see Xinhua, "Bombing at Urumqi South Railway Station solved (乌鲁木齐火车南站暴恐袭击案告破)," May 1, 2014, https://web.archive.org/web/20140903125343/http://news.xinhuanet.com/legal /2014-05/01/c_1110500096.htm. The author's assistant translated this title from Mandarin Chinese to English.

45. Andrew Jacobs, "In China's Far West, a City Struggles to Move On," *New York Times*, May 23, 2014, https://www.nytimes.com/2014/05/24/world/asia/ residents-try-to-move-on-after-terrorist-attack-in-china.html.

46. Leaked Chinese government documents in the possession of the author. Also see Ramzy and Buckley, "'Absolutely No Mercy.'"

Chapter 8. China's War on Terror

1. James Millward, "Violent Separatism in Xinjiang: A Critical Assessment," *Policy Studies* 6 (Washington, DC: East-West Center 2004), https://www.eastwest center.org/system/tdf/private/PS006.pdf?file=1&type=node&id=3200.

2. Interview with Yusuf Amet, former Chinese spy in Turkey.

3. Al Jazeera, "The Guantanamo 22," Al Jazeera, December 9, 2015, https:// www.aljazeera.com/program/featured-documentaries/2015/12/9/the-guantanamo -22/. The documentary *Uyghurs: Prisoners of the Absurd*, directed by Patricio Henriquez, is no longer available online. The full film is in the possession of the author. See also Richard Bernstein, "When China Convinced the U.S. That Uighurs Were Waging Jihad," March 19, 2019, https://www.theatlantic.com/international/ archive/2019/03/us-uighurs-guantanamo-china-terror/584107/.

4. Sean Roberts, *The War Against the Uyghurs: China's Internal Campaign Against a Muslim Minority* (Princeton: Princeton University Press, 2020), 110–11.

5. Al Jazeera, "The Guantanamo 22."

6. Also see Roberts, *The War Against the Uyghurs*, 70–71.

7. Al Jazeera, "The Guantanamo 22."

8. Roberts, *The War Against the Uyghurs*, 80–81.

9. Al Jazeera, "The Guantanamo 22."

10. US Department of State, "China: Country of Origin (COI) Report," Home Office of the United Kingdom, UK Border Agency, August 24, 2011, https://www.justice.gov/sites/default/files/eoir/legacy/2013/06/12/china-0811.pdf.

11. Al Jazeera, "The Guantanamo 22."

12. Nathan Vanderklippe, "After Guantanamo, Life on Pacific Island Was Difficult," *Globe and Mail*, June 28, 2015, https://www.theglobeandmail.com/news/world/after-guantanamo-life-on-pacific-island-was-difficult/article25172787/.

13. Interviews with three former Guantanamo Uyghurs in Turkey, April to July 2018.

14. Yusuf provided all of his WhatsApp conversations and voice recordings with Chinese intelligence in Xinjiang to the author. These files are in the author's possession.

Chapter 9. The Three Evils: Terrorism, Extremism, and Separatism

1. These Facebook messages are in the possession of the author.

2. "She Comes Not to Me," translated by Victoria Rowe Holbrook and Mücahit Kaçar, from Kaya Türkay, *Alî-Sîr Nevâyî: Bedâyiu'l-Vasat*, Üçünçi Dîvân (Ankara, Turkey: Türk Dil Kurumu, 2002), 441.

3. Amnesty International, "People's Republic of China: At Least 1000 People Executed in 'Strike Hard' Campaign against Crime," June 30, 1996, https://www.amnesty.org/en/documents/asa17/072/1996/en/.

4. Dozens of news articles have documented the government's early "trustworthiness" and related "credit ranking" systems rolled out mainly from 2015 to 2017. A dozen Uyghur and Kazakh refugees, however, told the author that they were subject to crude forms of the "trustworthiness" system even before that in Xinjiang, starting as early as 2014. The government released its first public paper outlining the social credit trustworthiness system in June 2014. See State Council of the People's Republic of China, "Planning Outline for the Construction of a Social Credit System (2014–2020)," June 14, 2014, https://chinacopyrightand media.wordpress.com/2014/06/14/planning-outline-for-the-construction-of-a-social-credit-system-2014-2020/.

5. Sarah Cook, "Islam: Religious Freedom in China," *Freedom House*, 2017, https://freedomhouse.org/report/2017/battle-china-spirit-islam-religious-freedom #footnote16_b6wryn6. For the estimate of 592 Uyghurs tried on security charges, Freedom House cites the *Dui Hua Human Rights Journal*, which made the estimate based on online government sources listed at https://www.duihuahrjournal .org/2015/03/xinjiang-state-security-trials-flat.html.

6. Joanne Smith Finley, "Securitization, Insecurity and Conflict in Contemporary Xinjiang: Has PRC Counter-Terrorism Evolved into State Terror?" *Central*

Asian Survey 38, no. 1, 1–26, https://www.tandfonline.com/doi/pdf/10.1080/02634937.2019.1586348?needAccess=true.

7. Human Rights Watch, "Timeline of Ilham Tohti's Case," September 15, 2014, https://www.hrw.org/news/2014/09/15/timeline-ilham-tohtis-case.

8. Interview with Jewher Ilham, June 2, 2020.

9. Radio Free Asia, "Uyghur Scholar Tohti Speaks about His Concerns before Detention," February 7, 2014, https://www.rfa.org/english/news/uyghur/interview-02072014182032.html.

10. Human Rights Watch, "Timeline of Ilham Tohti's Case." Also see People. cn, "Police: Ilham Tohti, Instructor from Minzu University of China, Is Involved in Separatist Activities (警方:中央民族大学教师伊力哈木从事分裂活动)," January 25, 2014, http://politics.people.com.cn/n/2014/0125/c1001-24226456.html. The author's assistant translated this title from Mandarin Chinese to English.

11. Human Rights Watch, "Timeline of Ilham Tohti's Case."

12. "Edward Wong, "China Sentences Uighur Scholar to Life," *New York Times*, September 23, 2014, https://www.nytimes.com/2014/09/24/world/asia/china-court-sentences-uighur-scholar-to-life-in-separatism-case.html.

13. Radio Free Asia, "Under the Guise of Public Safety, China Demolishes Thousands of Mosques," December 19, 2016, https://www.rfa.org/english/news/uyghur/udner-the-guise-of-public-safety-12192016140127.html. An investigation by the *Guardian* and the website Bellingcat further documented, through satellite imagery, two dozen religious sites that had been partly or completely demolished from 2016 to 2018. See Lily Kuo, "Revealed: New Evidence of China's Mission to Raze the Mosques of Xinjiang," *Guardian*, May 7, 2019, https://www.theguardian.com/world/2019/may/07/revealed-new-evidence-of-chinas-mission-to-raze-the-mosques-of-xinjiang.

14. According to the author's guide in Kashgar.

15. Nancy Shatzman Steinhardt, *China's Early Mosques* (Edinburgh, UK: Edinburgh University Press, 2015), 268–70.

16. Steinhardt, *China's Early Mosques*.

Chapter 10. People as Data

1. State Council of the People's Republic of China, "State Council Notice Concerning Issuance of the Planning Outline for the Construction of a Social Credit System (2014–2020)," June 14, 2014, https://chinacopyrightandmedia.wordpress.com/2014/06/14/planning-outline-for-the-construction-of-a-social-credit-system-2014-2020/. The original Chinese version is available at http://www.gov.cn/zhengce/content/2014-06/27/content_8913.htm.

2. Charlie Campbell, "How China Is Using 'Social Credit Scores' to Reward and Punish Its Citizens," *Time*, January 16, 2019, https://time.com/collection-post/5502592/china-social-credit-score/.

3. Celia Hatton, "China's 'Social Credit': Beijing Sets Up Huge System," BBC, October 26, 2015, https://www.bbc.com/news/world-asia-china-34592186.

4. Hatton, "China's 'Social Credit': Beijing Sets Up Huge System."

5. Louise Matsakis, "How the West Got China's Social Credit System Wrong," *Wired*, July 29, 2019, https://www.wired.com/story/china-social-credit-score -system/.

6. Ankit Panda, "The Truth about China's New National Security Law," *Diplomat*, July 1, 2015, https://thediplomat.com/2015/07/the-truth-about-chinas-new -national-security-law/.

7. President of the People's Republic of China, "National Security Law of the People's Republic of China (2015)," *China Daily*, December 11, 2017, http://govt .chinadaily.com.cn/s/201812/11/WS5c0f1b56498eefb3fe46e8c9/national-security -law-of-the-peoples-republic-of-china-2015-effective.html.

8. Edward Wong, "China Approves Sweeping Security Law, Bolstering Communist Rule," *New York Times*, July 1, 2015, https://www.nytimes.com/2015/07/02/ world/asia/china-approves-sweeping-security-law-bolstering-communist-rule .html.

9. ImageNet, "Large Scale Visual Recognition Challenge 2015 Results," http:// image-net.org/challenges/LSVRC/2015/results. Also see Kaiming He, Xiangyu Zhang, Shaoqing Ren, and Jian Sun, "Deep Residual Learning for Image Recognition," Cornell University, Science and Engineering Archive, December 10, 2015, https://arxiv.org/pdf/1512.03385.pdf.

10. "After thirteen amazing years at Microsoft Research, I have joined MEGVII Technology (also known as Face++, in July, 2016) as Chief Scientist and Managing Director of Research," personal homepage of Jian Sun, December 20, 2020, http:// www.jiansun.org/.

11. Yiting Sun, "Meet the Company That's Using Face Recognition to Reshape China's Tech Scene," *MIT Technology Review*, August 11, 2017, https://www.tech nologyreview.com/2017/08/11/149962/when-a-face-is-worth-a-billion-dollars/.

12. "Charles Rollet, "Infinova's Xinjiang Business Examined," IPVM, December 7, 2018, https://ipvm.com/reports/infinova-xinjiang.

13. Ryan Mac, Rosalind Adams, and Megha Rajagopalan, "US Universities and Retirees Are Funding the Technology behind China's Surveillance State," BuzzFeed News, May 30, 2019, https://www.buzzfeednews.com/article/ryanmac/us -money-funding-facial-recognition-sensetime-megvii.

14. Reuters, "China to Create $6.5 Billion Venture Capital Fund to Support Start-ups," January 15, 2015, https://www.reuters.com/article/us-china-venture capital-idUSKBN0KO05Q20150115.

15. Tom Mitchell, "China to Launch $6.5bn VC Fund for Emerging Industries Start-ups," *Financial Times*, January 15, 2015, https://www.ft.com/content/73f216c 8-9c97-11e4-a730-00144feabdc0.

16. Cory Bennett and Katie Bo Williams, "US, China Agree to Stop Corporate Hacks," *Hill*, September 25, 2015, https://thehill.com/policy/cybersecurity /254966-us-china-reach-common-understanding-on-hacking.

17. Robert Farley, "Did the Obama-Xi Cyber Agreement Work?," *Diplomat*, August 11, 2018, https://thediplomat.com/2018/08/did-the-obama-xi-cyber-agree ment-work/.

18. Since 2016, numerous studies have revealed broad consistencies with Irfan's and other Uyghur technology workers' testimonies gathered by the author.

See Jeffrey Knockel, et al., "We Chat, They Watch: How International Users Un-wittingly Build Up WeChat's Censorship Apparatus," Citizen Lab, University of Toronto, May 7, 2020. https://citizenlab.ca/2020/05/we-chat-they-watch/. In an Amnesty International 2016 survey of the world's most popular apps, WeChat got a score of zero out of one hundred for privacy, and ranked its owner, Tencent, last behind Facebook, Google, and Apple. Amnesty believed WeChat users had little or no encryption for their communications. The group also found that WeChat didn't disclose government requests for user data. See Amnesty International, "How Pri-vate Are Your Favourite Messaging Apps?" Furthermore, in September 2017, two years after Irfan said his office made the request for WeChat's data, and then again in 2020, WeChat changed its privacy policy, confirming privacy groups' suspicions. The new privacy policies revealed that WeChat gathered log data like search terms and profiles visited, along with metadata like call times, duration, and location information that could be disclosed to the Chinese government under Chinese law, which does not require a police warrant. See WeChat, "Privacy Policy," https://www.wechat.com/en/privacy_policy.html. Finally, see Cockerell, "Inside China's Massive Surveillance Operation." The article states that "in May 2014, the Chinese government enlisted a taskforce to stamp out 'malpractice' on instant messaging apps, in particular 'rumors and information leading to violence, terrorism, and pornography.' WeChat, alongside its rival apps, was required to let the government monitor the activity of its users."

Chapter 11. How to Rank Everyone on Their Trustworthiness

1. The system the government called "double-linked households," consisting of ten households that surveilled and reported on each other, began in 2014 in Ti-bet. Later on, in 2016, it spread in larger numbers to Xinjiang. However, Maysem and fifteen other Uyghur interviewees reported being subject to regular home in-spections and raids by their neighborhood committees as early as 2014. See Sarah Tynen, "I Was in China Doing Research When I Saw My Uighur Friends Disap-pear," *Conversation*, March 9, 2020, https://theconversation.com/i-was-in-china-doing-research-when-i-saw-my-uighur-friends-disappear-127166. Also see Nectar Gan, "Passports Taken, More Police . . . New Party Boss Chen Quanguo Acts to Tame Xinjiang with Methods Used in Tibet," *South China Morning Post*, December 12, 2016, https://www.scmp.com/news/china/policies-politics/article/2053739/party-high-flier-uses-his-tibet-model-bid-tame-xinjiang.

2. Human Rights Watch, "China: Visiting Officials Occupy Homes in Mus-lim Region," May 13, 2018, https://www.hrw.org/news/2018/05/13/china-visiting-officials-occupy-homes-muslim-region. The original Chinese-language source for Human Rights Watch's reporting has been taken down.

3. Human Rights Watch, "'Eradicating Ideological Viruses.'"

4. Human Rights Watch, "Eradicating Ideological Viruses."

5. *Xinjiang Daily*, "Xinjiang: 2017 Physicals for All Work Has Been Done (新疆: 2017年全民健康体检工作全部完成), November 2, 2017, http://www.gov.cn/xin

wen/2017-11/02/content_5236389.htm. The author's assistant translated the title from Mandarin Chinese to English.

6. Sui-Lee Wee, "China Uses DNA to Track Its People, with the Help of American Expertise," *New York Times*, February 21, 2019, https://www.nytimes.com /2019/02/21/business/china-xinjiang-uighur-dna-thermo-fisher.html.

7. Human Rights Watch, "China: Minority Region Collects DNA from Millions," December 13, 2017, https://www.hrw.org/news/2017/12/13/china-minority -region-collects-dna-millions.

8. Human Rights Watch, "China: Minority Region Collects DNA from Millions." See also Xinhua, "Healthy Xinjiang: Precisely Reacting to People's Health Expectations ("健康新疆": 精准对接群众健康期盼)," May 28, 2018, http://www .xinhuanet.com/local/2018-05/28/c_129881863.htm. The author's assistant translated the article from Mandarin Chinese to English. Xinhua reported that Physicals for All started in September 2016. The author interviewed a dozen Uyghur refugees who said they had been summoned to police stations and health clinics for medical examinations as early as June 2016. By the end of 2017, the authorities had completed two rounds of mass physicals and DNA collection for a total of 36.34 million people.

9. Human Rights Watch, "China: Minority Region Collects DNA from Millions."

10. Mark Munsterhjelm, interview with the author, January 29, 2020.

11. Mark Munsterhjelm, "Scientists Are Aiding Apartheid in China," *Just Security*, June 18, 2019, https://www.justsecurity.org/64605/scientists-are-aiding-apart heid-in-china/.

12. See Mark Munsterhjelm, *Living Dead in the Pacific: Contested Sovereignty and Racism in Genetic Research on Taiwan Aborigines* (Vancouver: University of British Columbia Press, 2014).

13. ALFRED, Yale University School of Medicine, https://alfred.med.yale.edu/ alfred/index.asp.

14. Munsterhjelm, "Scientists Are Aiding Apartheid in China."

15. Wee, "China Uses DNA to Track Its People."

16. Ailsa Chang, "How Americans—Some Knowingly, Some Unwittingly— Helped China's Surveillance Grow," NPR, July 18, 2019, https://www.npr.org /2019/07/18/743211959/how-americans-some-knowingly-some-unwittingly -helped-chinas-surveillance-grow.

17. Liu Caixia, Kenneth Kidd, et al., "A Panel of 74 AISNPs: Improved Ancestry Inference within Eastern Asia," *Forensic Science International: Genetics* 23, 2016, 101–110, https://pubmed.ncbi.nlm.nih.gov/27077960/.

18. Yinghong Cheng, "'Is Peking Man Still Our Ancestor?'—Genetics, Anthropology, and the Politics of Racial Nationalism in China," *Journal of Asian Studies* 76, August 2017, 575–602, https://www.cambridge.org/core/journals/journal-of -asian-studies/article/is-peking-man-still-our-ancestorgenetics-anthropology-and -the-politics-of-racial-nationalism-in-china/F7D479FC994A854400A53E0E1 B987236.

19. ALFRED, Yale University School of Medicine.

20. ALFRED, Yale University School of Medicine.

21. Kidd did not respond to the author's requests for comment, though he has told his story widely to the media, NPR, and the *New York Times*. See Wee, "China Uses DNA to Track Its People."

22. Thermo Fisher Scientific, "Thermo Fisher Scientific Reports Fourth Quarter and Full Year 2018 Results," January 30, 2019, https://ir.thermofisher.com/investors/news-and-events/news-releases/news-release-details/2019/Thermo-Fisher-Scientific-Reports-Fourth-Quarter-and-Full-Year-2018-Results/default.aspx.

23. Thermo Fisher Scientific, "Annual Report," 2017, https://s1.q4cdn.com/008680097/files/doc_financials/annual/2017/2017-Annual-Report-TMO.pdf.

24. Wee, "China Uses DNA to Track Its People."

25. Karen A. Kirkwood, Karen A. Kirkwood to Arvind Ganesan and Sophie Richardson, letter. From Human Rights Watch, June 20, 2017, https://www.hrw.org/sites/default/files/supporting_resources/thermo_fisher_response_.pdf.

26. He Wei, Ren Xiaojin, et al., "Xi's Speech at CIIE Draws Positive Reactions," *China Daily*, November 5, 2018, http://www.chinadaily.com.cn/a/201811/05/WS5bdfe891a310eff3032869d9_12.html.

Chapter 12. The All-Seeing Eye

1. Maysem did not have the form with her in our interview in Turkey, having left it in China. Dozens of other Uyghurs, however, kept this form and similar documentation, and showed them to the author. Snapshots of these forms are in the possession of the author.

2. Human Rights Watch, "China: Big Data Fuels Crackdown in Minority Region."

3. Human Rights Watch, "China's Algorithms of Repression," May 1, 2019, https://www.hrw.org/report/2019/05/01/chinas-algorithms-repression/reverse-engineering-xinjiang-police-mass.

4. The leaks released by the *New York Times* were reported by Ramzey and Buckley, "'Absolutely No Mercy.'" A different leak, the one that the author also obtained, was published at Bethany Allen-Ebrahimian, "Exposed: China's Operating Manuals for Mass Internment and Arrest by Algorithm," International Consortium of Investigative Journalists, November 24, 2019, https://www.icij.org/investigations/china-cables/exposed-chinas-operating-manuals-for-mass-internment-and-arrest-by-algorithm/.

5. The author is in possession of about four hundred pages of the leaked Xinjiang documents quoted here.

6. Catalin Cimpanu, "Chinese Company Leaves Muslim-Tracking Facial Recognition Database Exposed Online," ZDNet, February 14, 2019, https://www.zdnet.com/article/chinese-company-leaves-muslim-tracking-facial-recognition-database-exposed-online/.

7. Victor Gevers, Twitter post, February 13, 2019, 6:13 P.M., https://twitter.com/0xDUDE/status/1096788937492840451.

8. Arjun Kharpal, "Microsoft Says That Facial Recognition Firm That Beijing Allegedly Uses to Track Muslims Is Lying About a 'Partnership,'" CNBC, March 15, 2019, https://www.cnbc.com/2019/03/15/microsoft-facial-recognition-firm-sense nets-lying-about-partnership.html.

9. Shannon Liao, "An Exposed Database Tracked Whether 1.8 Million Chinese Women Were 'Breed Ready,'" *Verge*, March 11, 2019, https://www.theverge.com /2019/3/11/18260816/china-exposed-database-breedready-women.

10. Scilla Alecci, "How China Targets Uighurs 'One by One' for Using a Mobile App," International Consortium of Investigative Journalists, November 24, 2019, https://www.icij.org/investigations/china-cables/how-china-targets-uighurs-one -by-one-for-using-a-mobile-app/.

11. Li Zaili, "Religious Belief Is a Crime, Xinjiang Authorities Say," *Bitter Winter*, October 16, 2018, https://bitterwinter.org/religious-belief-is-a-crime-for -authorities/.

12. Alecci, "How China Targets Uighurs 'One by One.'"

13. Adam Lynn, "App Targeting Uyghur Population Censors Content, Lacks Basic Security," Open Technology Fund, August 31, 2018, https://www.opentech .fund/news/app-targeting-uyghur-population-censors-content-lacks-basic -security/.

14. Megha Rajagopalan, "China Is Forcing People to Download an App That Tells Them to Delete 'Dangerous' Photos," BuzzFeed News, April 9, 2018, https:// www.buzzfeednews.com/article/meghara/china-surveillance-app.

Chapter 13. Called to a Concentration Camp

1. Nectar Gan, "Passports Taken, More Police."

2. See the *Economist*, "Xinjiang: The Race Card," September 3, 2016, https:// www.economist.com/china/2016/09/03/the-race-card.

3. See Josh Chin and Clément Bürge, "Twelve Days in Xinjiang: How China's Surveillance State Overwhelms Daily Life," *Wall Street Journal*, December 19, 2017, https://www.wsj.com/articles/twelve-days-in-xinjiang-how-chinas-surveillance -state-overwhelms-daily-life-1513700355.

4. Cpcnews.cn, "Chen Quanguo CV (陈全国同志简历)," October 2017, http:// cpc.people.com.cn/BIG5/n1/2017/1025/c414940-29608824.htm.

5. Jun Mai, "From Tibet to Xinjiang, Beijing's Man for Restive Regions Chen Quanguo Is the Prime Target of US Sanctions," *South China Morning Post*, December 13, 2019, https://www.scmp.com/news/china/politics/article/3041810/tibet -xinjiang-beijings-man-restive-regions-chen-quanguo-prime.

6. In interviews with the author, dozens of Uyghurs described the same or very similar scenery when they checked into the reeducation camps, including Uyghurs interned in the same detention center as Maysem. Also see Killing and Rajago-palan, "Ex-Prisoners Detail the Horrors of China's Detention Camps."

7. In interviews, dozens of Uyghurs told the author that they were shuffled around between camps in the early, seemingly disorganized camp system of late 2016 and 2017. The reasons were not always clear to the interviewees, though

they assumed that overcrowding played a role. Also see Killing and Rajagopalan, "Ex-Prisoners Detail the Horrors of China's Detention Camps."

8. Almost all former detainees from Xinjiang told the author and other researchers that they were held in cells about the size of a living room, typically holding anywhere from fifteen to fifty cellmates monitored by two to four cameras. Also see US Department of State, "2019 Report on International Religious Freedom: China—Xinjiang," https://www.state.gov/reports/2019-report-on-inter national-religious-freedom/china/xinjiang/.

9. See Austin Ramzy and Chris Buckley, "Leaked China Files Show Internment Camps Are Ruled by Secrecy and Spying," New York Times, November 24, 2019, https://www.nytimes.com/2019/11/24/world/asia/leak-chinas-internment-camps .html.

10. The curricula of similar classes were described in the same detail by other Uyghur refugees interviewed by the author. Numerous news reports consist of similar stories. As of 2020, some testimony has emerged that suggests the teachers too may have been coerced or not fully informed they were being sent to teach inmates. At least one former teacher said she adopted a "double life," showing false loyalty in order to get out. Also see Ruth Ingram, "Confessions of a Xinjiang Camp Teacher," Diplomat, August 17, 2020, https://thediplomat.com/2020/08/confessions -of-a-xinjiang-camp-teacher/.

11. Interview with another former Uyghur inmate at Maysem's camp, September 2019.

12. For more information on overcrowding, see Killing and Rajagopalan, "Ex-Prisoners Detail the Horrors of China's Detention Camps."

13. For more information on how Xinjiang's authorities co-opt religious leaders to support the Communist Party, see Lily Kuo, "'If You Enter a Camp, You Never Come Out': Inside China's War on Islam," Guardian, January 11, 2019, https://www .theguardian.com/world/2019/jan/11/if-you-enter-a-camp-you-never-come-out -inside-chinas-war-on-islam.

Chapter 14. Mass Internment

1. Dozens of Uyghur refugees told the author that, in late 2016 and early 2017, they were allowed limited family visitations and occasionally allowed to leave the centers to meet family in their villages for short periods. It is unclear from the author's research whether the practice of visitations continues. See video footage of Uyghur inmates leaving their camp for the night at BBC, "Inside China's 'Thought Transformation Camps,'" June 18, 2019, https://www.youtube.com/watch?v=Wm Id2ZP3hoc.

2. Turkey is on the Chinese government's list of "26 sensitive countries" that make Xinjiang residents targets for surveillance and reeducation. See Human Rights Watch, "'Eradicating Ideological Viruses.'"

3. Interview with eight Uyghur refugees and one businessman still in Xinjiang, December 2017–February 2018.

4. Adrian Zenz, "China's Domestic Security Spending: An Analysis of Available Data," *China Brief* 18, no. 4 (March 12, 2018), https://www.researchgate.net/publication/343971146_China%27s_Domestic_Security_Spending_An_Analysis_of_Available_Data.

5. Adrian Zenz, "'Thoroughly Reforming Them towards a Healthy Heart Attitude': China's Political Re-Education Campaign in Xinjiang," *Central Asian Survey* 38, no. 1, 102–28, September 5, 2018. https://www.tandfonline.com/doi/abs/10.1080/02634937.2018.1507997?scroll=top&needAccess=tr&journalCode=ccas20. According to procurement documents gathered by Zenz, in 2016 one county government in Yuli—a poor region in the northern Taklamakan Desert nearby China's testing of nuclear weapons decades ago—reported on its website that 90 percent of almost two thousand people who took part in "transformation for education training classes" had been "transformed." Another county, Ghulja, said it had achieved a "transformation rate" of 85 percent. One bid that year called for the "construction of de-extremification transformation through an education base," requesting a teaching room, dining hall, guard room, and generator room for 2.5 million yuan (about $355,000). Another called for a video surveillance control room, police supervision office, dormitory, and dining hall for an unlisted price. And yet another wanted renovations and expansions, with an added security fence and surrounding wall, for 0.19 million yuan, almost $30,000. Other centers requested projects for anywhere up to 103 million yuan, or $14.7 million—the highest for a 377,000-square-foot facility, more than the size of five football fields, called a "legal system transformational center."

6. Adrian Zenz, "China Didn't Want Us to Know. Now Its Own Files Are Doing the Talking," *New York Times,* November 24, 2019, https://www.nytimes.com/2019/11/24/opinion/china-xinjiang-files.html.

7. Naubet Bisenov, "Kazakhstan-China Deportation Case Sparks Trial of Public Opinion," *Nikkei Asian Review,* July 26, 2018, https://asia.nikkei.com/Politics/International-relations/Kazakhstan-China-deportation-case-sparks-trial-of-public-opinion.

8. Sayragul Sauytbay, interview with the author, July 25, 2020. The author also obtained smartphone recordings of part of Sauytbay's court testimony as the defendant from her trial beginning in July 2018, for allegedly crossing illegally into Kazakhstan earlier that year. The testimony contains a multitude of information about her experiences as a teacher in a camp. For more reading, see Matt Rivers and Lily Lee, "Former Xinjiang Teacher Claims Brainwashing and Abuse Inside Mass Detention Centers," CNN, May 10, 2019, https://edition.cnn.com/2019/05/09/asia/xinjiang-china-kazakhstan-detention-intl/index.html.

9. Omir Bekali, interview with the author, September 2018. Omir Bekali was one of the first Kazakh citizens to come forward to the media with a detailed account of his time in the camps. Also see Gerry Shih, "China's Mass Indoctrination Camps Evoke Cultural Revolution," Associated Press, May 18, 2018, https://apnews.com/article/6e151296fb194f85ba69a8babd972e4b.

10. *Economist,* "China's Population: Peak Toil," January 26, 2013, https://www.economist.com/china/2013/01/26/peak-toil.

11. Lily Kuo, "China Transferred Detained Uighurs to Factories Used by Global Brands—Report," *Guardian*, March 1, 2020, https://www.theguardian.com/world /2020/mar/01/china-transferred-detained-uighurs-to-factories-used-by-global -brands-report.

12. Amazon, "Amazon's Updated Response to the Australian Strategic Policy Institute's Report on Forced Labour of Ethnic Minorities from Xinjiang," Business and Human Rights Centre, October 2, 2020, https://www.business-humanrights .org/en/latest-news/amazons-updated-response-to-the-australian-strategic-policy -institutes-report-on-forced-labour-of-ethnic-minorities-from-xinjiang/.

13. Eva Dou and Chao Deng, "Western Companies Get Tangled in China's Muslim Clampdown," *Wall Street Journal*, May 16, 2019, https://www.wsj.com/articles/ western-companies-get-tangled-in-chinas-muslim-clampdown-11558017472.

14. Foxconn, "Foxconn Walked into Xinjiang Kashgar to Help the Poor (助力精准扶贫 集团走进新疆喀什地区)," December 5, 2018, http://www.foxconn.com.cn/ ComDetailNews69.html. The author's assistant translated the title from Mandarin Chinese to English.

15. Ana Swanson, "Banned Chinese Companies Deny Allegations They Abused Uighurs," *New York Times*, July 21, 2020, https://www.nytimes.com/2020/07/21/ business/china-us-trade-banned.html. "Apple Cuts Off China's Ofilm over Zinjiang Labor," Bloomberg News. March 17, 2021, https://finance.yahoo.com/news/apple -said-cut-ties-china-053835604.html.

16. "Ainur Helps Family Realise 'Supermarket Dream' (阿依努尔助力家人实现'超市梦')," Hotan government (和田政府网), July 31, 2019, http://archive.ph/ DOUK3. Mandarin Chinese to English translations made by author's assistant.

17. Vicky Xiuzhong Xu, Danielle Cave, James Leibold, Kelsey Munro, and Nathan Ruser, "Uyghurs for Sale," Australia Strategic Policy Institute, February 2020, https://www.aspi.org.au/report/uyghurs-sale.

18. Dake Kang and Yanan Wang, "Gadgets for Tech Giants Made with Coerced Uighur Labor," Associated Press, March 5, 2020, https://apnews.com/article/3f9a92 b8dfd3cae379b57622dd801dd5.

19. William Yang, "Top Brands 'Using Forced Uighur Labor' in China: Report," *Deutsche Welle*, March 2, 2020, https://www.dw.com/en/top-brands-using-forced -uighur-labor-in-china-report/a-52605572.

20. Xu, Cave, Leibold, Munro, and Ruser, "Uyghurs for Sale."

21. "Nike Statement on Xinjiang," undated, https://purpose.nike.com/state ment-on-xinjiang.

22. Adrian Zenz, "Coercive Labor in Xinjiang: Labor Transfer and the Mobilization of Ethnic Minorities to Pick Cotton," Center for Global Policy, December 14, 2020, https://cgpolicy.org/briefs/coercive-labor-in-xinjiang-labor-transfer-and -the-mobilization-of-ethnic-minorities-to-pick-cotton/.

23. David Lawder and Dominique Patton, "U.S. Bans Cotton Imports from China Producer XPCC Citing Xinjiang 'Slave Labor,'" Reuters, December 3, 2020, https://www.reuters.com/article/us-usa-trade-china-idUSKBN28C38V.

24. National Retail Federation, "Joint statement from NRFA, AAFA, RILA, and USFIA on Reports of Forced Labor in Xinjiang," press release, March 10, 2020,

https://nrf.com/media-center/press-releases/joint-statement-nrf-aafa-fdra-rila
-and-usfia-reports-forced-labor.

25. Dake Kang and Yanan Wang, "China's Uighurs Told to Share Beds, Meals with Party Members," Associated Press, December 1, 2018, https://apnews.com/article/9ca1c29fc9554c1697a8729bba4dd93b.

26. People's Republic of China, "Full Text: Human Rights in Xinjiang—Development and Progress," Xinhua, June 1, 2017, http://www.xinhuanet.com/english/2017-06/01/c_136331805_2.htm.

27. Reuters, "China Official Says Xinjiang's Muslims Are 'Happiest in World,'" August 25, 2017, https://lta.reuters.com/article/us-china-xinjiang/china-official -says-xinjiangs-muslims-are-happiest-in-world-idUSKCN1B50ID.

28. Alim Seytoff and Paul Eckert, "UN Sidesteps Tough US Criticism on Counterterrorism Chief's Trip to Xinjiang," Radio Free Asia, June 17, 2019, https://www .rfa.org/english/news/uyghur/xinjiang-un-06172019173344.html.

29. Bloomberg News, "Face-Recognition Startup Megvii Said to Raise $100 Million," December 6, 2016, https://www.bloomberg.com/news/articles/2016-12-06/china-face-recognition-startup-megvii-said-to-raise-100-million.

30. Steven Millward, "Tencent's Biggest Investments This Year," Tech in Asia, December 28, 2016, https://www.techinasia.com/tencent-biggest-investments-2016.

31. Kai-fu Lee, AI Superpowers, 1–2.

32. James Somers, "The Friendship That Made Google Huge," New Yorker, December 3, 2018, https://www.newyorker.com/magazine/2018/12/10/the-friendship -that-made-google-huge.

33. Tim Bradshaw, "Google Buys UK Artificial Intelligence Start-up," Financial Times, January 27, 2014, https://www.ft.com/content/f92123b2-8702-11e3-aa31 -00144feab7de.

34. Amy Webb, The Big Nine: How the Tech Titans and Their Thinking Machines Could Warp Humanity (New York: PublicAffairs, 2019), 47.

35. DeepMind, "Match 1—Google DeepMind Challenge Match: Lee Sedol vs. AlphaGo," posted by YouTube user DeepMind on March 8, 2016, https://www .youtube.com/watch?v=vFr3K2DORc8&t=1670. This is the link to the first of five matches. From this link, readers can load and watch the other four matches too.

36. Kai-fu Lee, AI Superpowers, 1–2.

Chapter 15. The Big Brain

1. Koran 2:191.

2. See Noor Mohammad, "The Doctrine of Jihad: An Introduction," Journal of Law and Religion 3, no. 2 (1985): 381–97, https://www.jstor.org/stable/1051182 ?seq=1.

3. Megvii executive, interview by the author, May 31, 2020.

4. Sam Byford, "AlphaGo Beats Ke Jie Again to Wrap Up Three-Part Match," Verge, May 25, 2017, https://www.theverge.com/2017/5/25/15689462/alphago-ke -jie-game-2-result-google-deepmind-china.

5. Kai-fu Lee, *AI Superpowers*, 1–2.

6. Ministry of National Defense of the People's Republic of China, "The National Intelligence Law (中华人民共和国国家情报法)," June 27, 2017. http://www .mod.gov.cn/regulatory/2017-06/28/content_4783851.htm. The author used the English translation available at https://www.chinalawtranslate.com/en/national -intelligence-law-of-the-p-r-c-2017/. For an interpretation of Article 7 of the law, see Bonnie Girard, "The Real Danger of China's National Security Law," *Diplomat*, February 23, 2019, https://thediplomat.com/2019/02/the-real-danger-of -chinas-national-intelligence-law/.

7. Xi Jinping, "Secure a Decisive Victory in Building a Moderately Prosperous Society in All Respects and Strive for the Great Success of Socialism with Chinese Characteristics for a New Era," in *Terrorism: Commentary on Security Documents Volume 147: Assessing the 2017 U.S. National Security Strategy*, edited by Douglas C. Lovelace Jr. (Oxford: Oxford University Press, 2018), 253–304.

8. China Plus, "SenseTime Becomes Fifth Member of China's AI 'National Team,'" September 26, 2018, http://chinaplus.cri.cn/news/china/9/20180926 /188677.html.

9. Scott Pelley, "Facial and Emotional Recognition: How One Man Is Advancing Artificial Intelligence," *60 Minutes*, CBS News, January 13, 2019, https:// www.cbsnews.com/news/60-minutes-ai-facial-and-emotional-recognition-how -one-man-is-advancing-artificial-intelligence/.

Chapter 16. The Bureaucracy Is Expanding to Meet the Needs of the Expanding Bureaucracy

1. Sixteen former Uyghur and Kazakh refugees describe similar propaganda videos that denounced Ilham Tohti and other prominent people from Xinjiang.

2. In interviews, every Uyghur refugee the author spoke to who left China from late 2016 to 2017 spoke about mazes of paperwork they had to complete with numerous offices, before being granted the opportunity to leave China. In particular, the poet Tahir Hamut's dozens of hours of interviews with the author, carried out in the summer of 2018, provided insightful details about the bureaucracy and offices that needed signatures.

3. Xun Zhou, "The History of the People's Republic of China—Through 70 Years of Mass Parades," *Conversation*, September 30, 2019, https://theconversation .com/amp/the-history-of-the-peoples-republic-of-china-through-70-years-of-mass -parades-123727.

4. Maysem and the author decided to withhold and obscure key details about the route that Maysem used to escape China. Through her family connections, Maysem received help from many people in navigating her route and evading the authorities at great risk to themselves. Uyghur refugees, speaking with the author, also described various routes to India as difficult and dangerous at the time of Maysem's escape, but believed reaching India was not as risky as flying from Urumqi to Turkey. We do not want to endanger Maysem's brave helpers and have decided to use caution publishing the details of Maysem's route.

5. Agence France-Presse, "Wrecked Mosques, Police Watch: A Tense Ramadan in Xinjiang," June 5, 2019, https://www.bangkokpost.com/world/1689848. Satellite imagery gathered by the Earthrise Alliance, a nonprofit group, showed public gathering places built in place of razed mosques, cemeteries, and tombs.

Chapter 17. The Prison of the Mind

1. Maysem's friend in Ankara, Turkey, interviewed by the author, November 5, 2019.

2. Koran 2:156.

3. The messages are in the possession of the author.

4. Maysem showed the status updates to the author. Snapshots of the status updates are in the author's possession.

5. Maysem showed these WeChat messages to the author.

Chapter 18. A New Cold War?

1. Also see Republic of Turkey Ministry of Culture and Tourism, "Ankara— the Mausoleum of Ataturk," https://www.ktb.gov.tr/EN-114031/ankara--the-mauso leum-of-ataturk.html.

2. Shu-Ching Jean Cheng, "SenseTime: The Faces behind China's Artificial Intelligence Unicorn."

3. Cave, Ryan, and Xu, "Mapping More of China's Tech Giants."

4. IPVM, "Huawei/Megvii Uyghur Alarms," December 8, 2020, https://ipvm .com/reports/huawei-megvii-uygur.

5. Consumer Technology Association, "Huawei's Richard Yu Announced as CES 2018 Keynote Speaker," October 24, 2017, https://www.businesswire.com/ news/home/20171024005527/en/Huawei%E2%80%99s-Richard-Yu-Announced -CES-2018-Keynote.

6. Vlad Savov, "Huawei's CEO Going Off-Script to Rage at US Carriers Was the Best Speech of CES," *Verge*, January 9, 2018, https://www.theverge.com/2018 /1/9/16871538/huawei-ces-2018-event-ceo-richard-yu-keynote-speech.

7. "Indictment," *United States of America v. Huawei Device Co., Ltd. and Huawei Device USA, Inc.*, case no. 2:19-cr-00010-RSM (US District Court, Western District of Washington at Seattle), January 16, 2019, https://www.justice.gov/opa/press -release/file/1124996/download.

8. Hiroko Tabuchi, "T-Mobile Accuses Huawei of Theft from Laboratory," *New York Times*, September 5, 2014, https://www.nytimes.com/2014/09/06/business /t-mobile-accuses-huawei-of-theft-from-laboratory.html.

9. "Court's Verdict Form," *T-Mobile USA, Inc. v. Huawei Device USA, Inc.*, case no. 2:14-cr-01351-RAJ (U.S. District Court, Western District of Washington at Seattle), May 18, 2017, http://www.columbia.edu/~ma820/Huawei.484.pdf.

10. U.S. Department of Justice, "Chinese Telecommunications Device Manufacturer and Its U.S. Affiliate Indicted for Theft of Trade Secrets, Wire Fraud,

and Obstruction of Justice," press release, January 28, 2019, https://www.justice .gov/opa/pr/chinese-telecommunications-device-manufacturer-and-its-us-affiliate -indicted-theft-trade.

11. "Indictment," *United States of America v. Huawei Device Co., Ltd. and Huawei Device USA, Inc.*, case no. 2:19-cr-00010-RSM (US District Court, Western District of Washington at Seattle), January 16, 2019, 19–20, https://www.justice.gov/opa/ press-release/file/1124996/download.

12. Katie Collins, "Pentagon Bans Sale of Huawei, ZTE Phones on US Military Bases," *CNET*, May 2, 2018, https://www.cnet.com/news/pentagon-reportedly -bans-sale-of-huawei-and-zte-phones-on-us-military-bases/.

13. Michael Slezak and Ariel Bogle, "Huawei Banned from 5G Mobile Infrastructure Rollout in Australia," Australia Broadcasting Corporation, August 23, 2018, https://www.abc.net.au/news/2018-08-23/huawei-banned-from-providing -5g-mobile-technology-australia/10155438.

14. Tasneem Akolawala, "Huawei Says Shipped 100 Million Smartphones in 2018 Already, Aims to Cross 200 Million," *Gadgets 360*, NDTV, July 19, 2018, https://gadgets.ndtv.com/mobiles/news/huawei-100-million-smartphone-sales -2018-1886358.

15. Steven Musil, "Huawei Knocks Off Apple to Become No. 2 Phone Seller," CNET, August 1, 2018, https://www.cnet.com/news/huawei-knocks-off-apple-ip hone-to-become-no-2-phone-seller/.

16. Lucy Hornby, Sherry Fei Ju, and Louise Lucas, "China Cracks Down on Tech Credit Scoring," *Financial Times*, February 4, 2018, https://www.ft.com/content /f23e0cb2-07ec-11e8-9650-9c0ad2d7c5b5.

17. Lily Kuo, "China Bans 23M from Buying Travel Tickets as Part of 'Social Credit' System," *Guardian*, March 2019, https://www.theguardian.com/world/2019/ mar/01/china-bans-23m-discredited-citizens-from-buying-travel-tickets -social-credit-system.

18. Joe McDonald, "China Bars Millions from Travel for 'Social Credit' Offenses," Associated Press, February 22, 2019, https://apnews.com/article/9d43f4b 7426041179704ddd391c13d8.

19. Genia Kostka, "China's Social Credit Systems and Public Opinion: Explaining High Levels of Approval," *New Media & Society* 21, no. 7 (February 2019), https://journals.sagepub.com/toc/nmsa/21/7.

20. Heather Timmons, "No One Can Say for Sure What Trump and Xi Just Agreed To," *Quartz*, December 4, 2018, https://qz.com/1482634/no-one-knows -what-trump-and-xi-agreed-to-at-the-g20/.

21. Kate O'Keefe and Stu Woo, "Canadian Authorities Arrest CFO of Huawei Technologies at U.S. Request," *Wall Street Journal*, December 5, 2018, https://www .wsj.com/articles/canadian-authorities-arrest-cfo-of-huawei-technologies-at-u-s -request-1544048781.

22. Steve Stecklow and Babak Dehghanpisheh, "Exclusive: Huawei Hid Business Operation in Iran after Reuters Reported Links to CFO," Reuters, June 3, 2020, https://www.reuters.com/article/us-huawei-iran-probe-exclusive-idUSKBN 23A19B.

23. Vipal Monga and Kim Mackrael, "Court Filings Shed New Light on Arrest

of Huawei Executive," *Wall Street Journal*, August 23, 2019, https://www.wsj.com/articles/court-filings-shed-new-light-on-arrest-of-huawei-executive-11566581148.

24. Gordon Corera, "Meng Wanzhou: The PowerPoint That Sparked an International Row," BBC, September 27, 2020, https://www.bbc.com/news/world-us-canada-54270739.

25. Robert Fife and Steven Chase, "Inside the Final Hours That Led to the Arrest of Huawei Executive Meng Wanzhou," *Globe and Mail*, November 30, 2019, https://www.theglobeandmail.com/politics/article-inside-the-final-hours-that-led-to-the-arrest-of-huawei-executive-meng/.

26. Yong Xiong and Susannah Cullinane, "China Summons US, Canadian Ambassadors in 'Strong Protest' over Huawei CFO's Arrest," CNN, December 9, 2018, https://edition.cnn.com/2018/12/09/tech/huawei-cfo-china-summons-ambassador/index.html.

27. Keegan Elmer and Catherine Wong, "Canadian Michael Kovrig Held in China for Endangering National Security," *South China Morning Post*, December 12, 2018, https://www.scmp.com/news/china/diplomacy/article/2177585/chinese-state-security-behind-detention-canadian-former.

28. Agence France-Presse, "China Charges Canadians Michael Kovrig and Michael Spavor under National Security Law, 18 Months after Arrest," June 19, 2020, https://hongkongfp.com/2020/06/19/china-charges-canadians-michael-kovrig-and-michael-spavor-with-spying-18-months-after-arrest/.

29. Steven Lee Myers and Dan Bilefsky, "Second Canadian Arrested in China, Escalating Diplomatic Feud," *New York Times*, December 12, 2018, https://www.nytimes.com/2018/12/12/world/asia/michael-spavor-canadian-detained-china.html.

30. Gravitas Ventures, "Dennis Rodman's Big Bang in Pyongyang," January 2015.

31. Geoffrey Cain, "Watch Out, Kim Jong Un: Wrestler Antonio Inoki Is Bringing Slap to North Korea," *NBC News*, August 12, 2014, https://www.nbcnews.com/news/world/watch-out-kim-jong-un-wrestler-antonio-inoki-bringing-slap-n178396.

32. Lu Shaye, "On China, Has Canada Lost Its Sense of Justice?" *Globe and Mail*, December 13, 2018, https://www.theglobeandmail.com/opinion/article-on-china-has-canada-lost-its-sense-of-justice/.

33. Nathan Vanderklippe, "Two Canadians Detained in China for Four Months Prevented from Going Outside, Official Says," April 10, 2019, https://www.theglobeandmail.com/world/article-two-canadians-detained-in-china-are-prevented-from-seeing-the-sun-or/.

34. Author's interview with Canadian diplomat involved in the effort to release Michael Kovrig and Michael Spavor, April 14, 2019.

35. Darren J. Lim and Victor Ferguson, "Chinese Economic Coercion During the THAAD Dispute," *Asian Forum*, December 28, 2019, http://www.theasanforum.org/chinese-economic-coercion-during-the-thaad-dispute/.

36. *Korea Herald* and *Asia News Network*, "South Korea's Lotte Seeks to Exit China after Investing $9.6 Billion, as Thaad Fallout Ensues," March 13, 2019, https://www.straitstimes.com/asia/east-asia/south-koreas-lotte-seeks-to-exit-china-after-investing-96-billion.

37. Yonhap News Agency, "Lotte Group Hoping for Biz Comeback on S. Korea–China Thaw," November 1, 2017, https://en.yna.co.kr/view/AEN20171101003400320.

38. David Shepardson and Diane Bartz, "Exclusive: White House Mulls New Year Executive Order to Ban Huawei, ZTE Purchases," Reuters, December 27, 2018, https://www.reuters.com/article/us-usa-china-huawei-tech-exclusive-idUSKCN1OQ09P.

39. US Congress, Senate, A Bill to Establish the Office of Critical Technologies and Security, and for Other Purposes, S.29, 116th Congress, 1st session, introduced in the Senate on June 4, 2019, https://www.congress.gov/bill/116th-congress/senate-bill/29.

40. "Executive Order on Securing the Information and Communications Technology and Services Supply Chain," White House, May 15, 2019, https://www.whitehouse.gov/presidential-actions/executive-order-securing-information-communications-technology-services-supply-chain/.

41. Tom Warren, "Microsoft Allowed to Sell Software to Huawei Once Again," *Verge*, November 22, 2019, https://www.theverge.com/2019/11/22/20977446/microsoft-huawei-us-export-license-windows-office-software.

42. T. C. Sottek, "Google Pulls Huawei's Android License Forcing It to Use Open Source Version," *Verge*, May 19, 2019, https://www.theverge.com/2019/5/19/18631558/google-huawei-android-suspension.

43. Sean Keane, "Vodafone Found Hidden Backdoors in Huawei Equipment, Says Report," *CNET*, April 30, 2019, https://www.cnet.com/news/british-carrier-vodafone-found-hidden-backdoors-in-huawei-equipment-says-report/. The article reports on backdoors Vodafone found in Huawei's equipment as far back as 2011. Vodafone and Huawei claimed they had addressed the backdoors.

44. US Department of Justice, "Deputy Attorney General Rod J. Rosenstein Announces Charges against Chinese Hackers," press release, December 20, 2018, https://www.justice.gov/opa/speech/deputy-attorney-general-rod-j-rosenstein-announces-charges-against-chinese-hackers.

45. Adam Satariono and Joanna Berendt, "Poland Arrests 2, Including Huawei Employee, Accused of Spying for China," *New York Times*, January 11, 2019, https://www.nytimes.com/2019/01/11/world/europe/poland-china-huawei-spy.html.

46. The US Department of Justice filed the charges in two separate cases, one in New York City and one in Seattle, Washington. See "Indictment," *United States of America v. Huawei Technologies Co., Ltd., Huawei Device USA, Inc., Skycom Tech Co., Ltd., and Wanzhou Meng*, case no. 18-457 (S-2) (AMD) (U.S. District Court, Eastern District of New York), January 24, 2019, https://www.justice.gov/opa/press-release/file/1125021/download. Also see "Indictment," *United States of America v. Huawei Device Co., Ltd. and Huawei Device USA, Inc.*, case no. 2:19-cr-00010-RSM (U.S. District Court, Western District of Washington at Seattle), January 16, 2019, https://www.justice.gov/opa/press-release/file/1124996/download.

47. Dale Smith, "China's Envoy to Canada Says Huawei 5G Ban Would Have Repercussions," Reuters, January 17, 2019, https://www.reuters.com/article/us-china-canada-diplomacy/chinas-envoy-to-canada-says-huawei-5g-ban-would-have-repercussions-idUSKCN1PB2L2.

Chapter 19. The Great Rupture

1. US Congress, House of Representatives, Permanent Select Committee on Intelligence, Hearing: China's Digital Authoritarianism: Surveillance, Influence, and Political Control, May 16, 2019, https://intelligence.house.gov/calendar/event single.aspx?EventID=632.

2. John Bolton, *The Room Where It Happened: A White House Memoir* (New York: Simon and Schuster, 2020), 312. Also see Alan Rappeport and Edward Wong, "In Push for Trade Deal, Trump Administration Shelves Sanctions over China's Crackdown on Uighurs," *New York Times*, May 4, 2019, https://www.nytimes.com /2019/05/04/world/asia/trump-china-uighurs-trade-deal.html.

3. UK House of Commons, Science and Technology Committee, Oral Evidence: U.K. Telecommunications Infrastructure, HC 2200, June 10, 2019, http:// data.parliament.uk/writtenevidence/committeeevidence.svc/evidencedocument/ science-and-technology-committee/uk-telecommunications-infrastructure/oral /102931.pdf.

4. Nathan Vanderklippe, "Huawei's Partnership with China on Surveillance Technology Raises Concerns for Foreign Users," *Globe and Mail*, May 14, 2018, https://www.theglobeandmail.com/world/article-huaweis-partnership-with-china -on-surveillance-raises-concerns-for/.

5. Cave, Ryan, and Xu, "Mapping More of China's Tech Giants."

6. Cave, Ryan, and Xu, "Mapping More of China's Tech Giants."

7. US Department of Commerce, "U.S. Department of Commerce Adds 28 Chinese Organizations to Its Entity List," press release, October 7, 2019, https:// www.commerce.gov/news/press-releases/2019/10/us-department-commerce -adds-28-chinese-organizations-its-entity-list.

8. Bureau of Industry and Security, US Department of Commerce, "Supplement No. 4 to Part 744—ENTITY LIST," December 18, 2020, https://www.bis.doc .gov/index.php/policy-guidance/lists-of-parties-of-concern/entity-list.

9. Zhang Dong, "Xinjiang's Tens-of-Billion Scale Security Market, the Integration Giant Tells You How to Get Your Share," *Leiphone*, August 31, 2017, https:// www.leiphone.com/news/201708/LcdGuMZ5n7k6sepy.html. Jeff Ding, PhD candidate at the University of Oxford, translated the article for his *ChinAI* newsletter at https://docs.google.com/document/d/13GCpUPrJzu9ipZgPtFDrofTI1kyXk4 Op6qTUBhTSpqk/edit#.

10. Paul Mozur, "One Month, 50,000 Face Scans: How China Is Using A.I. to Profile a Minority," *New York Times*, April 14, 2019, https://www.nytimes.com /2019/04/14/technology/china-surveillance-artificial-intelligence-racial-profiling .html.

11. Chinese Security & Protection Industry Association (中国安防行业网), "Megvii (Face++) SkyEye System (旷视科技(Face++)天眼系统)," June 17, 2017, http://www.21csp.com.cn/zhanti/2017znfx/article/article_15000.html. The original link from 2016 was taken down and then reposted on January 17, 2017.

12. Naomi Xu Elegant, "China's Top A.I. Firms Land on U.S.'s Latest Blacklist," *Fortune*, October 8, 2019, https://fortune.com/2019/10/08/china-ai-us-entity-list/.

13. Charles Rollet, "Evidence of Hikvision's Involvement with Xinjiang IJOP

and Re-Education Camps," IPVM, October 2, 2018, https://ipvm.com/reports/hikvision-xinjiang.

14. Charles Rollet, "Hikvision Wins Chinese Government Forced Facial Recognition Project Across 967 Mosques," IPVM, July 16, 2018, https://ipvm.com/reports/hik-mosques.

15. Ben Dooley, "Chinese Firms Cash in on Xinjiang's Growing Police State," Agence France-Presse, June 27, 2018, https://www.afp.com/en/chinese-firms-cash-xinjiangs-growing-police-state.

16. Huawei, "5G Opening Up New Business Opportunities," Huawei white paper, August 2016, https://www.huawei.com/minisite/5g/img/5G_Opening_up_New_Business_Opportunities_en.pdf.

17. Stu Woo and Kate O'Keeffe, "Washington Asks Allies to Drop Huawei," *Wall Street Journal*, November 23, 2018, https://www.wsj.com/articles/washington-asks-allies-to-drop-huawei-1542965105.

18. Steve McCaskill, "US Wants to Help Ericsson, Nokia and Others Develop 5G Alternatives," *TechRadar*, February 17, 2020, https://www.techradar.com/news/us-wants-to-help-ericsson-nokia-and-others-develop-5g-alternatives.

19. Reuters, "U.S. Allied Firms Testing Alternatives to Chinese 5G Technology: Esper," February 15, 2020, https://www.reuters.com/article/us-germany-security-esper-5g/u-s-allied-firms-testing-alternatives-to-chinese-5g-technology-esper-idUSKBN2090A3.

20. Aimee Chanthadavong, "Huawei Australia Sees 5G Ban Start to Bite as Carrier Business Down 21% for 2019," ZDNet, May 1, 2020, https://www.zdnet.com/article/huawei-australia-sees-5g-ban-start-to-bite-as-carrier-business-down-20-for-2019/.

21. Fergus Hunter, "Huawei Ban a 'Thorny Issue' Hurting China-Australia Relations, Says Ambassador," *Sydney Morning Herald*, February 17, 2020, https://www.smh.com.au/politics/federal/huawei-ban-a-thorny-issue-hurting-china-australia-relations-says-ambassador-20200217-p541ic.html.

22. BBC Newsnight, "Hong Kong: Mass Protests Turn Violent but China Says Story Is 'Distorted,'" June 12, 2019, https://www.youtube.com/watch?t=1009&v=SMTc8ml5yoo&feature=youtube.

23. Katie Collins, "Huawei Gets 5G Go-Ahead in UK, with Some Hard Limits," CNET, January 28, 2020, https://www.cnet.com/news/uk-gives-huawei-green-light-to-build-countrys-non-core-5g-network/.

24. Ben Riley-Smith, "US Spy Planes Could Be Pulled from Britain as White House Conducts Major Huawei Review," *Telegraph*, May 4, 2020, https://www.telegraph.co.uk/news/2020/05/04/us-spy-planes-could-pulled-britain-white-house-conducts-major/.

25. Jonathan E. Hillman and Maesea McCalpin, "Watching Huawei's 'Safe Cities,'" Center for Strategic and International Studies, November 4, 2019, https://www.csis.org/analysis/watching-huaweis-safe-cities.

26. Sheena Chestnut Greitens, "Dealing with Demand for China's Global Surveillance Exports," Brookings Institution, April 2020, https://www.brookings.edu/wp-content/uploads/2020/04/FP_20200428_china_surveillance_greitensv3.pdf.

27. Yau Tsz Yan, "Smart Cities or Surveillance? Huawei in Central Asia," *Diplomat*, August 7, 2019, https://thediplomat.com/2019/08/smart-cities-or-surveil lance-huawei-in-central-asia/

28. Joe Parkinson, Nichola Bariyo, and Josh Chin, "Huawei Technicians Helped African Governments Spy on Political Opponents," *Wall Street Journal*, August 15, 2019, https://www.wsj.com/articles/huawei-technicians-helped-african-govern ments-spy-on-political-opponents-11565793017.

29. Samuel Woodhams, "Huawei Says Its Surveillance Tech Will Keep African Cities Safe but Activists Worry It'll Be Misused," *Quartz Africa*, March 20, 2020, https://qz.com/africa/1822312/huaweis-surveillance-tech-in-africa-worries -activists/.

30. Brahma Chellaney, "China's Debt-Trap Diplomacy," *Project Syndicate*, January 23, 2017, https://www.project-syndicate.org/commentary/china-one-belt-one -road-loans-debt-by-brahma-chellaney-2017-01.

31. Nicholas Casey and Clifford Krauss, "It Doesn't Matter If Ecuador Can Afford This Dam. China Still Gets Paid," *New York Times*, December 24, 2018, https:// www.nytimes.com/2018/12/24/world/americas/ecuador-china-dam.html.

32. BBC News, "Kazakhstan's Land Reform Protests Explained," April 28, 2016, https://www.bbc.com/news/world-asia-36163103.

33. Daniel C. O'Neill, "Risky Business: The Political Economy of Chinese Investment in Kazakhstan," in *Journal of Eurasian Studies* 5, no. 2 (July 2014), 145–56, https://www.sciencedirect.com/science/article/pii/S1879366514000086.

34. Eleanor Albert, "The Shanghai Cooperation Organization," Council on Foreign Relations, October 14, 2015, https://www.cfr.org/backgrounder/shanghai -cooperation-organization.

35. Interviews with Sayragul Sauytbay, Serikzhan Bilesh, and one other former Atajurt member from January to July 2020. This story is also told in Ben Mauk, "Diary: Prison in the Mountains," *London Review of Books*, August 2018, https:// www.lrb.co.uk/the-paper/v41/n18/ben-mauk/diary.

36. Kiran Stacey, "Pakistan Shuns US for Chinese High-Tech Weapons," *Financial Times*, April 18, 2018, https://www.ft.com/content/8dbce0a0-3713-11e8-8b98 -2f31af407cc8.

37. Henney Sender and Kiran Stacey, "China Takes 'Project of the Century,' to Pakistan," *Financial Times*, May, 17, 2017, https://www.ft.com/content/05979e18 -2fe4-11e7-9555-23ef563ecf9a.

38. Stacey, "Pakistan Shuns US for Chinese High-Tech Weapons."

39. Frankopan, *The New Silk Roads*, 12–13.

Chapter 20. You're Not Safe Anywhere

1. Ministry of Foreign Affairs of the Republic of Turkey, "Statement of the Spokesperson of the Ministry of Foreign Affairs, Mr. Hami Aksoy, in Response to a Question Regarding Serious Human Rights Violations Perpetuated against Uyghur Turks and the Passing Away of Folk Poet Abdurehim Heyit," February 9, 2019, http://

www.mfa.gov.tr/sc_-06_-uygur-turklerine-yonelik-agir-insan-haklari-ihlalleri-ve
-abdurrehim-heyit-in-vefati-hk.en.mfa.

2. Carlotta Gall and Jack Ewing, "Tensions between Turkey and U.S. Soar as Trump Orders New Sanctions," *New York Times*, August 10, 2018, https://www .nytimes.com/2018/08/10/business/turkey-erdogan-economy-lira.html.

3. Masanori Tobita, "China Money Flows into Turkey as Crisis Creates Opening," *Nikkei Asian Review*, August 22, 2018, https://asia.nikkei.com/Politics/Inter national-relations/China-money-flows-into-Turkey-as-crisis-creates-opening.

4. Kerim Karakaya and Asli Kandemir, "Turkey Got a $1 Billion Foreign Cash Boost," Bloomberg News, August 9, 2019, https://www.bloomberg.com/news/arti cles/2019-08-09/turkey-got-1-billion-from-china-swap-in-june-boost-to-reserves.

5. The newspaper is in the possession of the author.

6. Ayla Jean Yackley and Christian Shepherd, "Turkey's Uighurs Fear for Future after China Deportation," *Financial Times*, August 24, 2019, https://www.ft .com/content/caee8cac-c3f4-11e9-a8e9-296ca66511c9.

7. United Nations Human Rights Council, "Letter Dated 8 July 2019 from the Permanent Representatives of Australia, Austria, Belgium, Canada, Denmark, Estonia, Finland, France, Germany, Iceland, Ireland, Japan, Latvia, Lithuania, Luxembourg, the Netherlands, New Zealand, Norway, Spain, Sweden, Switzerland and the United Kingdom of Great Britain and Northern Ireland to the United Nations Office at Geneva Addressed to the President of the Human Rights Council," 41st session, agenda item 2, July 23, 2019, https://ap.ohchr.org/Documents/E/ HRC/c_gov/A_HRC_41_G_11.DOCX.

8. United Nations Human Rights Council, "Letter Dated 12 July 2019 from the Representatives of Algeria, Angola, Bahrain, Bangladesh, Belarus, the Plurinational State of Bolivia, Burkina Faso, Burundi, Cambodia, Cameroon, Comoros, the Congo, Cuba, the Democratic People's Republic of Korea, the Democratic Republic of the Congo, Djibouti, Egypt, Equatorial Guinea, Eritrea, Gabon, the Islamic Republic of Iran, Iraq, Kuwait, the Lao People's Democratic Republic, Mozambique, Myanmar, Nepal, Nigeria, Oman, Pakistan, the Philippines, the Russian Federation, Saudi Arabia, Serbia, Somalia, South Sudan, Sri Lanka, the Sudan, the Syrian Arab Republic, Tajikistan, Togo, Turkmenistan, Uganda, the United Arab Emirates, Uzbekistan, the Bolivarian Republic of Venezuela, Yemen, Zambia, Zimbabwe and the State of Palestine to the United Nations Office at Geneva Addressed to the President of the Human Rights Council," 41st session, agenda item 3, July 12, 2019, https://ap.ohchr.org/Documents/E/HRC/c_gov/A_HRC_41_G_17.DOCX.

Coda. Stop the Panopticon

1. Aldous Huxley, *Brave New World* (London: Chatton and Windus, 1932).

2. George Orwell, *1984* (London: Secker and Warburg, 1949).

3. John Brunner, *Stand on Zanzibar* (New York: Doubleday, 1968).

4. Ray Kurzweil, "Singularity Q&A," Kurzweil Library, September 2005, https://www.kurzweilai.net/singularity-q-a.

5. Natasha Singer and Cade Metz, "Many Facial-Recognition Systems Are Biased, Says U.S. Study," *New York Times*, December 19, 2019, https://www.nytimes .com/2019/12/19/technology/facial-recognition-bias.html. The full report is available at Patrick Grother, Mei Ngan, and Kayee Hanaoka, "Face Recognition Vendor Test (FVRT): Part 3: Demographic Effects," National Institute for Standards and Technology at the US Department of Commerce," December 2019, https:// nvlpubs.nist.gov/nistpubs/ir/2019/NIST.IR.8280.pdf.

6. Mark Puente, "LAPD Pioneered Predicting Crime with Data. Many Police Don't Think It Works," *Los Angeles Times*, July 3, 2019, https://www.latimes.com/ local/lanow/la-me-lapd-precision-policing-data-20190703-story.html.

7. World Health Organization, "Pneumonia of Unknown Cause—China," January 5, 2020, https://www.who.int/csr/don/05-january-2020-pneumonia-of-unkown -cause-china/en/.

8. "The Coronavirus Didn't Really Start at the Wuhan 'Wet Market'," Live Science, May 28, 2020, https://www.livescience.com/covid-19-did-not-start-at-wuhan -wet-market.html.

9. Aylin Woodward, "At Least 5 People in China Have Disappeared, Gotten Arrested, or Been Silenced after Speaking Out about the Coronavirus—Here's What We Know About Them," *Business Insider*, February 20, 2020, https://www.business insider.com/china-coronavirus-whistleblowers-speak-out-vanish-2020-2.

10. Jeff Kao, Raymond Zhong, Paul Mozur and Aaron Krolik, "Leaked Documents Show How China's Army of Paid Internet Trolls Helped Censor the Coronavirus," *ProPublica* and *New York Times*, December 19, 2020, https://www.pro publica.org/article/leaked-documents-show-how-chinas-army-of-paid-internet -trolls-helped-censor-the-coronavirus.

11. Associated Press, "China Delayed Releasing Coronavirus Info, Frustrating WHO," June 3, 2020, https://apnews.com/article/3c061794970661042b18d5 aeaaed9fae.

12. Steven Erlanger, "Global Backlash Builds against China over Coronavirus," *New York Times*, May 3, 2020, https://www.nytimes.com/2020/05/03/world/ europe/backlash-china-coronavirus.html.

13. US Consulate General in Guangzhou, People's Republic of China, "Event: Discrimination against African-Americans in Guangzhou," April 13, 2020, https:// china.usembassy-china.org.cn/health-alert-u-s-consulate-general-guangzhou -peoples-republic-of-china/.

14. Lijian Zhao, Twitter post, March 12, 2020, 10:37 P.M. Beijing time, https:// twitter.com/zlj517/status/1238111898828066823.

15. Selam Gebredikan, "For Autocrats, and Others, Coronavirus Is a Chance to Grab Even More Power," *New York Times*, March 30, 2020, https://www.nytimes .com/2020/03/30/world/europe/coronavirus-governments-power.html.

16. Krystal Hu, "Exclusive: Amazon Turns to Chinese Firms on U.S. Blacklist to Meet Thermal Camera Needs," Reuters, April 29, 2020, https://www.reuters.com/ article/us-health-coronavirus-amazon-com-cameras-idUSKBN22B1AL.

17. Sam Biddle, "Police Surveilled George Floyd Protests with Help from Twitter-Affiliated Startup Dataminr," *Intercept*, July 9, 2020, https://theintercept

.com/2020/07/09/twitter-dataminr-police-spy-surveillance-black-lives-matter -protests/.

18. IBM, "IBM CEO's Letter to Congress on Racial Justice Reform," June 8, 2020, https://www.ibm.com/blogs/policy/facial-recognition-sunset-racial-justice -reforms/.

19. Amazon, "We Are Implementing a One-Year Moratorium on Police Use of Re-Kognition," June 10, 2020, https://www.aboutamazon.com/news/policy-news-views/ we-are-implementing-a-one-year-moratorium-on-police-use-of-rekognition.

20. Jay Greene, "Microsoft Won't Sell Police Its Facial-Recognition Technology, Following Similar Moves by Amazon and IBM," *Washington Post,* June 11, 2020, https://www.washingtonpost.com/technology/2020/06/11/microsoft-facial-recog nition/.

21. Javier C. Hernández, "China Locks Down Xinjiang to Fight Covid-19, Angering Residents," *New York Times*, August 25, 2020, https://www.nytimes.com /2020/08/25/world/asia/china-xinjiang-covid.html.

22. Dake Kang, "In China's Xinjiang, Forced Medication Accompanies Lockdown," Associated Press, August 31, 2020, https://apnews.com/article/309c576 c6026031769fd88f4d86fda89.

23. Bloomberg News, "Huawei Sees Dire Threat to Future from Latest Trump Salvo," June 8, 2020, https://www.bloomberg.com/news/articles/2020-06-07/hua wei-troops-see-dire-threat-to-future-from-latest-trump-salvo.

24. Zhaoyin Feng, "Chinese Students Face Increased Scrutiny at US Airports," BBC Chinese Service, September 4, 2020, https://www.bbc.com/news/world-us -canada-54016278.

25. Ishan Banerjee and Matt Sheehan, "America's Got AI Talent: US' Big Lead in AI Research Is Built on Importing Researchers," MacroPolo, June 9, 2020, https://macropolo.org/americas-got-ai-talent-us-big-lead-in-ai-research-is-built -on-importing-researchers/?rp=m.

26. Michael Zennie, "Hong Kong Democracy Activist Jailed after Pleading Guilty to 2019 Protest Charges," *Time*, November 23, 2020, https://time .com/5914785/joshua-wong-jailed-hong-kong/.

27. Yimou Lee, David Lague, and Ben Blanchard, "Special Report: China Launches 'Gray-Zone' Warfare to Subdue Taiwan," Reuters, December 10, 2020, https://www.reuters.com/article/hongkong-taiwan-military-idUSKBN28K1GS.

28. Karen Leigh, Peter Martin, and Adrian Leung, "Troubled Waters: Where the US and China Could Clash in the South China Sea," *Bloomberg,* December 17, 2020, https://www.bloomberg.com/graphics/2020-south-china-sea-miscalcula tion/.

29. David Crawshaw and Miriam Berger, "China Beat Back Covid-19 in 2020. Then It Really Flexed Its Muscles at Home and Abroad," *Washington Post*, December 28, 2020, https://www.washingtonpost.com/world/2020/12/28/china-2020 -major-stories/.

30. Michelle Toh, "China's Tariffs Slam Door Shut on Australian Wine's Biggest Export Market," CNN.com, November 30, 2020, https://edition.cnn.com/ 2020/11/30/business/australia-china-wine-tariffs-intl-hnk/index.html.

31. Shorhet Hoshur, "Self-Proclaimed Uyghur Former Spy Shot by Unknown Assailant in Turkey," Radio Free Asia, November 3, 2020, https://www.rfa.org/english/news/uyghur/spy-11032020175523.html.

32. Helen Davidson, "Pressure on Turkey to Protect Uighurs as China Ratifies Extradition Treaty," *Guardian*, December 29, 2020, https://www.theguardian.com/world/2020/dec/29/pressure-on-turkey-to-protect-uighurs-as-china-ratifies-extradition-treaty.

33. Victor Ordonez, "Chinese Embassy Tweet about Uighurs and Birth Rate Draws Instant Condemnation," ABC News, January 8, 2021, https://abcnews.go.com/International/chinese-embassy-tweet-uighurs-birth-rate-draws-instant/story?id=75118569.

34. Edward Wong and Chris Buckley, "U.S. Says China's Repression of Uighurs Is 'Genocide,'" *New York Times*, January 19, 2021, https://www.nytimes.com/2021/01/19/us/politics/trump-china-xinjiang.html.

35. Matthew Hill, David Campanale, and Joel Gunter, "'Their Goal Is to Destroy Everyone': Uighur Camp Detainees Allege Systemic Rape," BBC News, February 2, 2021, https://www.bbc.com/news/world-asia-china-55794071.

36. Leyland Cecco, "Canada Votes to Recognize China's Treatment of Uighur Population as Genocide," *Guardian*, February 22, 2021, https://www.theguardian.com/world/2021/feb/22/canada-china-uighur-muslims-genocide.

Acknowledgments

1. Ohm Youngmisuk, "LeBron James: Daryl Morey Was 'Misinformed' before Sending Tweet about China and Hong Kong," ESPN, December 14, 2019, https://www.espn.com/nba/story/_/id/27847951/daryl-morey-was-misinformed-sending-tweet-china-hong-kong.

2. Tim Bontemps, "NBA, NBPA announce playoffs to resume Saturday, new initiatives," ESPN, August 28, 2020. https://www.espn.com/nba/story/_/id/29759939/nba-announces-playoffs-resume-saturday. Patrick Brzeski, "It's Official: China Overtakes North America as World's Biggest Box Office in 2020," *Hollywood Reporter*, October 18, 2020, https://www.hollywoodreporter.com/news/its-official-china-overtakes-north-america-as-worlds-biggest-box-office-in-2020.

3. BBC News, "Censored Bond film *Skyfall* Opens in China," January 21, 2013, https://www.bbc.com/news/world-asia-china-21115987.

4. BBC News, "Disney Criticised for filming Mulan in China's Xinjiang Project," September 7, 2020, https://www.bbc.com/news/world-54064654.

5. Jonathan Shieber, "Zoom Admits Shutting Down Activist Accounts at the Request of the Chinese Government," *TechCrunch*, June 11, 2020, https://techcrunch.com/2020/06/11/zoom-admits-to-shutting-down-activist-accounts-at-the-request-of-the-chinese-government/.

6. Nicole Hong, "Zoom Executive Accused of Disrupting Calls at China's Behest," *New York Times*, December 18, 2020, https://www.nytimes.com/2020/12/18/technology/zoom-tiananmen-square.html.

Index

About the Author

Marion Ettlinger

Geoffrey Cain is an investigative journalist and technology writer who reported from Asia and the Middle East for twelve years. He's contributed to the *Economist*, *Time*, the *Wall Street Journal*, and dozens of other magazines and newspapers. His first book, *Samsung Rising: The Inside Story of the South Korean Giant That Set Out to Beat Apple and Conquer Tech*, was long-listed for the Financial Times and McKinsey Business Book of the Year award. A Fulbright scholar, he studied at London's School of Oriental and African Studies and George Washington University, and is a term member of the Council on Foreign Relations.

PublicAffairs is a publishing house founded in 1997. It is a tribute to the standards, values, and flair of three persons who have served as mentors to countless reporters, writers, editors, and book people of all kinds, including me.

I. F. STONE, proprietor of *I. F. Stone's Weekly*, combined a commitment to the First Amendment with entrepreneurial zeal and reporting skill and became one of the great independent journalists in American history. At the age of eighty, Izzy published *The Trial of Socrates*, which was a national bestseller. He wrote the book after he taught himself ancient Greek.

BENJAMIN C. BRADLEE was for nearly thirty years the charismatic editorial leader of *The Washington Post*. It was Ben who gave the *Post* the range and courage to pursue such historic issues as Watergate. He supported his reporters with a tenacity that made them fearless and it is no accident that so many became authors of influential, best-selling books.

ROBERT L. BERNSTEIN, the chief executive of Random House for more than a quarter century, guided one of the nation's premier publishing houses. Bob was personally responsible for many books of political dissent and argument that challenged tyranny around the globe. He is also the founder and longtime chair of Human Rights Watch, one of the most respected human rights organizations in the world.

．　　　．　　　．

For fifty years, the banner of Public Affairs Press was carried by its owner Morris B. Schnapper, who published Gandhi, Nasser, Toynbee, Truman, and about 1,500 other authors. In 1983, Schnapper was described by *The Washington Post* as "a redoubtable gadfly." His legacy will endure in the books to come.

Peter Osnos, *Founder*